# A River of Stories

## *It's Been Quite a Ride*

## Also by Jim H. Ainsworth

### Novels
*Rails to a River: A Long Awakening*
*Firstborn Son*
*Go Down Looking*
*Home Light Burning*
*Rivers Ebb*
*Rivers Crossing*
*In the Rivers Flow*
*Rivers Flow–2nd Edition*

---

### Business • Financial Planning • Financial Services
*How to Become a Successful Financial Consultant*
First Edition 1997 • Second Edition 2013

---

### Memoir
*Biscuits Across the Brazos*

# A River of Stories

## *It's Been Quite a Ride*

### A Collection of Stories

Jim H. Ainsworth

Copyright © Jim H. Ainsworth 2014

All rights reserved. No part of this book may be reproduced in any form or by any electronic or mechanical means, including information storage and retrieval systems, without permission in writing from the publisher, except by a reviewer why may quote passages in a review. For permission, go to www.jimainsworth.com or write the publisher at the address below.

First Edition

ISBN 978-0-9904628-0-4

Library of Congress Control Number: 2014911872

Design by Vivian Freeman, *Yellow Rose Typesetting*

Printed in the United States of America

Season of Harvest Publications
2403 CR 4208
Campbell, Texas 75422

*For my family—who stayed with me through many mistakes on this long ride and who will be with me to the end—no matter what.*

# What booklovers are saying about Jim Ainsworth's writing:

*Jim Ainsworth has a better grasp of the English language than any author that I have ever read. When he writes a scene or a situation he describes it in terms that put you inside the pages of the book—you see, feel and touch the moment.*
—Charlie Smith

*Ainsworth's real-life experiences are exceptional-read his bio.*
—Larry Whitlock

*Jim Ainsworth's deep, quiet voice rumbles around your chest. We all hear the music inside and it resonates straight into our hearts.*
—Author Donna G. Paul

*Ainsworth's deft words encapsulate reflective thought; deep empathy; life recalled; lessons learned; vagaries and truths of relationships. Reading Ainsworth is a joy.*
—Trice Lawrence

*Excellent lessons for all men and women about devotion, character, and a little thing called integrity.*
—Stephanie Bertani

*I have said it before and will say it again. I believe Jim is one of our great American storytellers.*
—Rosalie Oliver

# A Note from the Author

I HAVE BEEN FORTUNATE, I THINK, to have engaged in many careers in my life. I have been other things, but now, I am a novelist. This is not a novel. I have written nonfiction books before, but only on subjects where I held some expertise and experience. The stories and essays in the first part of the book are true. I know because I was there or I have firsthand experience and expertise. But in the last part of the book, the part about "Believing in a Grand Thing," I have crossed the Rubicon, the point of no return. There is at least one essay in this book that explains why I write fiction, but I think writing that last part revealed another, possibly more influential, reason. That reason is that I was afraid to write anything but fiction. When I was in the financial services business, a buzz phrase was popular. "Open the Kimono" meant to reveal everything, to be forthcoming with clients, open the books, hold nothing back. Throughout the years-long process of putting this book of stories and reflections together, I struggled with reticence, with a reluctance to peel back layers of privacy and expose my innermost thoughts and habits. So in the last part, I forged ahead, revealing opinions and feelings. But I wrote as an admitted novice, hoping that my struggles might strike a chord with readers grappling with the same issues. I considered deleting it many times, but on the final page, I reveal one more God wink that convinced me to leave it in.

# A River of Stories

## It's Been Quite a Ride

# Contents

## Introduction
Seventy Years of Stories     3
The Eulogy I Never Delivered     5

## Friends Matter
His Dog Knows Me     15
Hosses and Bosses     17
CT and Me     20
The Cowhill Council     26
The Circle Is Unbroken     29

## A Tribute to Animal Friends
Cowboys Don't Know How to Say Goodbye     35
Men and Cats     39
Why I Ride     42

## Authors, Singers, and Songwriters
Searching for a Reclusive Author     49
Golightly, Annie     55
Life Is a Stallion     59
The Bard and the Balladeer     63
Visiting with a Living Legend and a Poet Laureate     69
Tom T. Hall Comes Home     72

# Ranching, Cowboys, and the Saddles They Ride

| | |
|---|---|
| Two Days in Albany | 77 |
| A Voice from the Past | 81 |
| A Visit to the Who Knows Ranch | 84 |
| A Panhandle Test of Mettle and Murder on the High Plains | 88 |
| A Breakfast I Will Never Forget | 91 |
| Roundup on the Quien Sabe and a Sad Goodbye | 94 |
| Old Tascosa, the Mother Road, the Bent Door | 98 |
| Getting Ready for the Last Roundup | 101 |
| Heading for the Last Roundup and a Horse Love Affair | 103 |
| Cowboy Rituals at Dawn | 108 |
| Riding the Breaks | 111 |
| The Last of the Last Roundup | 114 |
| A Saddle with a Story | 116 |
| The Old Roper | 118 |

# Checking Off the Bucket List

| | |
|---|---|
| Falling Down a Mountain | 125 |
| The Old Hag Arrives | 130 |
| The Stranger in the Mirror | 133 |
| Meeting the Marlboro Man | 135 |
| The Sunrise Side of the Mountain | 138 |
| True Unity | 140 |
| The Straight Story | 142 |

# Writing, Reading, Readers, and Why Fiction Matters

| | |
|---|---|
| We Read to Know We Are Not Alone | 147 |
| Buyers, Readers, Fans, and Evangelists | 150 |
| A Sign…a Whisper…a Nudge | 153 |
| The Blurry Line Between Fiction and Truth | 158 |
| Why I Write Fiction | 162 |

# The Healing Power of Family Stories

| | |
|---|---|
| A Christmas Star and Scar | 169 |
| Under the Porch | 172 |
| The Chance He Never Had | 175 |
| For Eddy Boy | 179 |
| George Clooney, Johnny Cash, Jimmie Rodgers, and Daddy | 181 |
| Granny's Buttons | 184 |
| Reflection: The Art of Looking Back | 186 |
| Fiction, Truth, and Families | 189 |
| Taking Down the Jelly Bean Jar | 191 |

# How Stories Heal the Fear of Public Speaking

| | |
|---|---|
| There's Something about Old Country Graveyards | 201 |
| Going Home Again | 207 |
| Picking up the Fork and Spoon | 213 |
| Formulas, Secrets, and Universal Truths | 219 |

# Lines that Rhyme

| | |
|---|---|
| Unworthy | 229 |
| The Wedding Dress | 230 |
| Boots with Soul | 231 |
| Unseen Things | 233 |
| A Quilt for Papa Jim | 235 |
| A Boy, a Man | 237 |

# Life's Final Songs

| | |
|---|---|
| High Plains Tribute | 239 |
| Aunt Hido | 242 |
| She Kept Going | 245 |
| Last Trip to Klondike | 248 |
| The Treasure | 252 |

| | |
|---|---|
| A Bright Torch | 256 |
| The Man Had Sand and Salt | 259 |
| She Rode to the Whistle | 262 |
| Riding a Fine Horse in New Country | 264 |
| A Country Funeral | 268 |
| The Jerry Don Test | 271 |
| Not Ordinary | 277 |
| He Made All Things Seem Possible | 280 |

## Believing in a Grand Thing

| | |
|---|---|
| When the Student Is Ready, the Master Will Appear | 289 |
| Is There Evidence of Life After Death? | 293 |
| Why Does God Let Bad Things Happen? | 296 |
| Why Me, Lord? | 299 |
| Self-Help vs. God's Help | 304 |
| Free Will vs. God's Will | 306 |
| How and Why Do We Pray? | 309 |
| The Bible in a Few Words | 312 |
| Final Thoughts | 318 |

## Index

# Introduction

Little wonder then that we seek to share our stories with others: our brains are hard-wired to construct and absorb stories. Our love of story is what makes us human.... Until the day we die, we are living the story of our lives. And, like a novel in process, our life stories are always changing and evolving, being edited, rewritten, and embellished by an unreliable narrator. We are, in large part, our personal stories.

*The Storytelling Animal: How Stories Make Us Human*
Johnathan Gottschall, scientist and scholar

# Seventy Years of Stories

*To be told before I'm too old*

JOHN PIPER, IN HIS BOOK *Don't Waste Your Life,* says reading C. S. Lewis taught him "newness is no virtue and oldness is no vice. Truth and beauty and goodness are not determined by when they exist. Nothing is inferior for being old and nothing is valuable for being modern."

I think a lot about the past these days. Living seven decades causes one to do that. But surprisingly, I think almost as much about the future. I wonder a lot about what I learned, what I accomplished, how much time I wasted, and how much I used wisely. I practice and have almost mastered the ability to spend less time thinking about mistakes I made so I can be more aware of the short amount of time I have left and try to make the best use of that time. I constantly seek but only occasionally seem to find my real purpose in life, my reason for being.

I have included many of my favorite stories in this book. Most of them were written to stand alone as articles, posts or part of an anthology. A few have not been seen before. They are in no particular chronological order, but I did my best to categorize them in the table of contents. I hope you will forgive when you see some portion of one story appear in a second or even third story. I can only say that this affirms my belief that stories are the threads that sew our lives together. Important events (stories) usually thread their way into other important events many years later.

Writing enables me to appreciate these incredible connections. In an article for *In Touch Magazine,* Jamie Hughes asks, *"Why can we experience the same story a thousand different ways and never get tired of it?"* Perhaps it's because the storyline appeals to a deep-seated need we all share: a desire to be rescued from the world we know is deeply flawed...something elusive and ineffable that dances just beyond our grasp...and we get to experience it vicariously through a story."

I often wonder why I and so many others fail to notice when we are happy, and why it takes a catastrophe or misfortune in our lives or the life of someone we know to make us appreciate our own blessings. Reading and writing stories has helped to instill in me a deep sense of gratitude. And writing has helped me to look back, review and even discover the best lessons I have learned and how I learned them. I discovered that growing up poor was an advantage, not a disadvantage. Those experiences instilled in me a deep acceptance of personal responsibility. I also have a much deeper understanding of the people, family, friends, and others who have exerted strong influence on my life.

We learn, of course, by doing, and I learned a lot through hard knocks and making mistakes, but I also learned a lot by listening to great mentors and reading their works. Through writing, I discovered almost everything I learned came from a story or involved a story. Life...*is* a series of stories. Life is a gift to us, and the way we live our lives is our gift to those who come after. I still often have doubts about why anyone would be interested in my stories, but I have learned readers find their own stories in mine. I have been a recipient of many such story-gifts and I want to pass those gifts on to others. Stories heal us and bind us together.

The first story involves many gifts I received from one person. I hope you will see not just the man I describe here, but that special man you knew that was like the one I describe. And I know there were many others like him. I also hope you forgive my putting this tribute first, because this book is not about death, it's about life and living; about how stories heal; about how life is lived forward, but understood backward; about how stories allow us to reflect, to understand, to give meaning. This never-delivered eulogy explains better than anything I could say how stories influence our lives and why we should all embrace our own stories and the stories of others.

# The Eulogy I Never Delivered

DADDY DIED A WEEK AFTER MY TWENTY-SIXTH birthday. My mother, sister, brother and I knew death was coming, but we were not really prepared. I guess it's impossible to prepare for the death of a spouse, parent, or child. Daddy's death brought a rush of decisions to be made at once. I like to think we handled his final affairs pretty well after his funeral. With help from family and friends, we gathered his small herd of livestock, his pickup, tools and farm equipment at the house and held an auction. We sold the house and land and found Mother a place in town. All of this was heartbreaking, and I look back on it with sadness, but also with fond, poignant memories. Daddy's funeral, however, has never been a proud memory for me.

My siblings and I had never had complete responsibility for arranging a funeral. Maybe we all thought of funerals as necessary but painful experiences to be borne—something to suffer through, get over and done with as soon as possible. And that is what we had. The preacher read Daddy's obituary and list of survivors, preached a too-long sermon without mentioning the kind of man my father had been. He didn't ask beforehand, and I was not mature enough to pull him aside and tell him.

I will always be grateful for the quartet (all very fine men) that sang *The Old Rugged Cross*, but truth be told, they were several years past their prime and out of sync with the piano player.

At home that night, when it was just us, I realized we had made a terrible omission. By changing a few words in the obituary, the funeral might have served as well for a complete stranger. The celebration of Daddy's life had been a ritual (and a ragged one). When Mother and I were alone,

I said, "Somebody should have stood up. Nobody said anything personal about Daddy." I could see in Mother's eyes that she was thinking the same thoughts. In that instant, I knew that "somebody" should have been me. I went outside, sat down against a tree, and cried.

When I stopped crying, I started making excuses. The decade of my twenties is still sort of blurred for me. I had a small family, a mortgage, car payments and a succession of jobs I really disliked. I don't like to admit it, but I was immature and prone to feeling sorry for myself. I was running fast, but on a treadmill.

Eulogies, especially by family members, were rare in our part of Northeast Texas back then. In my ignorance, I thought only preachers or church elders stood behind pulpits during funerals. I thought that the stories I could tell about my father might have seemed out of place, even irreverent, in a church. And I might have cried. Survivors had to make do with a preacher who would say a few kind words about the departed. But our preacher had not said those words.

I think I heard Daddy's voice that night as I lay awake. He told me to pull myself together; that a eulogy at his funeral was not what mattered most; that his life story would be told by how his wife and children comported themselves after his death; that we had many things to handle quickly so Mother could go on with her life. And he forgave me, forgave us all.

I can hardly speak a sentence today about my father without my voice breaking. There were so many things I did not get to tell him, so many conversations I never got to have man-to-man, mostly because I was still a self-centered kid when he died. Since I have become a writer, I have tried to tell Daddy's story through a series of novels. I have shown him as a flawed man, because he was, just as I am. I knew on some level, of course, that he was a great father, but I never knew how great until I began collecting my own memories and those of others and writing stories.

Yes, I know a lot of us look back with rose-colored glasses at our parents and our past. Many, of course, look back with anger and bitterness. So go back with me now to 1970, to the First Baptist Church in Klondike, Texas, and allow me to give my father the eulogy he deserves.

Daddy's life span included two world wars. He was a tenant farmer starting a family during the Dust Bowl days and the Great Depression era. He farmed his own land during the six-year drought of the fifties.

I can't recall Daddy ever telling me he loved me but once, and that was from his deathbed. He was a strict disciplinarian, expected a lot, and I considered him to have a pretty quick temper when I was a boy. My respect for him was tinged with fear. He liked the taste of whiskey and sometimes drank too much. He gave me at least two razor strap whippings (I deserved both). And Daddy was unsuccessful by almost any material or financial standard. Sounds terrible, doesn't it?

My father was less vain than any man I have ever known. Clothes served only utilitarian purposes for him and were chosen solely for practicality, not style. Almost all of his shirts had long sleeves and were gray or khaki. He wore only one brand of faded overalls, one color and type of brogans. He had one hat and one cap. He cut his own hair into a burr during summers because short hair was cooler and less trouble.

As I began reconstructing memories and researching his life and my childhood in order to write about them, I discovered I was wrong about several things. For example, did he really have a quick and hot temper? Oh, I saw him angry plenty of times, but only after he was provoked for long periods. And his anger was usually righteous. I clearly recall his agony before, during, and after those razor strap whippings. He never struck me in anger; never condescended to me; never disparaged my clumsy efforts at things he was good at. I never saw him show cruelty to man or animal. When I recalled the stressful events and pain that might have dominated his life, he showed patience and calmness that were, well, more than I could have managed when I was his age.

But what about the other things? He did expect a lot from me, my sister, and my brother.

But, to the end of his days, he inspired us all to be better than we thought we were capable of being. He set the bar high and made us believe we could reach it. I remember standing in our old farmhouse with rain leaking through the roof while he patiently showed me how to field a ground ball, how to affect a proper batting stance, or how to hold and release the basketball to shoot a free throw. I don't recall his telling me I would have a house much nicer than the one we lived in or have more money than him, but like many things about my father, he had a gift of expressing a message without giving it voice.

For example, I never doubted, not for a second, his love for me, even though he never expressed it verbally when I was a boy. His most affectionate gesture was a hand on my head or an arm across my shoulders (I have a picture of us like that). I don't remember many hugs. I recall standing mute beside him at ballgames or school functions, waiting to get his attention when he was talking to someone (I did not dare interrupt by speaking). He would glance at me, dig in his pocket and come out with whatever change he had. He let me take what I needed from his open palm. I always took only what I needed, but when it was all of it, he never complained. He trusted me that way. Actions like that instilled his unconditional love deep within me without saying the words.

But how could he be both gentle and stern? I think my siblings and I owe a debt of gratitude to the brother we never knew. Daddy and Mother lost their first son before he turned two. He was their only child at the time. Such a devastating event destroys many marriages and a lot of parents. They somehow changed it into a positive—a deep appreciation of the sacredness of life and the preciousness of children. I think that is the primary reason they showed their unconditional love for us without expressing it verbally. Ten years later, Mother almost died giving birth to stillborn twins. Still, they held the family together.

Daddy knew instinctively that praise owes its value to scarcity. I wanted to please him more than any person on earth. That sounds unfair to Mother, but, like most good moms, praise flowed easily from her lips, sometimes to the point of embarrassing me in front of others. Not Daddy. Words of praise from him were rare, but were a soothing balm to my soul. I knew I had earned it when he gave it voice. I especially loved it when I overheard him praising me to others.

That's the kind of father he was. How about the kind of person he was? He skipped his last year of high school, but always seemed well-informed. He was a jack-of-all-trades. I know that description is usually followed by "master of none," but that didn't apply so much to daddy. One of his nicknames was Doc, because he was the man folks called when they needed a veterinarian but could not afford one. I have seen him perform surgery on cattle, dogs, pigs, and horses as well as deliver many foals and calves. He was a plumber, electrician, mechanic, horseman, cattleman, farmer, heavy equipment operator, and he could measure acreage. Neighbors sometimes dropped by to get him to figure interest on a loan. He helped me with a high school science project by accurately identifying all the varieties of trees in our county.

I have seen him get up in the middle of a meal at our table many times to thaw out an elderly couple's frozen water pipes, replace blown fuses and plugs, get a stranded farmer's pickup or tractor started, or get a mother cow back on her feet. I have seen him wire houses from scratch when electricity first came into rural areas. I watched him do it, wondering how he knew about wiring, meters and plugs at a time when many did not even have electricity.

The rest of us would be a little peeved when someone called him away from our family meals, but I don't recall Daddy ever complaining. He probably did, but I can't remember it.

Daddy did all those things, but was unsuccessful by most standards. We were always broke. Our house needed paint and repairs, and we drove old cars. The fifties' drought brought our family to our financial and prayerful knees. Part of the problem was his medical bills. He was sick and in pain for the better part of two decades with a malady misdiagnosed as cancer, gallstones, ulcers, etc. When they finally found the problem and corrected it with surgery, damage had already been done to vital organs. He had digestive problems all of his life.

And he did all that plumbing, electrical, vet, mechanical and other work with sight in only one eye. He lost sight in the other when an errant nail put out one eye, leaving him with severe headaches for the rest of his life. The aftermath of that accident reveals my father as a brave and heroic man, but I never heard him tell the story (I learned it from others). He never mentioned being blind in one eye, but he could not hide the headaches.

One more thought about his role as my father. When I think of him back in those days, I remember the times when he was there when I needed him most—like the night of the biggest disappointment in my ten-year life, the night I did not make the Little League all-star team. Daddy had asked my coach and knew in advance I had not been voted in. Mother could not stand to see the pain and embarrassment she knew I was going to suffer, so she went home before they made the announcements over the loudspeaker. Daddy stayed. He walked me back to the car, hand on my shoulder. He reassured me of my skills, but discouraged any talk of unfairness.

At home, he stood helplessly in the yard as I rushed into the house, covered my head with pillows so nobody could hear, and cried the biggest cry of my life. The next day and for days afterward, he made sure I understood he was disappointed not *in* me, but *for* me, and let me heal on my own.

When I played sports, I always looked in the stands, or in the case of baseball, out behind the fences for Daddy. He would usually be there, sitting on a tailgate or leaning against the fence, in his overalls and brogans. I learned from others that he had once been a gifted athlete.

There were many occasions when he got me out of self-inflicted jams, stood up for me when I was naïve enough to let others take advantage of me, fixed things I broke. When I resisted, he told me to take the chance he never had and go to college, saying I would have to help, but he and mother would somehow manage my tuition. Money and the obvious strain they endured to send me to school were never mentioned again. But on my first day of college, I bought some used textbooks that I discovered were missing several pages. I was furious with myself and the student who sold them to me. On the way home, I saw a shadow of something crossing the road in front of me and hit it before I could stop. I suspected it might be my neighbor's dog, but hoped it was a coyote. I didn't stop to find out. When I was asked about hitting our neighbor's baby calf, I denied it. Hours later, I confessed to my father, told him and the neighbor I was ashamed. Daddy nodded and said, "Guess it's my fault for not being the type of father a son can come to when he makes a mistake." But the fault was all mine, and it took me years to live down my cowardice. I will never forget the lesson he taught me that night.

We had one more conflict during my first semester in college, a time when I was feeling the pressure of school and work. A huge pile of scrap lumber appeared next to our house one day. It grew the next day, and on the third day, a used door appeared on top of the pile. I got an axe and determined to chop up the lumber and burn it. I was in full backswing on the door when I felt his hand on my wrist. "I might use that door," he said.

I complained the pile of old wood made the place look junky and was embarrassing. He said that was his lookout, not mine, that our home belonged to him and Mother, not me. Then he brought up a trip to town I had taken in the family car during an ice storm after being told not to go. One thing led to another, and pretty soon, I drew back my fist. He dropped both arms and stared at me. "You gonna hit me, son?" That was the end of it, of course. A month later, he had turned that pile of scrap lumber into a one room shack in our back yard, complete with a small porch—a place where I could study in peace and quiet. How many fathers would do that?

Mother, by the way, never forgot that we failed to give Daddy a proper goodbye. Until the day she died, she frequently asked me to say something nice about her at her funeral. And I did. But if I had delivered Daddy's eulogy when I was twenty-six, I would probably have been clumsy, definitely bashful and probably inarticulate. Maybe it worked out best this way. Daddy, I am sure, understood.

Does Teadon (his other nickname) sound like a great father, even a great man? I think so. But when I was a kid, I am ashamed to admit I didn't always think he was. I admired his skills, loved him, but I also knew he didn't have a high school diploma. I knew he was poor and that we were poor, that we lived in a big shack, drove old cars. I was never ashamed of his being poor or dressing in overalls and brogans, but I wanted to do better. And, he disappointed me a few times. Once, I recall being ashamed of him.

Only when I started writing novels based on real lives and events did I learn what a great father I had. Not an easy thing to admit, but there it is. Only when I began to closely examine and write about those memories, the things he did, the pain he endured, the mistakes he made, did I finally understand him (even the time I was ashamed), to appreciate his patience, his ability to inspire, to express his love in so many ways that words were not required. Hearing sincere words of love is never a bad thing, but showing it is even better, and that made Richard, Doc, Teadon and RA a great father and a great man. I wish I could have told him.

# Friends Matter

I'm a really lucky guy. When I need help, I have a close family I can count on to come running every time. And I'm lucky to have a lot of friends. But I also have a few friends who are almost like family. I'm talking about the kind of buddies that would come running with hacksaws, chisels, shovels, chains and pulleys to get me out of whatever ditch I may have gotten myself into. They would be ready to ruin their best pair of boots, their Sunday-best clothes, mess up their new pickups, and empty their pockets to get me out of a jam. They would believe in my innocence if I proclaimed it in the face of evidence to the contrary. And even if I was guilty, they would still stick by me. They humble me, and I only hope I would be strong enough to do the same for them.

# His Dog Knows Me

I MEET REGULARLY WITH A GROUP of seasoned gentlemen in a grain silo with a brick floor out in the country. We drink gourmet coffee and occasionally cappuccino because our host, Jerald Thomas, is in the coffee business. Almost every morning for more than a decade, my arrival greeting was always a head nod and tongue-lolling smile from Nugget, Jerald's yellow Lab. The dog knew me, knew my Jeep, recognized it as soon as I turned off the highway. We have known each other since he was a pup. Everyone who has ever had a pet knows that comforting feeling that comes when a dog, cat, or horse recognizes you and looks at you with those friendly, welcoming eyes—eyes that say come over and put your hand on my head—eyes that say "I'm glad to see you." It starts the day out right.

One morning, on the eve of Christmas Eve, Nugget was not waiting for me. I was late and had other things on my mind, including some repair work at my office, and regret I didn't think much about his absence. Nugget had spent his life on a small acreage next to a state highway and had to be kept up for his own safety. He was allowed to run free, but only under Jerald's supervision. Jerald had to be there to call him back when Nugget as much as glanced toward the highway.

But early that morning, Jerald was not there when Nugget decided to run like he had when he was young, free as the wind. When Jerald arrived and found him gone, he tried to follow, but Nugget circled back and headed home, happy to have his master follow him in a playful game. But he was old and his reflexes had slowed. He probably never saw the eighteen-wheeler.

As I turned the key in my Jeep to leave that morning, my recently acquired Tom T. Hall CD played "Old Dogs and Children and Watermelon Wine." Tom said, *"Old dogs care about you, even when you make mistakes."* Jerald's heart is broken over the loss of his loyal companion and I will certainly miss my old friend. I like to think Nugget would have wanted to leave us this way, running free. He had serious health problems that were not going away. Maybe he knew it was time to go and wanted it to be on his own terms. Still, it's hard to say goodbye.

# Hosses and Bosses

WE ALL SAT AT BOOTHS AND TABLES in the new trendy cafe in a building a few feet away from the campus of Texas A&M-Commerce (formerly known as ET). We were within sight of a multitude of memories for all of us. Most had frequented the same building when it housed different enterprises during college days decades ago. The occasion was a celebration of Dr. Fred Tarpley's eightieth birthday. He had been a Tejas sponsor as far back as 1957.

We had difficulty deciding who should sit where, but finally settled in. Music blared from two different sources (with two different songs) and we had a little trouble hearing ourselves talk. Settled in, we perused our menus. We laughed when asked to produce drivers' licenses in order to buy beer or wine. My good friend Jace Carrington asked the young waitress if she was joking.

Just about the time we finished placing our orders, the annoying recorded music suddenly changed. A real band scheduled to perform that night (we were there around 5 P.M.—yes, we do eat early) had arrived to "test the sound system." Their sound came through with perfect clarity and pitch. Wife Jan noticed the sudden change in the gathering of thirty or so lifelong friends before I did. Looking back, I think the shift in the room's atmosphere was similar to a hypnotic regression without benefit of a hypnotist. We were transported back in time without thinking about it.

Fingers drummed on tabletops in time with the beat, eyes brightened, feet tapped, heads nodded, and butts squirmed in time with the music. The few still standing swayed with the rhythm. The jitterbug or the push was definitely about to erupt. I wanted them to.

*You got me runnin', you got me hidin'*
*You got me run, hide, hide run*
*Anyway you wanna let it roll*
*Yeah, Yeah, Yeah...*
*You got me doin' what you want me*
*Oh baby, why you wanna let go?*

The tune-up for the band with this 1959 Jimmy Reed classic didn't last long, but it was enough to refresh some memories of the way this fun-loving, caring group of people used to be and still are. It brought a feeling. I came along only a few years behind them, but Jan and I felt we had caught a really good glimpse of what it must have been like to have been part of this fine group of people we have so much respect and admiration for during the fifties, a great decade. They remain youthful in appearance and especially in manner, but time seemed to reverse as we swayed to the beat of that old classic.

I started to title this The Brotherhood, but that would not give due credit to the Bosses. I know in advance I will get a fact or two wrong on this piece and I know I will be quickly, but kindly, corrected. There were thirteen social clubs on the campus of ET during the forties and fifties. The Tejas Club was formed in 1946 and affiliated with Sigma Phi Epsilon Fraternity thirteen years later.

I never joined a fraternity. I am reminded of what Groucho Marx said, "I don't care to belong to any club that will have me as a member." But that doesn't explain why I was not a joiner. I had plenty of excuses: no money, part time job, I was a commuter, etc. But many of the Tejas guys had the same circumstances. They didn't let a few obstacles stand in the way of forming bonds that have lasted a lifetime.

Many of the Hosses are country boys like me. Most had to struggle to pay for tuition and books; many left college or enrolled for the first time after serving their country. Many would not have been in college had it not been for the GI Bill. All have Tejas nicknames. At least, the ones I know do. I knew many by name and reputation but knew little about their group until Jan started working with them through her campus job. We were honored with invitations to many of their social functions. As we left the home of John and Peggy Moss in Pecan Gap one evening a few years back, I asked Jan if she had ever seen a finer, more fun-loving, successful, warm group of people in her life. Both of us appreciated being included.

When my first novel, *In the Rivers Flow*, was published in 2003, Hoss Jace Carrington (another Delta County boy) sent a copy to Kendall Wright (a Cooper native), a Hoss who lives in Alabama. Many scenes in the novel occur in Delta County. Jake Rivers, my protagonist, plays on a baseball team the first year Little League came to Northeast Texas. I did not know that Kendall, in college then, was an assistant coach for one of the teams. Even though I had changed character names, he sent me a letter identifying every one of the characters by their real names, which team they played for, what positions they played, and even where they are today. He even brought me a photo of all the coaches during that wonderful era.

I am not only impressed with the kindness, generosity, warmth and friendliness of this group, but would be remiss if I failed to mention their leadership. There may be exceptions, but this group is made up of successful folks, not only in wealth, but in life. They formed an endowment for ET and quickly grew it to one of the largest on campus. They served and continue to serve in leadership positions all over the country, and I am sure I don't know the half of it. I am privileged to be included as an honorary member.

You say I didn't explain who the Bosses are? You must not be married.

# CT and Me

## *An Apology to an Old Friend*

OUR FRIENDSHIP GOES BACK TWENTY-FOUR years, so recollections and the exact sequence of events have grown fuzzy, but the character and actions of my friend remain crystal clear. Telling a story about him is the best way I know to describe the man he was.

"What the hell are you doing answering the phone there?" A sense of relief spread over me as I recognized CT's raspy chuckle. He always made me laugh and I needed a good laugh. A sneaky constable had just served me with lawsuit papers.

I could not manage even a chuckle. "Believe me, I've been asking myself that same question." I glanced at the papers lying on the table next to the phone. It was not my office, not my table, not my phone, not my chair, yet the process server had tracked me here.

CT and I had been friends about seven years back then. We lived three hundred miles apart and could not have been more dissimilar, but we hit it off right away. We had met while working as registered representatives (stockbrokers) for the same broker-dealer. Those had been the good old days—days before I took an inside job as vice-president of that BD—days before things began to unravel.

There had been contentious stockholder meetings, resignations, replacements, a new president, lawsuits and threatened lawsuits; a friend of ours had been fired. What started out as bright and shiny had become tarnished for CT and me. When they fired the new president, a man I had come to respect, I resigned.

I knew a lot of other reps and they kept the phone lines hot speculating about my next move. More out of curiosity and a haunting feeling of unfinished business than anything else, I visited an associate at his fledgling BD and wound up spending the day, then the next. I had been there about two weeks when CT called.

I asked him, "How did you know how to find me?"

CT's voice still had a smile in it. "Just a lucky guess. You staying there?"

"Seems too late to turn back now. People like you and me don't like to be told we can't do something—especially by lawyers."

Another throaty laugh. "I'll call back when you make up your mind."

When he called back a few weeks later, I was president of that tiny new BD. President of three people including myself. The throaty voice laughed. "I see you're still answering the phone. How are you holding out?"

The little triangle closet I was in had a metal desk and a phone with a shoulder rest to ease the neck crick I was getting from talking eight hours a day. We had been sued because we were competing, told to cease and desist, and had been warned that our phones were tapped and that private investigators followed us everywhere we went. I did not believe that, and besides, what did it matter now? I was neither happy nor invigorated about all of it, but I had to be energized or lose everything I owned. "Hanging in there, barely."

"Got enough money?"

"Never enough."

"I could float you a loan."

"You can't do that. You can't even talk to me. I'm told our phones are tapped."

"How would it be if I came over and brought my clients?"

I waited a long time to answer. My heartbeat stepped up a notch or two thinking of having my old friend with me again. Not only would he make things more fun and interesting, we also badly needed someone who could generate revenues. And CT could generate revenues better than a slot machine. "You know the answer to that, but I can't ask you to do it. You know I got sued. With your production and reputation with other reps and in the industry, you will be, too."

"Who was it said people like us don't like to be told what we can and can't do?"

It's a simple story to this point, one that some people won't see as significant. But CT knew its significance, and so did I. CT was a major stockholder in the company that was suing me. It made sense for him to go on his merry, profitable way and stay where he was. We would still have been friends. He really had no reason to come over, other than our friendship and his trust in me.

Of course, CT liked the thrill of it all. The challenge. He was willing to roll the dice, risk everything, and spend who-knew-how-long-or-how-much defending himself and his family against a lawsuit, all for the sake of friendship and to show folks he was in charge of his own destiny. Not many men left like CT.

He did join us; he did get sued; he did become our top producer. Since CT's integrity was beyond reproach throughout the industry, his stamp of approval meant many more reps would follow. He brought our fledging firm legitimacy we might never have attained without him.

Other reps were extremely important to our success; reps with integrity and clout I am proud to call friends and colleagues; reps who showed courage and faith by joining a startup. They would all agree, however, that CT was the catalyst.

When I discovered he was not cashing his commission checks, I called and asked why. He said he figured we could use a little float. I told him the checks were good, but he delayed cashing them anyway. "Don't need the money," he said.

At our conferences, I made sure a spot was reserved

for CT in a good location, a place that he could reach easily and sit comfortably for twelve-hour stretches. Yes, for twelve hours a day, four or five days in a row, sometimes longer, CT would commiserate with fledgling and successful reps, explaining how to succeed in the business of financial planning and selling stocks, bonds, mutual funds, annuities, and insurance.

CPAs, CFPs, CFSs, lawyers—all licensed stockbrokers, sat in rapt attention interspersed with lots of laughter as the man with a tenth-grade education explained the secrets of his success. There was really only one secret—well, maybe two. CT always stated them like this: "Number one, never put your interests ahead of your clients'. Number two, your job is to help people." CT had a gift for illustrating these simple secrets with anecdotes (stories) the most inexperienced rep could understand. I liked to watch the lights come on in their eyes. I called those gatherings The University of CT.

People soon forgot that CT was handicapped. He had the appearance of a strong, athletic and virile man—a real outdoorsman. He was all those things, but an accident crippled him in his early adulthood, forcing him to wear a brace and walk with a crutch. He used a motorized cart when the pain got too bad. And yes, there was a lot of pain—constant for over four decades.

After the accident, he started over in new jobs and professions and failed several times. Finally, he pulled himself up by his bootstraps and his one good leg and embarked on a journey of self-education. He started a new business. This one worked.

I never knew about the pain until I had known him about five years. He suffered in silence. He took me deep sea fishing in his own boat and spent the better part of the trip patiently untangling my reel. We sat in a little seaside bar somewhere (Padre Island, I think) and had rum and Coke. We never discussed constant pain. When I told him I was leaving the business to pursue the next chapters in my life, he understood, never accusing me of abandoning the ship he had risked everything to come aboard.

We remained friends after I left the business. I have been in his home many times and know his family. He and Maggie Jo made a six-hour, pain-filled journey to my home to help me celebrate the launch of my first novel after all business connections between us were in the past. Not many friends like that. My books occupy an honored location on a shelf in their living room.

Two years ago, painkillers ate a hole in his digestive organs and he almost died from kidney failure. I did not know until he was out of the hospital. We talked a few times each year on the phone and exchanged a few e-mails, but all those years on the phone had given me phone-phobia and he had the same distaste for e-mail, though he was technologically advanced. If we had not lived six hours apart, we would have had coffee every day, I think. But there was that six-hour distance. When he recovered from the near-death experience and his fishing friend died, putting his boat in the water became onerous and painful, so he took up hog and deer hunting, mostly hogs.

He promised to take me because I really wanted to see how a man with only one good leg could manage successful hog hunts. He did manage, however, with the same gumption he managed everything else. What I really wanted to do most was to come to the little house he had on Padre Island and ride down the coastline in his Jeep.

Seventeen years after he called me that day to ask what I was doing at the new BD and twenty-four years into our friendship, Maggie Jo called to tell me CT was dying. Cancer. I was having coffee with a new friend when she called. I am sure the new friend was shocked at the look that came over my face and the clouds in my eyes. I told Maggie I would need time to absorb that, to get my arms around it. Forty-eight hours later, I was on his doorstep.

We talked for hours—with him still remaining calm and poised in this crisis to end all crises. There was a pain pump, installed after that episode two years earlier. I had not known. He was upbeat and his voice was strong, but his eyes reflected the hurt. Even CT was having trouble managing this level of pain. When he tired too much and it was time for me to go, I knew it might be the last time I saw him alive and I wanted to cross that bridge that men seldom set foot on, that chasm between what we feel in our hearts versus what comes out of our mouths.

I am sure my effort was stumbling, inept, as I struggled to say what this friend had meant to me and how much I admired him, to form into words the sum of a man's life from the viewpoint of someone other than family.

He set the bar high; he served without expectation of reward; he was humble; he was prosperous without losing frugality; he was generous without taking credit; and he knew the value to oneself that comes from helping others. To me, he was a true, good, and loyal friend. They should build monuments to people like CT.

CT died a few days later. (Feb. 8, 2009) I am so very sorry we never made the hog hunt and that Jeep trip along the coast.

# The Cowhill Council

COWHILL COUNCIL MEETINGS ARE pretty much always offbeat. We don't keep records, so I have to rely on memory, which is fading. I don't expect to be contradicted by any of the council members because their memories are equally poor or worse. Also, we don't really have any members—just regular guests. Nobody wants the group to be official. We do have lots of rules. In fact, we usually make new ones at least once a week. That's so we can have something to break.

Cowhill Council had no official beginning. The seeds were planted back in 1992, but didn't really take root until about 1996-1997, with irregular meetings of Jerald Thomas, Pop Thomas, and me. Jerald was and is the nucleus of the group. When Jerald went along on our covered wagon and horseback trip across Texas, the campfire gatherings every night and morning implanted the value of regular meetings back home.

We usually met on what Jerald calls The Five Acres out on highway 24/50, but just as often in his downtown coffee shop. When Pop died, Jerald's brother Ricky (disabled from a construction injury) moved out to the five acres and the meetings became regular. The Five Acres is known for being pleasant in the summer with large oak trees and a cool breeze off a small pond.

When cold weather and rain crowded us into a one room house, Jerald dragged up the top half of an old grain silo, installed windows, a brick floor, and two woodstoves (one for heat and one for cooking). My wife, Jan, made pillows for our chairs. The grain bin came complete with black marks similar to ones used to keep score in domino games. We joke that the marks represent stories told more than twice.

Imagine this—a bunch of well-seasoned gentlemen sitting under oak trees watching ducks swim on the pond or inside a grain silo drinking cappuccinos—the aroma of biscuits cooking on a woodstove—smoke billowing from the stovepipes. Soon, Jerald was bringing eight to ten drinks a day from his coffee shop and cooking biscuits for an erratic crowd. At one point, we decided the downtown square needed more cars and people and moved back to the coffee shop. One of our members (I won't say which one) cautioned us to clean up our language since we were no longer in the country. He used four expletives. We soon moved back to the country life.

The Cowhill Council is, if anything, eclectic. They say if you build it, they will come. And they did. A plumber, sales manager, housing director, builder and re-furbisher of skyscrapers, a CPA, antique dealer, coffee shop proprietor, teachers and professors, two artists, a tractor and farm equipment dealer, photographers, ministers, a novelist, financial aid director, hall of fame athlete, evangelists, team ropers, stockbrokers, fundraisers, car salesman, financial planner, psychologist, newspaper editor, authors, columnists, wannabe and real cowboys, Harley riders, carpenters, cattle ranchers, a Texas Rehab executive, real estate salesman, champion turkey caller, western wear store proprietor, bankers, lawyers, a world renowned authority on cotton gins and ginning, a drywall and ceiling tile man, a traveling evangelist, a chemical salesman, a trucking salesman, an avid hunter (with bows, arrows, and ammo), a builder of churches on at least two continents, two draftsmen, farmers real and wannabe, and several real and wannabe musicians. We were visited once by a former pro baseball player. A soon-to-be U.S. Congressman was a recent guest. We maintain his election victory was due to the visit.

Sound like a big group? Nope. Less than ten guys who had several careers and businesses—trying to find something we were good at. On a good day, five or six of us might show up. But we have been visited (more than once) by two Pulitzer Prize winners (John Knaur and Skeeter Hagler), dozens of photography students, two syndicated columnists (one several times), and two radio personalities (Tumbleweed Smith and Enola Gay). At least three of us have been featured in a Tumbleweed Smith column and/or a radio broadcast.

Last year, we lost Ricky (Jerald's brother) and two of us were involved in car wrecks. I know what you are thinking, but other drivers were at fault in both instances. I walked away unscathed from mine. Paul was not so lucky. A pickup rammed his tractor from behind as he was driving it home after doing work for his church. He was thrown from the tractor and sent skidding down the highway on his ear (literally). After two emergency helicopter flights, a couple of surgeries, and a long rehab, he's back fit as a fiddle. We are thankful the only council member who has been shot with an arrow and almost died from a deer stand fall is a survivor not only by instinct, but practice (I know you expect to hear a great hunting story about being shot with an arrow. Sorry, but he was shot on an urban street). And he says he didn't fall from that deer stand. The ladder broke.

We don't do much cooking anymore and the cappuccino was traded for coffee after Jerald closed his coffee shop. Biscuits are cooked elsewhere and warmed in the microwave. Yes, there is a microwave in the feed silo. Political candidates come (during campaign season only, of course) looking for votes, not advice. A city hall controversy brought the city manager, mayor and council members a few years back.

Some of our meetings are well, boring. Some are even sad. We talk a lot about politics, local, statewide and national. We even venture into religion on occasion, holding the contrarian belief that those are the two subjects we need to talk about most, not avoid.

Seldom do feelings get hurt. Meetings without a meaningful exchange of worthy information outnumber those where we learn valuable insights. More often than not, when Jan asks what I learned, I say, "Nothing." Of course, that could be because what happens at Cowhill Council stays at Cowhill Council.

# The Circle Is Unbroken

AS THE FOUR OF US SAT TOGETHER in Chili's I tried to visualize us as we were when we first became friends, but could not. We've all changed too much. We get together at least once a year, sometimes more. Jake lives the farthest away, so I see less of him. He grew up in Klondike, a small town that used to be much larger, but has hovered just over a hundred in population for as long as I can remember.

John is from the Shiloh community (smaller than Klondike) and has returned to his childhood home to spend the rest of his days after years in the Metroplex. I lived between Shiloh and Klondike near the old West Delta School and now live outside of Commerce about fifteen miles from our old homeplace. Charles grew up in the big metropolis of Cooper (around 2000 folks) and moved to Winnsboro many years ago. John, Jake and I went to West Delta School and we all went to high school in Cooper.

Jake and I have been friends since first grade. Our mothers worked in the sewing factory together and were also close friends. Our fathers were drinking buddies. His brother dated my sister. Another older brother was a friend of my older brother. I attended a particular church for a period of time simply because I knew Jake went there and he made me feel like I belonged when I came back from the Panhandle. We played Little League baseball together (though on separate teams). He had a terrific curve ball and was an all-around gifted athlete. You get the picture. We have history and it goes back to our beginnings.

John came along a few years later fresh from living in Italy and Japan as his family traveled with his Army father. I thought living in a whole 'nother country was pretty exotic because I had never been out of Texas but John never boasted about his world travels. We quickly became best friends. We sometimes walked the ten or twelve-mile round trip between our houses to get into mischief together or to swim in snake-infested country pools.

I had to rise most mornings before dawn to help in our dairy. John sought and took a job doing the same thing despite my warnings. We bought mopeds (a bicycle with a motor) at the same time. We talked a lot. John is irreverent and possessed of a dry wit that kept me laughing then and now. I borrowed a horse for John so he and I could play hooky on April Fools' Day and ride all the way to Pecan Gap when we were about twelve. We sometimes raced home in our cars after going out on separate dates in Cooper (not recommended).

Charles and I were enemies in high school, but became close friends about a decade later. On a wild and mischievous night when I was a senior, he threw a fist to my face that sent me tumbling and blackened the whole side of my face. His nickname in high school was Moose, for good reason. Thirty-six years later, we traveled across Texas together with him driving a covered wagon and cooking while Cousin Marion and I rode horses. He was also a client of my CPA firm and my western wear store until I sold them. He designed and built the sign that hangs at my little acreage. When he traveled with his father Dutch on another covered wagon journey to the Fort Worth Fat Stock Show, he wore a hat I had worn for months. We have history, and it's all good after we got over our high school feud.

My family moved to the Panhandle when I was a freshman, and when I came back two years later, West Delta School was closed and Jake and John had moved on with their lives at Cooper High School. They were friendly and welcoming, but things would never quite be the same.

I am the oldest of the bunch, but not by much. I graduated a year ahead of them, and we lost contact for a while after high school, although John used to fill in for me when I needed to be away from my college job as a delivery boy for City Pharmacy. After that, they went their separate ways and I went mine. Let's just say they had a lot more fun in those post high school years than I did and leave it at that. Ironically, Charles and I were the first to establish a new, adult friendship.

Among the four of us, only one parent remains. Chrystelle, John's mother, is ninety-seven. In addition to our parents, Jake lost two brothers and I lost one, all at young ages. John lost his wife, a brother, his dad, and two sisters-in-law. Charles lost both parents.

When John moved back here, he, Jake and I made a couple of trips to the State Fair, trying to rekindle boyhood memories of Rural Youth Day at the fair. It wasn't the same. As we walked the fairgrounds, one vendor beckoned us to try the newest gadget, a magnetic bracelet. He told us all the players on one super bowl team were going to wear the bracelets during the big game. The bracelets were supposed to improve balance.

He coaxed Jake and me to stand on one leg with our arms forward and one leg back with and without the bracelet. I'm not sure the bracelets made any difference, but I'm sure Jake and I looked pretty foolish. When the vendor asked John to try it, he replied with his usual dry wit, "No thanks, I don't do much of that kind of thing anymore." You had to be there to appreciate the humor.

About three years back, Charles was shredding along his pool bank when his tractor turned over and pinned him in the mud underneath—an accident that would have killed most men. He was flown to a hospital and kept unconscious for several weeks so his collapsed lungs could function again and his ribs heal. John took a picture of him in that hospital bed and sent it around to several people. When I saw it, I asked, "You take that with a phone or camera?"

He said, "Phone. Why?"

"You might want to hide it because if Charles ever sees that picture, you might have that phone shoved where the sun don't shine."

Charles said he heard angels' wings when he was down in that mud with a tractor on top of him. He appears completely healed now, but I think the brush with death somehow changed him, made him more retrospective, more aware of the fragility of life. I now have a row of weeds and grass along the bank of my pool that I call my Moose row. I no longer try to get down there with a tractor and shredder. Who knows? Maybe his accident saved my life.

So now we are what we used to consider old men. When we get together, I want to talk about what we are doing right now and what we going to do with the rest of our days to make our lives more meaningful and interesting. I fret about that more than I should, I guess. They usually want to talk over old times and laugh a lot. We have come almost full circle, so to speak. And yet, our friendships have endured. I value that.

# A Tribute to Animal Friends

The Healing Power of True Unconditional Love

> *Until one has loved an animal, part*
> *of their soul remains unawakened.*

Ever tried to sit for five minutes and think about nothing? I know the value of meditation and clearing the mind. I have been trying to get better at it for a quarter century. I have read many articles and books on the subject. The most recent one advised writing a complete description of your perfect place of peace and tranquility, recognizing that everybody's will be different, then visualizing that place each time you want to reach a meditative state. I thought about it a lot and came up with my own place.

I decided not to share everything about my special place (it's too private). I can hint there is a mountain stream and a cool, soft breeze that stirs aspens and tall pines. As I wrote my idea of a bucolic and peaceful scene, I was surprised when it included a red-tailed hawk, a crow, and almost every dog, cat, and horse I have ever owned. There are no people. It sounds like chaos, but it's not. I suppose the animals are there and not people because animals come closer than humans possibly can to perfect, unconditional love. They are just happy to be around us and expect almost nothing in return. I am happy to be loved unconditionally and to love other people unconditionally, but us humans can't reach the pinnacle of perfection. Humans can't escape (and probably shouldn't) having some expectations from other humans, no matter how much we love them. Animals come closer. I hope the following stories illustrate that.

> *There is nothing better for the inside*
> *of a man than the outside of a horse.*
>     Winston Churchill, Will Rogers,
>     Ronald Reagan and many more

# Cowboys Don't Know How to Say Goodbye

I HAVE DREAMED ABOUT YOU EVERY NIGHT since you left without my telling you goodbye. I saw you inside a trailer, looking over your shoulder at my waving, sobbing grandchildren. The miles pass, carrying you farther and farther away from your home. In my dreams, you ask me, "What did I do to deserve this? Why did you send me away with strangers? Didn't I deserve to spend the rest of my days with you?"

I don't have good answers to your questions, of course. Truth is you did everything I ever asked you to do—most of it willingly. You do deserve a good life. But you were visiting my son's family when I was asked if you were for sale. You were close enough for me to see occasionally, but not close enough for me to have to look you in the eye when I said yes. I chose pragmatism over what I saw as sentimentality. My son seemed to understand when I didn't have the courage to see you leave and didn't call until you were already gone.

Growing up on a farm, I saw lots of births and deaths: cattle, pigs, chickens, dogs, cats, you name it. I learned to suck it up and go on. My father and grandfather always told me living and dying and buying and selling are part of life, even horse life. My grandfather also said a horse that isn't being ridden needs a new home. That, if anything, is my excuse for letting you go.

You see, you and I are getting old. Yes, I know seventeen is not necessarily old for a horse, but it is me that is getting too old (or too lazy) to keep you exercised, groomed and busy. The kids weren't riding you anymore, and I was taught that a horse should never be allowed to get bored or fat. The people who bought you plan to ride and rope. I like to think you will enjoy that—that you will be healthier in your old age if you keep exercising.

Just after you left, I decided to travel back down a trail that you and I traveled together more than twelve years ago—a trip that changed my life for the better. I owe you for that ... and for so much more. As I looked at the landmarks along that trail, I had visions of you and me traveling there more than a decade earlier. Stirring those memories probably started the dreams. I have not forgotten you carried me on that long trip across part of Texas, leading a covered wagon and other riders.

You walked so fast we had to stop and wait on the others. On most days, we rode ahead to find a camp for the night and returned, making the miles you traveled more than the other horses and mules. I hobbled you at night, but you soon got the hang of hobbles and could travel with them on. But you never went far from my bedroll. I awoke most mornings to your nicker or the sound of your grazing. You could have stepped on my bedroll (and me) anytime, but you never did.

I also remember that hot day on the trail when you tried to follow me into an air-conditioned store in downtown Decatur. I remember when trucks honked as we traveled down a busy highway. You eyed them with disdain, never acknowledging their efforts to frighten you with as much as a swish of your tail. Just like when you and I and a grandkid or two rode in those parades.

And yes, I remember those earlier team penning days. During our first competition, I rode you so hard you began to shake. You stumbled and almost fell in the arena. You leaned against the side of the trailer all the way home to keep from falling. I apologized for that, but please let me say I'm sorry again.

I remember the night you had colic and fell against the barn door. I got you up and walked you into the wee hours. And when you got an infection from a shot, I trotted beside you for two miles every day for a month. But, of course, that pales when compared to what you have done for me.

Right after that trip across Texas, you and I started team roping. I could almost hear you talking way back then. You said I was too old to team rope. People told me I needed a trained roping horse if I was ever going to learn the sport. Green ropers and green horses don't mix. But I said you and I would learn together or we wouldn't learn at all. And we did.

I don't think you really liked roping, especially in those early days. But that makes it all the more important that you learned for me. I remember pulling wet pads and blankets from your back hundreds of times. I remember those moonlit nights when we crossed the creek bridge after roping under arena lights. I was angry with you on many of those nights. There was a lot of rearing and acting up on your part. You never threw me, but I did fall off once and had more than one steer drag me off. I blamed you most of the time. I belatedly learned those things were my fault, not yours. That's when we started to win.

And how about that night I left you ground-tied in the arena as we pulled horn wraps off the roping steers? You were tired and hot and decided to head to the house without me. I whistled as you headed down the lane. You stopped. I yelled, "Back up," and you retreated to the spot where I had left you. My chest swelled with pride. Who says horses can't understand humans?

I remember the look in your eyes the night we won our first saddle. You looked sort of silly, standing there with two saddles on your back. I just know you asked me, "Are you satisfied? Can we quit roping now?"

Remember that spring roundup on the great Moorhouse Ranch? We got to see real cowboys in action. You made great friends with your trailer buddy on the way out to the ranch and wouldn't let that smaller gelding out of your sight. When we threw you and the little gelding in with the Moorhouse remuda, you circled your buddy all through the night, ears pinned, daring any other horse to bite or kick your friend. As recently as a year ago, you protected the mare you shared a pasture with from a runaway stud and got yourself all cut up in the effort.

My daddy and granddaddy said every man has a right to own one really good horse in his lifetime. I have had horses almost continually since I was nine. I have never owned a perfect one. A perfect horse can spin both directions on a dime, do effortless rollbacks, stick his tail in the ground on a slide, squat like a cutter when looking at a cow, and come at a gallop every time I whistle. And the mane should always lie in place on the left side.

You weren't perfect, but you came closer to a perfect horse than I ever came to being a real cowboy. You were and always will be my great horse of a lifetime. And you helped to raise my grandkids. I have pictures of you in the book we share, and there is a nice painting of you and me on my wall. I look at that painting most days and remember. I will never forget.

Goodbye, old friend.

I found some solace and assuagement of guilt in these words from Waddie Mitchell, cowboy bard—when he performed with Don Edwards and the Fort Worth Symphony Orchestra. The CD is called *A Prairie Portrait*.

> *For horses and dogs and good cowboys have hearts*
>    *full of gumption and try,*
> *They're chuck full of grit and don't know how to quit*
>    *but they don't know the concept goodbye...*
> *For horses and dogs and good cowboys don't know*
>    *how to tell you a lie*
> *Just don't take it wrong when one day they're gone*
> *Tain't in 'em to tell you goodbye.*

# Men and Cats

SHE HAD A ROUGH START IN THIS LIFE—her mother killed by a car—she and her siblings forced to fend for themselves before they were finished nursing—hiding in abandoned buildings, crossing dangerous alleyways, depending on bag ladies and the kindness of strangers for sustenance.

Then she came to us. Jan had been after me to get her a pet. I had my horse, after all, and our dog Rivers had been gone for a few years. Friend Jerald captured her in one of his downtown buildings. Said she was the pick of the litter because she was a tuxedo cat—black with a white tie at her throat and a spot of white on her belly. He brought the kitty to us in a box. I knew next to nothing about cats and neither did Jan. I have always been a horse and dog person and Jan a dog person. We had cats when I was a boy, but they were barn cats. My contacts with them only came when I milked our jersey and the barn cats begged me to send a spray or two their way. They followed me and the milk bucket back to the house, but at a respectable distance. Touching one would get you scratched.

No animals of any kind were allowed in our house when I was growing up. Jan was unsure about this little kitty and I was highly reluctant. I intended to ignore the situation as much as possible and hope she didn't disrupt my life too much. We agreed that we would put her on the covered porch in a little house we bought for her and let her stay outside as soon as she was big enough to fend for herself. Because of her green eyes, Jan named her Jade.

I read somewhere that a woman can pet a horse and her heartbeat will match the horse's within ten seconds. Jade worked the same magic on Jan right away. She was a calming influence and Jan loved everything she did. There were a few problems with owning a cat in the beginning, but nothing serious. She usually ate inside, but quickly asked to be let out. When the first catfight occurred in the dark, we moved her into the utility room at nights.

When she was still a kitten, I came home one night green with nausea and a bad headache and went directly to bed. In a few minutes, I felt something under the covers with me. I knew it was her, and that she was not allowed on the bed, but was too sick to do anything about it. Jade made her way to the top, stuck her head out, laid it down in the hollow of my neck, and purred. I think she knew I was sick.

The next morning, she lay down on my bare feet when I was shaving. I knew she had me then. The head butts and rubbing against my leg cemented it. When Jan told friends and family the cat had captured my heart, I told them it was hard not to love something that seemed to love you. I referred to her as a wily seductress, a regular femme fatale.

During the first year, I would see her peeking out from the shrubbery or ground cover as I drove off in the mornings. I couldn't shake the feeling it might be the last time I ever saw her. Jan felt the same way. Jade takes risks and loves the outdoors. But her early life prepared her for survival.

She likes dark, tight, and protected spots, so she spends a lot of time under our old barn, in trees, and hidden in the weeds along our fence line. She befriends skunks, possums, raccoons and some stray cats (fighting or

running from others). We were outside one day when she walked alongside a mother raccoon as she moved her young ones from the barn to a tree nest. Jade repeated the trip with each new baby.

She likes to go out before daylight and come back in after dark. We worry when we hear coyotes howl as she steps out, wondering if she will return. The first night she did not come home, Jan fretted by the window until close to midnight. Jade finally limped home. She had apparently been trapped by a predator and had to leap from barn rafters to escape.

I never knew before Jade that cats growl. Jade growls when any strange animal enters anywhere on our nine acres. She knows where the fence lines are and never ventures far outside them. She is very afraid of strangers and hides outside when we have guests. If she gets trapped inside when they arrive, she stays under the bed until the guests leave.

Our friends, and especially our children, are amazed I allow this cat in the house. During one holiday celebration, she stayed under the bed about as long as she could, finally emerging before our family left. She slinked her way around the perimeter of the room to reach my chair and jumped on my knee. I imagined her announcing to the others, "I belong to him. So don't mess with me." I only learned later she was saying, "He belongs to me."

Her conquest of me is now complete. She usually finds me when I go outside, turns on her back in front of me for a belly rub. I can't get past her, so her request for affection forces me to pause and be tender. Jan loves the time Jade spends with her in her quilt house, but much to her chagrin, Jade seems to prefer my lap when she's in the living room, probably because I have saved her from so many catfights and predators. And she almost always responds (eventually) to my whistle when it's time to come home.

She comes and goes as she pleases now, but still spends most days outside. She knows how to ask to get out and which door she prefers. She asks that you accompany her to the utility room to eat. She does all sorts of endearing things, like slapping my cheeks with her paws when I do sit-ups.

I don't know if cats can experience the true emotion of love, but it's a sure thing they can experience trust. Jade trusts me and that gives me a warm feeling. I won't let her down.

# Why I Ride

### *Shooter's Story*

AS I WAS STRUGGLING THROUGH *Why I Write* by George Orwell, someone thought I said "why I ride" when I mentioned the book's title. Almost daily, I ask myself why I write, but I also ask myself why I ride. On hot August mornings, that question comes up as I struggle up the small incline leading from the creek to the stalls and barn, leading Shooter with a piece of string. I taught him not to run away when I approach (the carrot helps), but he only occasionally comes when I whistle. He knows it's too hot to ride and won't run up and volunteer.

So why do I do it? I have all sorts of answers, but none satisfy me. The truth is; I dread it, especially on cold or hot mornings and on mornings when I have low energy or hurt in the wrong places. I try to be thankful that I can still walk up that hill and keep pace with Shooter. When I swing the saddle across his back, trying to ignore the pain in my left arm and shoulder, I feel a little better. When I step in the stirrup and throw my leg across the saddle, better still.

But the next day, I dread it again. And if I skip two days, it's drudgery to go back. So why? First, there's the thing about taking care of animals you own. It always bothered me to see a young horse just stand in the pasture and get fat. Their manes and tails usually need attention, their coats get dull, flies and other pests fly around their eyes and leave welts. They get stiff. They turn into decorations rather than useful companions. And of course, horseback riding is good exercise for me. But I could burn an equal amount of calories in the time it takes to catch him, groom him, saddle and bridle him, bathe and feed him.

I can also hear my Papa Hiram (yes, he's Papa Griff from the *Follow the Rivers* series of books) asking from long, long ago, "*Ride that horse today, Bolivar?*" And then there's Teadon (Daddy, yes, he's Rance) saying, "*A man does what he knows is right, whether he feels like it or not.*" When I ride, I remember them both and think about the sacrifices my parents must have made so that I could have a horse as a boy.

And then there are the saddles. I rode bareback as a boy and wanted a saddle so much it hurt. I fear it has made me gluttonous about them. I own too many. Like old men, saddles crack and get stiff from lack of use. Riding keeps them supple and moist and it's a lot more pleasant to clean and oil a saddle that's used than one that's not (it's another strange mental thing).

I wouldn't even have a horse if things had gone as planned. Still in grief over losing Rowdy, I thought I had owned my last one, but a friend needed a place to wean a colt with good bloodlines. I volunteered. It was good weather, and I soon began to teach him to lead, then to lunge in a round pen, and pretty soon I knew I had to finish one last horse. Before he wore his first saddle, I owned him.

He's pretty enough as horses go, got good conformation. He's not the most athletic or talented horse I've ever owned, but he is the most affectionate. He likes people and sometimes I think he especially likes me. Neighbors bring him apples on their daily walks. He's obedient; stands where he's left without being tied. I never tie him to saddle and brush him and I leave him totally naked while I put up the tack. He turns, stands in the right spot, and waits patiently for his bath, then follows me to the open gate without as much as a string. I feel better as I see him walk out into the pasture, all clean from a bath, "legged up" and muscled out, his eyes clear, his coat glossy, doctored for flies and pests.

But he's a strange combination of gentleness and spookiness. He's afraid of the oddest things. Big trucks; yard windmills that make loud noises; cars honking; no problem. But chickens scare him and we pass by a chicken ranch on one the many routes we take. I think it's sensory overload. First the smell, then the shallow creek we have to cross, the overhanging branches, then a sea of chicken tents. Yes, I said tents—big white ones. Who wouldn't be frightened?

He's also scared of puddles left after a rain, any movement in woods or weeds made by things unseen by me, little blue flowers, and anything that wasn't there the last time we came that way. I finally cured him of his fear of big rolls of hay (yes, he was afraid of the big bales).

He knows every detail of every trail. If anything is askew, added, or out of place, he comes to a dead stop and wants to turn back home—quickly. This can be disconcerting when you are in a pretty fast lope and he comes to a quick stop on his front feet without warning. I have never fallen, but have found myself across his neck or shoulder more than once if I don't see the object before he does. I hope Jan is not reading this.

In my younger days, it would have embarrassed and irritated me to no end that a horse I trained acted this way. He would have been punished until he learned to behave. I tried that. But I have decided that Shooter simply cannot help being afraid. When I first started training him, I kept a log as a reminder of the steps he needed to complete so he could be a finished horse. It gave me a sense of accomplishment as I checked off leading, lunging, saddling, mounted walking and loping, jumping barrels and rails, sidepasses, backing up, etc. But when we went outside our pasture, it was like starting all over again.

Because of the log, I know he has ridden by the chicken ranch more than three hundred times, but he's still a little skittish every time we pass.

He no longer comes to a stop and tries to turn back, but if someone has left a stack of wood beside the road or a limb has fallen, look out. I think only age will cure his fright.

When I first started my riding ritual, I was terribly bored (Shooter's skittishness did not relieve boredom). I blame team roping and team penning. After you have competed using a horse and rope with cattle, ridden across Texas, participated on short roundups and cattle drives, riding alone down the road ain't much. Sorta like giving up. Growing old.

But now, I try to put a different spin on it. For one thing, I have discovered about a dozen alternate routes to ride. Thanks to a friendly neighbor, I ride in wooded areas a lot. I know most of the trails my neighbor has cut through the deep woods. I can ride all the way to the river, see lots of wild animals, even a few I can't identify, but mostly pigs and deer, even an occasional fox (Shooter is alert to them, but they don't bother him as much as blue flowers or lizards).

Yes, Jan frets, and I guess I think about it a little, being out there all alone where vehicles could not reach me in case of emergency. Heck, it might take a day or two and a few good bloodhounds to find me.

Then there are those rare days when I feel myself "take a deep seat" in the saddle—the times when I return to those days of yore when I was nine; when I rode my little mare bareback; the days when I discovered I could control her with my seat, thighs, calves, and heels and by little flicks of three fingers of each hand on the reins; that she and I could lean into the turns together and I felt as if I could scoop up Mother Earth with a free hand; the days before I developed a fear of falling; the days when I achieved what Tom Dorrance called "true unity."

Of course, I was too young to know what I had achieved. I felt like Little Beaver, but I wanted a saddle so I could emulate great cinema cowboys like Joel McCrea, Ben Johnson, and my mother's favorite (yes, she's Mattie in my books), Dale Robertson. Remember *Tales of Wells Fargo* and that commercial he did for Pall Mall where he rides up fast and steps off his horse? "That's my horse. That's Jubilee." Many decades later, a little filly was born on my place. I named her Jubilee. I met Dale in Ruidoso a few years ago. He was selling autographed photos of his Wells Fargo days. We lost him a few months back.

When I return home, I take Shooter through a few rituals. He backs pretty good, can spin reasonably well both ways, is clumsy on rollbacks, and he knows the last thing we do is to run full speed to the barn and make a good stop on his back feet beside the horse stall we never use. That's when I start to feel good—when it becomes worthwhile. I think he feels better, too. When we miss a few days, he comes up and hangs his head over the fence and stares at me. Of course, that could be for a carrot.

And I occasionally ride the four miles to Cowhill Council, where a few well-seasoned friends gather for coffee by a pond with ducks, under big oaks. I have also discovered a few hidden meadows in other pastures, places where one can commune with nature.

I presented a program about my books a few months ago and someone in the audience asked if I still rode. I told them most of what I just told you. I told them it was an almost daily ritual. As I was leaving that evening, a lady about ten years my senior rushed to open the door for me. She gave me a penetrating, almost disconcerting look and said, "It's not a ritual thing; it's a spiritual thing. I see you taking off your hat and putting it over your heart, getting down on one knee all alone in those woods, and talking to Jesus."

Now how did she know that?

# Authors, Singers, and Songwriters

*Balance—the Elusive Elixir of Life*

During the decades I spent trying to build muscle in the left side of my brain, I always admired those who were strong on the other side, the creative side. When I began to write, I noticed songwriters and poets could tell a story in seventy words that might take me seven hundred or more (and their words rhymed). When their words are set to music, it seems a writer like me is unable to compete. Of course, this was back in the good old days when songs did tell stories.

As I try to build mind pictures for my readers, I often hear inspiring background music in my head and wish I could put that music in my words. When I see a book converted to a movie done well, I envy the music and cinematography that can thrill us, inspire us, fill us with emotion and make us overflow. Writers only have the written word on a printed page, and nowadays, on the screen of the latest gadget.

Remember that sweeping panoramic view of Montana mountains and valleys at the end of *The Horse Whisperer* as Tom Booker watches Annie Maclean drive away to music that tugs at our heartstrings? We writers try to achieve that affect in at least one or two scenes (some try to do it on every page), but we just don't have the visual effects and the sound. Still, if there had been no novel, no screenplay, there would have been no movie, no soundtrack, no music. Words always come first, and we can take comfort in that.

Writing has introduced me to a lot of authors and people who spent their lives concentrating on the right side, the creative side. Many were born with a strong right brain and sometimes, they let the left atrophy. But I also found many old cowboys, drywall men, painters, and other sorts we usually think of as left-brained and pragmatic, writing, reciting and singing poetry and songs. I seem to always seek these folks out. It seems to me they may have found balance, the elusive elixir of life.

# Searching for a Reclusive Author

### *Notes from My Journal about a Trip I Made to Tennessee*

LEFT IN JEEP WITH THE TOP DOWN IN JULY heat headed for Hohenwald, Tennessee. I hoped to meet and visit with author William Gay. I read his *Provinces of Night* and was mesmerized. When I saw a photo of the author beside a crude painted poster of Jimmie Rodgers, I knew there had to be some type of connection between us. I had heard he was somewhat reclusive, so my chances were doubtful. To give my pragmatic left brain an excuse for chasing such a wild goose, I told it I was going to do some family history research. My maternal great-grandparents came from Maury, Tennessee.

Spent first night in a real fleabag motel. A driving overnight rainstorm (6 inches) filled the Jeep floorboards overnight. Yes, I had a cover, but it just served as a funnel to pour water inside the Jeep. I pulled into a covered service station bay and managed to get the top up and Velcro the side windows in the pre-dawn dark.

Jeep windows fogged up quite a bit as the temp dropped about thirty degrees when I headed into the mountains. Discovered ballpoint pens had rolled off and blocked defroster. Smoke boiled out of tall trees as temperature dropped. Road very winding, up and down and I was constantly threatened with log trucks, but held my own. Jeep handled well. Kudzu everywhere. Must have crossed six or seven rivers including the Beech. Crossed the Tennessee River on Alvin York Bridge (hero of First World War) from Tennessee. Over Coon Creek, Rushing Creek, etc.

Finally made it to Hohenwald and checked into only motel in town. Pretty crummy and worn out, but paradise compared to first night. Took the precaution of examining the room before I gave up my credit card this time. Also checked for ice machine, which was second only to cleanliness in importance. Don't need chocolates on my pillow, but I require ice.

Next morning, I drove down to old house that had been converted into coffee shop/bookstore just off the square. Looked for William Gay's books and did not find a one. Asked owner about him and the guy turned up his nose and told me to ask his wife. When I did, she just said, "He's a hermit." They told me he had moved to another part of the county. Hohenwald is in Lewis County (named for Explorer Meriwether Lewis, who is buried here).

Went to Chamber of Commerce and picked up some info. and maps. Nice lady there said Gay comes to library quite often, but is reclusive and strange. Of course, I already knew that from seeing pictures of him and from reading his stuff. Made me want to meet him even more. Said she would give my cell number to lady at library when she returned. Maybe she could help.

I drove up to Columbia, Tennessee, county seat of Maury County, where my maternal grandmother was born. Had to almost strip and give up my pocket knife to get into courthouse where county clerk (called by different title there) seemed unfamiliar with the concept of marriage licenses and birth certificates. Finally, someone told me archives were kept in the old jail across the street. Great old restored building and helpful people there. Found marriage license for great-grandparents. Their old farm is now a state park in Maury County and in Marshall County, (Lewisberg County Seat), Nathan Bedford Forrest (Civil War Hero) memorial is also on their old farm. Satisfied to have accomplished at least something, I headed back to Hohenwald, taking a little side trip on Natchez Trace Parkway. Very, very, nice Jeep ride. Close to Choctaw country and more ancestors.

Back in Hohenwald, I learned it's common practice to name roads for residents, so I located William Gay Road in late afternoon. Only one house on the road's dead end. BEWARE OF DOG and TRESPASSERS WILL BE SHOT AND SURVIVORS PROSECUTED signs. Dogs would not let me get out and knock. They literally tried to chew the tires off my Jeep and tried to jump inside (the top was down), so I turned around and came back disappointed. Wish I could have taken a picture, but camera was back in motel room. The house was built with rough-hewn timber, not logs, and had several different types of rusted sheet metal on the roof. Gay was a carpenter by trade, so I wondered if he had built it. Interesting place. Would love to have seen the inside. I settled for a Jeep ride through Tennessee Hill Country and lucked on Grinders Creek, a place mentioned often in Gay's novels. Looks just like he described in his book.

The next day, I walked downtown to the chamber again and found the librarian had called Gay on my behalf. The reclusive author told her he might call me. Went to library and the librarian gave up his correct number (after I gave her one of my own books.) I called. He confirmed he had tried to call me but lady had given him one digit wrong on number. Told me to drive on out to his house. Seems his wife divorced him and took the house on William Gay Road.

Followed his directions to Little Swan Creek. His house is up a slight hill before the bridge that crosses the creek. He shares a road with other folks that live up the hill behind him. William Gay looks like what he was most of his life, a drywall man who may have drunk and smoked a little too much. However, this drywall man is brilliant. Hair hangs in ringlets as if it had never seen a comb, over his collar but not as long as I have seen in pictures of him.

House is logs with red metal roof. Nice enough, but he has not abandoned his hillbilly heritage. An abandoned pickup sits in front of a small shop, the bed full of V-8 cans and assorted trash. Think he was sipping V-8 the whole time I talked to him, alternating with drags on cigarettes. Said he and his son are trying to quit. Interesting that I also consume a lot of V-8. End of his left index finger has been pinched off. Mine, too.

Room filled with books. Hundreds. Fireplace and woodstove in the room, but no overhead light. Room very dark (just like I like my office). Paintings scattered here and there. (Yes, he paints, too.) A few guitars and a few books on how to compose music. Big books on Van Gogh art and lots of DVDs and all kinds of art books. While he talked on phone to his daughter, I perused the shelves and found our tastes a lot alike, especially in movies. (I offered to leave so he could talk in private, but he motioned for me to stay).

I kept offering to end my intrusion on his privacy, but he urged me to stay and talk. We talked about his writing and some funny stories. I told him the scene with Albright and the hog was the funniest I ever read. Asked him about characters in *Provinces of Night,* Fleming, E. W. and Boyd, etc. Told me he was a little bit Fleming (a seventeen-year-old boy), a little bit Boyd (the boy's father), and a little bit E. W. (the grandfather). Same answer I give when people ask me if I am Jake in my books.

He had a director's chair with the name of his

book of short stories on it. They made a movie recently based on one of the stories in *Hate to See That Evening Sun Go Down.* Hal Holbrook plays the old man. I have since seen the movie and really enjoyed it.

He got a call from his agent while I was there about another book *Twilight.* It has been optioned for a movie, also. Don't like it as well as *Provinces,* but still a very good read. After my visit, I learned *Provinces* would be made into a movie starring Kris Kristofferson called *Bloodworth.* I also learned his publisher for *The Lost Country* is having trouble and holding up its publication.

I told him I had written him in the first part of 2007 after reading

*Provinces.* Said that was about the time his wife kicked him out and he never got the letter. He seemed impressed I brought along a copy. He's won numerous prestigious awards, primarily for his magazine short stories, but also for his books. He's a visiting writing scholar at Sewanee, University of the South. *Oxford American* magazine commissioned him to write an article about his experiences going to a college campus as a scholar when he never attended college. He has read himself into brilliance. Though I expect there was something genetic going on, too.

A lady in town asked him if he got help with his writing. He asked, "What kind of help?"

She said, "Well, your people was never very smart and you wasn't either. Figured you got some help."

Based on his stories, his family was both poor and violent, doing everything wrong to excess. Although he had a huge appetite for books and magazines and regularly entered writing contests, he followed the same path as the rest of the family for most of his life until he started winning competitions for his stories.

I was a reader as a kid, but always felt guilty about it and never read any heavy stuff unless I had to. Wish someone had told me reading was never a waste of time. I recall reading a comic book (we called them funny books) when Daddy ran a service station in Commerce. I was about ten and was supposed to watch the front while daddy did some mechanic work in the garage behind. A customer went to get him because he could not get my attention to take his money. Daddy had to shake me I was so engrossed in reading what was probably a comic book. Don't think that has happened before or since, but I get the impression William Gay lived his life inside books because his outside life was so bad.

I praised him for the dialect in his writing because I consider it perfect. He said he listened to folks around there a lot. Recently, a man on a construction job complained, "My old lady ain't put a hot meal on the table in weeks. The bitch will be laying on her ass when I get home tonight." When asked what he would do if she did have a hot meal, he replied. "I won't eat a damn bite." I found that hilarious and so typical.

I told him I had met Flannery O'Connor once when she came to ET. He asked which year and I said 62 or 63. I think he was trying to catch me in a made-up story, because he knew she died in 64 at 39. He asked if she was frail when I saw her. He said he had always wanted to meet her. He told me of many writers who had influenced his writing and life, including a fellow who wrote stories for the *Progressive Farmer* magazine. Gay has an incredible memory for authors and book titles. Wish I did. I can remember details inside books, but have trouble with titles and authors.

I left after a couple of hours and drove up the Natchez Trace toward Nashville. Got off a little early and headed toward Grinders Switch (home of Minnie Pearl). There is a water tower and an abandoned depot, but little else there. Really great Jeep ride though the winding hills and across winding railroad track. Back down through pretty mountain scenery and to Hohenwald by bedtime. A good day.

---

William Gay first came to the Sewanee Writers Conference in 1999 as a Tennessee Williams Scholar. Later that year, Gay published his first novel, *The Long Home*, which received the James A. Michener Memorial Prize. Gay returned to Sewanee in 2000 as a Walter A. Dakin Fellow and served as the Tennessee Williams Fellow for the 2000-2001 academic year. Gay then published another novel, *Provinces of Night*, and a collection of stories, *I Hate to See That Evening Sun Go Down*, which contained stories that had been published in the *Missouri Review*, *Georgia Review*, *Oxford American*, *Atlantic Monthly*, and *Harper's*. His stories have also been anthologized in *Best American Short Stories*, *New Stories from the South*, *O. Henry Awards Prize Stories*, *Best New American Voices*, and *Best American Mystery Stories*. In 2006, he published his third novel, *Twilight*, and was named a USA Ford Foundation Fellow by United States Artists. In 2010, MacAdam/Cage will publish his new novel, *The Lost Country*.

---

NOTE: Gay died before his last novel was published. Nobody has found his last manuscript (or will admit to it.)

# Golightly, Annie

I HAD HEARD OF HER BEFORE, BUT THE first time I saw her was in my yard on a warm summer day. She walked around, casting a critical but not judgmental eye on our place in the country that we call Bar Nun Ranch. It's not really a ranch, of course. Not big enough. But I think Annie liked what she saw. I was expecting her and hailed her from the metal-roofed building I call my office. Jan calls it the White House.

She drove the few yards in her new bright-red Ford half-ton with fancy wheels and all the accessories that cowboys tend to prefer. I found out later her hair had been jet black, but it was now white and pulled back in a severe pony-tail. Tall, but beginning to stoop slightly, she wore jeans and a white western shirt and ivory ostrich boots with riding heels. I don't pay much attention to jewelry, but I recall she had on a lot of turquoise. When she extended her hand and shook mine firmly and warmly with a bright smile, I knew we would be friends, but I didn't know the half of Annie's story. Still don't, but I know more than some.

Her reputation preceded her. My in-laws knew her and a lot of folks just older than me remembered growing up with her around Fairlie, Yowell, and Commerce. The mere mention of her name to any of those people always elicited a smile and a story or two of her young and wild days as Ann Milford. Her brother was the famous Dallas weatherman and later congressman, Dale Milford. Everybody around here was proud that he was one of our own when we saw him on television every weeknight. But five minutes into our conversation, I suspected Annie was nothing like her brother.

Annie loved my rustic office because, of course, it is about as cowboy as I could make it. She handed me a business card that said, "Painter of Portraits, Poet/Writer, Umbrella Fixer, Goat Roper, Fry Cook, Grandma, Bootlegger, Part Time Cab Driver, Full Time Texan." I thought it was a joke, but it wasn't. I was particularly interested in that part about painting. The red pickup just happened to hold a couple of large portraits she had painted. One was of a 911 first-responder that would bring tears to a grown man's eyes. I'm no art critic, but I knew she was talented. That first meeting planted the seeds of a friendship that has blossomed over the years. I knew she had owned at least two night clubs, but did not know she had performed in "The Best Little Whorehouse in Texas" at Casa Manana and that she was a nominee for the Cowgirl Hall of Fame.

Annie was coming to see me about a manuscript she had written. Terry Mathews, now Arts and Entertainment Editor for the *Sulphur Springs News Telegram*, caused our paths to cross. Annie had participated (that word is too lightweight) in what became known as the Great American Cattle Drive of 1995. Her manuscript told of her adventures as the only woman drover on the drive. She had held her own with cowboys (all younger than her) all the way from Fort Worth, Texas, to Miles City, Montana, a journey of some eighteen-hundred miles and six months. As a veteran of my own horseback and covered wagon trip across Texas, I was impressed. We had traveled less than a quarter of that distance and we didn't have 300 head of longhorn cattle and over a hundred horses to keep moving. And Annie was nearly sixty-four when the drive began.

I suspected her drive was well-financed and the participants were borderline coddled on the trip. I learned better. They endured rain, sleet, hail, high winds, a tornado, extremes of both heat and cold, and lack of funds. Worse, they endured homesickness, frustration, disappointments, and dissension. We had none of the latter and few of the former on our trip. Bad weather pales in comparison to dissension. But Annie persevered.

Annie is an unabashed lover of cowboys and everything remotely related to their lifestyle—makes no bones about it. She told me later that such unconditional love had delivered a lot of joy but also more than a few heartaches and trouble. I learned that she was once-divorced and twice-widowed. Done with changing her last name, she took the name Golightly on a dance-floor whim. I don't recall who her dance partner was when she made that decision. She lost one house by flood, another by fire, but still managed to get all five kids raised.

During the time we worked together on her book, I learned she was not only famous in our small corner of Northeast Texas, but it seemed almost everyone in the town "Where the West Begins" knew her, too. Her father was Cherokee and the heritage is so evident she became known in Fort Worth as "The Singing Savage." She had performed for two American Presidents and two foreign ones, Governor and Mrs. John Connally, Arnold Palmer, Nelson Rockefeller, Gene Autry, Roy Rogers, Slim Pickens, Chuck Connors, to name a few. She had performed with Tom T. Hall, Rex Allen, Rosemary Clooney (for you young folks—that's George's aunt), Ace Reid, Arthur Duncan, among others. She completed her degree in English and Creative Writing at Texas Wesleyan University at age sixty-three.

She was also one of the most cooperative authors I ever worked with. And she knew how to market her work. Her friend Mike Cochran wrote the foreword to her book. Mike is a journalist retired from Associated Press and the *Fort Worth Star-Telegram* who has been nominated for the Pulitzer three times, authored five books, won six Headliner awards, and the Texas Institute of Letters Stanley Walker Journalism Award (twice). Another friend of Annie's and columnist for the *Star-Telegram*, the late Jim Trinkle, said of Annie, "There is a happy, vibrant quality to songs as Annie sings them. Audiences...are moved by her personal magnetism."

When *Dreams and A White Horse* was published less than a year after that first meeting, I learned Annie knew folks at Billy Bob's (world's largest honky-tonk) and managed to arrange a signing there. She generously requested (make that insisted) that I bring along my own books to sell. I needed no persuading. I had listened to her CDs, but finally cajoled her to sing a song or two that night in Billy Bob's, a night I will never forget.

It was to be the last time I would hear her sing and play. A stroke stopped all that. It affected her peripheral vision and she had to stop driving. She had trouble with one arm working like it used to. She had to give up the pickup of her dreams and leave her beloved Fort Worth to be near her daughter. She can no longer paint and has to hunt and peck on the keyboard.

I dropped by to see her in Corsicana a short while back and spent a terrific afternoon. She talked frankly about her health problems but refused to let them get her down. She was filled with gratitude for the life she had and the life she had left, for the love and support of family and friends. She still possessed the dogged determination that caused her to rise to the challenge of participating in a long trail drive after being told women would not be allowed to serve as drovers.

And did I mention she's a good cook? I keep a jar of her plum jelly in my office refrigerator, saving it only for special occasions because Annie told me there would not be any more. I hope she's wrong about that.

---

POSTSCRIPT: I write my postings days, sometimes weeks, even months, in advance of publication. I wrote the rough draft of this one on February 24, 2012. I added the final touches to it at 3:30 P.M., February 28. I planned to call Annie and read it to her before posting the first week of March. At 5:22 P.M. on February 28, I got an e-mail that appeared to be from Annie, a very rare occurrence. It was her address, but not from Annie. The e-mail was from Annie's family. She died at 3:23, seven minutes before I finished the final edits on the article. She insisted that there be no funeral, no memorial service, only to be remembered by family and friends. She will be. She donated her body to science. That's so Annie. She knew, I expect, when she told me there would be no more jelly.

# Life Is a Stallion

## She Rode to the Whistle

I FIRST SAW THE ATTRACTIVE YOUNG WIFE of a new doctor in town when I was working my way through college as a soda jerk and delivery boy at City Pharmacy in Commerce. She came in fairly often with a few of her friends to have a mid-afternoon coffee or cherry Coke.

I don't recall when I learned she had been stricken with a terrible disease, but I do recall being told she was only expected to live a few years. I remember the morbid prophesy, "She won't ever see forty." Whoever said that didn't really know Brenda Black White.

I had no contact with Brenda after I finished college, even though I eventually returned to Commerce. Decades passed before she was kind enough to call me one day after *Biscuits Across the Brazos* was published. She had a lot of nice things to say about the little book and I could tell I was talking to a sassy, but classy lady. But she was in a wheelchair by then.

She came to one of the outdoor stews we had on our little ranch and that was the first time I saw what scleroderma had done to her. A character in my second novel is afflicted with the disease and I did a lot of research on this cruel malady that has no known cause or cure. It usually attacks the skin, making the face appear as a taut mask, but it also attacks the organs, leads to respiratory problems, bone and muscle pain, digestion difficulties, and dental problems.

Brenda endured most, if not all, that scleroderma inflicts. She was confined to a wheelchair and had to use the eraser end of a pencil to turn pages in a book or type on her computer. But she fought with all the weapons available to her. She did her research, and knew what those weapons were.

When I began writing in earnest, my friend and mentor Fred Tarpley got me into several projects I never intended to pursue (most of which I am grateful for). One of those was publishing. Publishing novels and memoirs was one thing, but if anyone had ever told me I would publish a book of poetry, I would have laughed. Not because I have an aversion to poetry, but because I know little about it, certainly not how to edit it. Fred assured me we could handle it.

He put me in touch with Brenda again. I hadn't seen her in five or six years, and didn't know she was a published poet who had achieved notoriety by reading her work in places as far away as New York. I read her *Callahan County* book of poems. Her often edgy, sometimes humorous, frequently dark, always deeply felt verses provoke a range of emotions. And you knew every word came from her heart. One line would make you laugh, the next might make you cry or cringe.

She invited me over for tea one afternoon and I'm ashamed to admit that I dreaded it. I told her I didn't drink much hot tea, so she lured me with key lime pie. Her disabilities embarrassed me at first, but five minutes after I sat down, she had me laughing. I forgot her severe handicaps. She asked what kind of music I liked, what books I read. The conversation was stimulating and punctuated with a lot of laughter. When I left, she gave me a card with her doctrine for living expressed in her poem called "Life."

> *Life is a stallion*
> *And I'm on a real bitch.*
> *The ride would be smoother*
> *If he didn't buck and pitch.*
> *But I'm on till the whistle*
> *And tied to the hitch.*
> *And I'll ride this wild bastard*
> *Till he throws me in the ditch.*

A week later, she downloaded about three dozen songs she thought I would like to three CDs. I dropped by for the CDs and some ice cream chocolate pie.

Brenda and Fred organized another book of her poems. When we began the publishing process, I could never get her to agree on a cover. The image, of course, was a table set up for tea. With each interpretation offered, Brenda found something not to like. The tablecloth was a quarter inch too short, the flowers not just right, the color not rich enough. I pushed her at first, but finally stepped back and let her work with the designer and gave them a deadline. They met it. Her book is called *The Thing About Me.* She planned another tea party to celebrate.

Fred referred to her gatherings as "High Teas." I will never forget the last one. Dr. Michael Johnson, an author and speaker Brenda simply called Cowboy arrived with me. It was hot, and I wore one of my best colored t-shirts, Wranglers faded and washed to a nice softness, and well-broken-in boots.

Michael had on a dusty black cowboy hat and his usual starched jeans and shirt with boots, of course. When we walked in, Brenda was already holding literary court with Dr. Fred Tarpley, well known author, editor, linguist and professor (and my publishing partner and editor). Also present was professor, author and publisher Dr. Charles Linck. When Dr. James Conrad arrived, we all congratulated him on his award from the Texas Institute of Letters for his most recent book. I felt a little rough-around-the-edges in this gathering of literary legends.

Brenda offered us vanilla-rum tea and our choice of key lime pie, chocolate ice cream pie, or cheesecake. Victoria, her caregiver, served it all accompanied by a rather stern visage. Michael excused himself and I smiled as I watched him (from my seat at the literary table) lean over the bathroom sink to wash the snuff out of his mouth. I felt out of my element, but comfortable because Brenda was there and I knew my presence as her publisher was a command performance.

I remember looking around the room and trying to imagine what this eclectic group might have looked like in a situation comedy. What a sight we must have made with our vastly different backgrounds and interests, sipping tea, eating pie and cookies, all under Brenda's watchful eye. She brought us all together, stimulated the conversations, directed the event as if it were a stage play.

The title poem's first lines tell a lot about Brenda.

> *The Thing about me*
> *Is that I'm always falling in love*
> *With men, women, little kids, everybody and everything*
> *Butterflies, sunsets, clouds, daisies*
> *Birds, books, music, movies*
> *But mainly people.*

When *The Thing About Me* was ready for print, I wrote this message in the front as a note from the publisher:

> *Brenda Black White faces more adversity in a day than most of us do in a lifetime. She does it with aplomb and raw courage. When much is taken away, much is given in return. The bucking and pitching of her life has given Brenda a wider range of sensitivity and experience. In her own words, she is "on till the whistle and tied to the hitch," and her poems reflect tenderness and deep awareness of the blessings and curses of an unusually wild ride. Brenda says, "I'll ride this wild bastard till I'm thrown in the ditch"... and she will. Brenda's poems are full of grit and sass expertly blended with romance and a deep appreciation of everyday life. Her writing can be tender and gentle, but also raw, gutsy, and lusty. Be ready.*

# The Bard and the Balladeer
## God Winks

I OCCASIONALLY PRESENT A PROGRAM called "When Coincidences Ain't." Squire Rushnell has written a series of books about *When God Winks*. This story is about a series of coincidences that weren't, or Godwinks. It begins like most good stories do—a good friend or loved one does or says a little something that makes your life better in a small or big way. I have discovered it may be weeks, months or even years before we realize the full positive impact of a small good deed. That's the case of my relationship with the Bard and the Balladeer.

Friend Jerald Thomas brought me a CD (or was it a cassette?) back in the early nineties from Canton, his home away from home and location of the world's largest flea market. The album was titled *Saddle Songs* and featured the voice of Don Edwards. I had never heard of him, but I pitched it onto the console of my pickup so I would be reminded to play it.

I was a road warrior in those days, spending a lot of time in cars and airplanes, so I listened to a lot of music as I traveled. I looked forward to hearing what I hoped might be at least one good cowboy song on this new album. Though I had enjoyed cowboy music since I was a child listening to my grandfather play the fiddle, the genre had always been a distant second to old country. And I mean old country going all the way back to Jimmie Rodgers. The cowboy songs I grew up with had too many clichés like "git along little doggie." More importantly, they often didn't tell a story. And I always covered my eyes when Gene or Roy or Rex broke into song when they should have been doing more manly things.

New country has almost no appeal to me. It no longer reflects its rural roots and too many songs just repeat the same tired verses. I have supplanted new country with mountain music. But Don Edwards's songs were different—a combination of Eddy Arnold's yodel (Don can do *Cattle Call* as well as Arnold could) and a voice that reminds many of Marty Robbins. And Don's songs tell stories. My little cassette suddenly became a treasure. But little did I realize that Jerald's small gift would bring about a series of what Squire Rushnell calls Godwinks.

Corporate life and being confined in various airplanes and large cities had me yearning for my roots and I longed to get back to a semblance of the cowboy lifestyle. I knew that was not in the immediate future, so I did the next best thing. I subscribed to a lot of cowboy magazines and whenever possible, I arranged my schedule to be in places where I could connect to cowboy-dom. You know, places like Wyoming, Montana, Colorado, Utah, Idaho, New Mexico, even Nevada, where cowboy poet Waddie Mitchell (the Bard part) hails from. Some of these are buckaroo states. Of course, the top places for cowboys are still Texas and Oklahoma.

One of the magazines I subscribed to was *Cowboy*. Yep, just Cowboy. The first Godwink came with my initial issue of the magazine in the summer of 1995. There, on the front cover, was a painting by Bob Moline called *The Minstrel of the Range*. The subject was Don Edwards. What a coincidence. I had no idea at the time that the artist, Bob Moline, did more than paint.

The painting on the magazine cover introduced an article titled *Too Good for the Mainstream* about Don Edwards. By this time, I knew Don had grown up in New England. He was not a real cowboy, but had adapted the cowboy lifestyle well, even trying his luck at rodeos before deciding that playing and singing suited him better. In the article, he explained what cowboy music is:

> The best explanation I've heard was by the famous old-time cowboy Andy Adams. "There is no such thing as cowboy music. It is a hybrid between the weirdness of an Indian cry and the croon of the darky mammy. It expresses the open, the prairie, the immutable desert."

In a footnote to the article, Don said this about the above statement:

*I refuse to succumb to the mindless stupidity of political correctness. This is a direct quote from Andy Adams back in the later 1800s and not meant to insult the red man or the black man, both of whom played monumental roles in the making of western history. I hold all peoples of the West in the highest esteem, regardless of race, color or creed. If anyone reading this has a problem with this colorful and picturesque language of the old-time masters, then all I will say in the matter is lighten up, grab holt of yourself and get a life.*

Attaboy, Don. I was beginning to like this balladeer more and more. But the Godwinks were just beginning.

Another cowboy magazine back in those days was called *Yippy Yi Yea*. Sounds corny, I know, but it was a good magazine that did an excellent job of covering the real western lifestyle. No glamour shots of models wearing so-called cowboy gear. When models don't normally dress western, they always look like the hats on their heads and the boots on their feet are garish costumes. My first issue had Buck Taylor on the cover over a caption that said, "From *Gunsmoke* to Brushstroke." Buck, best known at the time for his role as Newly O'Brien on *Gunsmoke* and Turkey Creek Johnson in *Tombstone*, was doing more paintings than movies then and I was interested in his transition. Also, I had been mistaken for Buck on at least one occasion and more were to come. Sorta hurts my feelings, because he is a lot older.

The Godwink came inside, however, where I found a feature article on Bob Moline (remember the guy who painted Don's portrait for the cover of *Cowboy?*) Are you following the trail here? From *Saddle Songs* to seeing Don in *Cowboy* magazine and then seeing a feature article on Bob Moline (the guy who drew Don's portrait for *Cowboy*) in my first issue of *Yippy Yi Yea* that had Buck Taylor (my sometime twin) on the cover. Stay with me. We're all going to wind up in Commerce at my old roping arena and the saloon that Jerald built (yes, the guy who gave me the CD that started it all).

Along comes another issue of *Cowboy*. A painting of Waddie Mitchell (the Bard in Bard and Balladeer) graced the cover. Inside, Waddie, a veteran Nevada buckaroo, tells us the difference between buckaroos and cowboys. He, along with Utah folklorist Hal Cannon, established the first cowboy poetry gathering in Elko, Nevada, in 1985. *Yippy Yi Yea*'s next issue came along only a few days later. There was a beautifully tooled saddle on the front and an inset picture of Don Edwards. Inside was an article, complete with pictures of Don and his Sevenshoux Ranch in Weatherford. The saddle on the cover sat in his living room. Guess who made it? Bob Moline. There is also a picture of the Wrangler award Don received from the Cowboy Hall of Fame. On one of his walls hangs a rawhide riata made by his friend and traveling partner, Waddie Mitchell.

In the article, Don refers to himself as a cowboy Leon Redbone. I learned he once played at Six Flags Over Texas when it first opened and was a regular and former part-owner of the White Elephant Saloon, one of my favorite watering holes. I am not there often, but I try to visit whenever I am in the Fort Worth Stockyards area. A mural of Don is painted on one of the walls in the saloon.

I admit that I may be making too much of a series of coincidences, and I did not think much about what was happening at the time. I did feel that I needed to meet Don Edwards. But I wasn't sure how that would come about. I chalked it all up to fortuitous events and moved on with business as usual. Then someone put a flier on my desk in my Dallas office about the Fort Worth Cowboy Gathering organized primarily by Red Steagall. Don Edwards was on the flier. I met Don briefly at the Fort Worth gathering and found him friendly and down to earth. I had the feeling this would not be our last encounter.

At the time, annual conferences and training for the financial services firm where I worked was under my purview. I began to look at the stockyards through new eyes. Plans began to formulate for the next conference. Cowboy poetry was just taking off in those days, and guys like Waddie Mitchell and Baxter Black were appearing on late night talk shows after appearing at gatherings like the ones in Elko, Nevada, or Alpine, Texas.

I asked my associate Greg Aden to look into booking The Bard and the Balladeer. I made a little research trip to Fort Worth, checking out ways we could entertain a bunch of guys and gals (registered representatives) who hailed from all over the country. There was a large group from the Baltimore area and a few from California and other places that

I feared might not appreciate my bringing them into the cowboy lifestyle for a business conference. Some of our reps were reluctant when we announced Fort Worth was the site for our next conference (one said it was not a "destination city"), but their doubts quickly dissipated about five minutes into Don and Waddie's exclusive performance at the Worthington Hotel for our company. I got to know them better and also got to meet Rich O'Brien, famous in his own right as a musician and producer.

Three years later, I left my old job and sold my interest in the financial services company to pursue a few of those cowboy dreams. One of the first was a trip across Texas from Ranger in Eastland County to Cooper in Delta County by covered wagon and horseback to retrace the journey my ancestors made eighty years earlier. I rode a saddle made by Bob Moline (the story of the saddle is told later). In Decatur, I left my horse outside and walked into an art gallery featuring the work of Buck Taylor. One of the employees mistook me for Buck. The same thing happened a few years later at a Fort Worth Stockyards restaurant.

Two years later, I was on the committee to plan a United Way concert here in Commerce. I contacted The Bard and The Balladeer. They came, saw and conquered. Waddie spent the night at our house. Don signed my movie poster of the *Horse Whisperer* where he appeared as ranch foreman Smokey. By this time, he had been Western Music Association Artist of the Year for two years running. He had performed for Ronald Reagan when he was president and George Bush when he was governor.

I began team roping in 1998 using Bob's saddle. Team roping is hard on a saddle. I took it into Oxbow Saddle Shop in Fort Worth, Bob's new shop. They oohed and aaahed at the saddle Bob had made before he opened the saddle shop, then made it look like new.

A few months later, I received an invitation to attend a performance by Don at his old hangout, The White Elephant Saloon in the Fort Worth Stockyards. Waddie was not there, but Rich O'Brien and Don treated Jerald and I like old friends. In 2001, Waddie was featured on the front page of the travel section of the *Dallas Morning News*, telling tales at the National Storytelling Festival in Jonesborough, Tennessee. Nine months later, Don Edwards was the subject of the feature story in the "High Profile" section of the *Dallas Morning News*.

In 2010, someone sent me an article by e-mail from *Western Horseman* called "Off the Grid." It was a story about Waddie (otherwise known as Bruce Douglas Mitchell) and his wife Lisa (the daughter of comedian Buddy Hackett) and their five-thousand-square-foot home and seven-hundred-twenty-acre ranch (Half Circle One) outside Elko, Nevada. The morning after he stayed at our house, he told me about his dream of owning such a place.

In the April/May 2012 issue of *American Cowboy*, there is a story about Don called "At Home with Don Edwards." He has moved away from Weatherford to Hico. In the article, I learned that *Saddle Songs* is now included in the Folklore Archives of the Library of Congress. Remember that *Saddle Songs* was that little cassette that Jerald gave me? That's what started it all. Still think it's a series of coincidences?

# Visiting with a Living Legend and a Poet Laureate

AFTER MY STAY AT THE QUEIN SABE RANCH (more about that later), I headed for the Ambassador Hotel in Amarillo with the manuscript of my first novel in hand. I signed up for a preconference workshop for beginning writers. I checked into my room and barely made it down in time for the first preconference session. The instructors treated us not like beginning writers, but like small children. I was discouraged a little as I heard college professors rattle off rules I had already broken. My left brain that likes to abide by rules battled with my right brain that likes to break them. I hoped for better days ahead at the main conference.

On Saturday, my first sessions were almost as bad as the preconference, but I did get to spend an hour and a half in an informal conversation with Elmer Kelton. Kelton was probably the best living author of westerns at the time, a consummate gentleman who imparted more information during that time than I had received in all my previous sessions combined. He told me how he wrote, correcting and editing each page before he goes on to the next one. It was not a method I adopted, but he was clear it was not a rule, just a preference for him. My favorite story was of his by-pass surgery. As he came out of the effects of anesthesia, he hallucinated and imagined himself to be Huey Callaway, one of the characters in *The Good Old Boys* and *Smiling Country* who was hurt while riding a bronc. He said he was pretty sure the pain he was experiencing was from a bronc, not surgery. Elmer Kelton and I crossed paths a few more times before he passed away. One of the nicest people I have ever met. Years later, Sam Brown, a high school friend, ranch cowboy, poet and author, told me that Kelton agreed to read his first book and advised him on getting published. I know he did the same for many authors.

Naturally, I was flattered, when seven years later, this review appeared:

> *Jim Ainsworth is a master storyteller. He is cut from the 'old rock,' the stone of Kelton and Dobie. He is able to weave a story that can transport the reader to a different time and place.* Home Light Burning *is a well written page-turner with crisp prose and dialogue that flows like a spring from a limestone bluff.*
> —*Plainview Daily Herald*, December 24, 2009.

Then later, this review on Amazon for *Go Down Looking*: "This is one of the best pieces of fiction since Elmer Kelton died."

Okay, I don't claim to be in the same class as Kelton, but the comparisons were nice and much appreciated. Even if the first day had been a disaster, I knew I would always cherish that short time with Kelton, even if I never wrote another word. By late afternoon of the last day, I was disappointed I was not taking something more concrete away from the conference. I found it in the last two sessions.

Jane Kirkpatrick, author of several books, was down to earth, humorous and an all-around excellent speaker. My ears perked up when she said she had grown up on a dairy farm in Wisconsin and now lived in a remote part of Oregon called Starvation Point. She had come all the way to Amarillo to speak to a writers' conference. In the final session, I met Jan Epton-Seale from the Rio Grande Valley of Texas. Like Kirkpatrick, she had traveled far to speak in Amarillo. She spoke about writing memoirs and creative writing. She has written several volumes of poetry and published fiction and nonfiction. She was later named Texas Poet Laureate in 2012. But she made a big mistake when she hinted that she also did professional editing.

I approached her at the end of the seminar and asked if she would read my manuscript. She asked how long it was and I said about 425 pages. She frowned at the length but still quoted a price. I went to my car to retrieve the nice manuscript box holding the manuscript of *In the Rivers Flow*, my first novel. When she opened the box, she frowned again. "This is single spaced."

"I double spaced it when I wrote it, but changed it to single so it would fit in the box." She smiled and said the price would be a little higher. To her credit, she did not double the fee.

I left the seminar feeling pretty good and had a relaxing trip home. Something had been accomplished, maybe something substantial. I had experienced working roundup and branding on a huge Texas ranch, reconnected to a friend from long ago, visited my old home and had hired an accomplished, unbiased author to read and critique my first novel. I mentally charged my batteries all the way home, giving myself pep talks. When I arrived home by one in the morning, I was charged. Jan and I talked till three.

I didn't hear from Jan Epton-Seale for several weeks. She called the house on a Sunday afternoon and my Jan answered. I was team roping that day, so I will probably never know exactly what Jan said to Jan. I am sure it was more critical than my wife said. However, when I received her written critique and marked-up manuscript the next week, the first sentence began... *First, you can write.* Excellent criticism and suggestions followed, but that first sentence was what I needed. Jan Epton-Seale, South Texas editor for *Texas Books in Review*, knew that. Someday, I'll write about a surprise meeting with her eleven years later in a Highland Park mansion.

# Tom T. Hall Comes Home

WE FORGET WHAT WE HEAR, REMEMBER what we see, and understand what we do. Reading fiction allows us to hear, see and do. I have many friends, mostly men, who have not read a book since high school. They say they can't stay awake or, "I'll wait till the movie comes out."

That's because they only read words. They haven't taught themselves to hear, see and do right along with the characters in books. When they learn to do this, they read faster and begin to understand the meaning of stories and begin to enjoy one of life's greatest pleasures.

Writing novels has also given me a renewed appreciation for songwriters. They often say as much in one page as I do in three hundred. So I thought it might be fun to try this hear, see and do thing with a few words from famous songwriter, Tom T. Hall. Who doesn't remember "The year that Clayton Delaney Died"? In another song, "Homecoming," Tom tells the story that covers several decades in one page, about six hundred words. And he does it with only one character speaking.

Humor me. See if you can see what Tom is telling us in the first verse, only fifty-two words, four lines.

> Guess I should've written Dad, to let you know that I was coming home
> I've been gone so many years, I didn't realize you had a phone
> Saw your cattle coming in, boy, they're looking mighty fat and slick
> Saw Fred at the service station, told me his wife is awful sick

What do you see in your mind's eye with each line?

I saw a son returning after being away for many years with no contact.

We know the approximate era because the dad did not have a phone when the son left. Daddy's a farmer/rancher—but the bigger issue is the son making small talk to avoid speaking about the invisible barrier between them—his prolonged absence and his guilt. Fred is probably a brother who has a sick wife. The brother has stayed behind with his father.

Do you have a vision of the father and son meeting for the first time in years? Where are they? What are they wearing? I see the father in overalls and one of those Hank Williams hats, the son in a loud western shirt with the top two or three snaps undone. The father is on the porch and the son is at the porch steps of a little farm house with a fig tree in the yard and a swing on the porch, a vine grows up a trellis. He has one boot on the first step. Do you see the cattle? What kind are they? See the old service station?

Now skip to the fourth verse.

> *I'm sorry I couldn't be here with you all when Momma passed away*
> *I was on the road, and when they came and told me, it was just too late.*
> *I drove by the grave to see her; boy, that sure is a pretty stone*
> *I'm glad that Fred and Jan are here, it's better than you being here alone.*

Can you see the gravestone, the little country graveyard? The anguish on the son's face, the disappointment and grief on the father's? And now we know that Fred is a brother.

Now the final verse (we're skipping several good ones).

> *Well, Dad, I gotta go; we got a dance to work in Cartersville tonight*
> *Let me take your number down, and I promise you I'll write*
> *Now you be good and don't be chasin' all those pretty women that you know*
> *And, by the way, if you see Barbara Walker, tell her that I said hello.*

We're back to the guilty small talk, the awkward departure in order to return to a life the father does not approve of. And, of course, the old flame the son left behind. See the sweetheart's face? See the forced smile on the son's face disappear and a deep sadness fill his eyes as he mentions his old heartthrob?

Now, go read. Oops. I forgot the ones who need to read this don't read. I am preaching to the choir. Marcel Proust called the moments of unity between writer and reader "that fruitful miracle of a communication in the midst of solitude." To my readers, I say thanks for that fruitful miracle. And thanks for your kind comments.

# Ranching, Cowboys, and the Saddles They Ride

The top shelves in my office are adorned with coffee table type books that tell the story of Texas and her great ranches and the cowboys who made them work in words, paintings and photographs. Books like *Historic Ranches of Texas, Texas Cattle Barons, Cowboy Gear, Texas Cowboys, The Love of Horses, A Cowboy's Faith.*

In my former profession as a CPA and Financial Planner, clients were often surprised, even shocked, to see me in jeans and boots in a cowboy office. I got a lot of referred clients because people in Dallas went home and talked about their "cowboy CPA." Poet and singer Annie Golightly said she could almost smell a cowboy's sweat and hear cattle calls as she gazed around the office where I write. I can't explain my love for all things cowboy. I am not now nor have I ever laid claim to being a real cowboy, but that doesn't keep me from loving the history, the lifestyles and the stories of cowboys and ranches. And it is definitely in my DNA, passed down for three generations. I hope you enjoy the following stories about my experiences on some of the great ranches of Texas as well as with horses, cattle and saddles.

# Two Days in Albany
## The Lambshead Ranch

LONG BEFORE LUCAS BLACK HAD HIS *Seven Days in Utopia*, I had my two days in Albany. One of the more memorable events in my life began in 1989 when I read *Watt Matthews of Lambshead* by Laura Wilson (she's the mother of the Wilson brother actors). David McCullough (before he won the Pulitzer and became world famous), wrote the introduction to the book. Watt was ninety when the book was published, but still stood at the branding chutes and applied his iron to 2000 calves during spring roundup. But what really struck me was that this wealthy man still lived in a small bunkhouse on the ranch with a concrete floor and no central A/C and only a fireplace for heat; slept on an iron bed; took noontime naps on a wooden bench without benefit of a pillow; and ran his 45,000 acres from an open corner in the cook shack.

Though Watt's father feared Princeton would be bad for his character, his mother insisted that he attend. He graduated in 1921. The four years he spent there were the only four years he did not live on Lambshead Ranch. The Princeton class directory listed him as "Rancher, Box 636, Albany, Texas." And Princeton did not harm his character. Bill Cauble, a Lambshead cowboy, said, "To me, that's the real character of a man, when he could have anything he wanted, but didn't want anything."

I made an entry on my goals list: *Meet Watt Matthews*. I couldn't really see how that would come about, but I wanted it to. After writing that goal, Watt seemed to show up in about half the magazines and newspapers I picked up—two time winner of Golden Spur Award, Charles Goodnight

Award from National Cutting Horse Association, and many others. He was invited to be inducted into the Cowboy Hall of Fame, but asked that his mother be inducted instead. She was, but he was inducted later.

Two years after setting my goal to meet Watt, I made a career change that took me in a direction I never imagined. I co-founded a small financial services firm. Our niche was in training CPAs to be financial planners. Four years later, one of our CPAs invited me to San Angelo, fairly close to Watt. I put him off. A family friend invited me to Ranger. Too

*Watt Matthews with sister Lucille on her 100th birthday.*

busy. A Sweetwater CPA invited me out. All close to Albany, but the head-slapping moment came when an Albany CPA that I did not know called me. A deep voice said, "How many hints do you need?"

I made business stops in Abilene, San Angelo, Sweetwater, and spent the night in little Albany, a town of about two thousand. The CPA I came to visit sent me to the First National Bank, where Watt had been a director for over sixty years. A pair of his old boots and spurs and a hat were in a glass display in the lobby. A teller gave me directions and I drove thirteen miles to the ranch, then fifteen more on a ranch road until I found headquarters. I checked the outbuildings and all seemed deserted. I just couldn't bring myself to knock on the door of a small cottage in the middle of headquarters. What would I say to a man now ninety-six? "Hi, I'm a tourist. Would you sign my books?"

Tail between my legs, I returned to town. I visited the Matthews room in the Old Jail Art Museum. In the local bookstore, I bought *Interwoven*, a book written in 1936 by Sally Reynolds Matthews, Watt's mother. Watt was the youngest of her nine children. The bookstore owner laughed when I told her about my hapless trip to the ranch. She called and got Watt's caregiver on the phone. She invited me to come back out.

Watt and his caregiver and about ten cowboys were in the cook shack when I arrived. "Get a plate," he said. I politely declined, apologized for bothering the great man. When he repeated the invitation more firmly, I got in line behind the last ranch hand, heaven for this wannabe cowboy. The meal was great ranch fare, tasty and hearty. After an hour of conversation, I presented my books. He asked the nurse for a pad and pen. He wrote on the yellow pad and handed it to me.

> *Thanks to Jim Ainsworth for bringing this book to Lambshead for me to sign.*
> *Sincerely, a new friend.*
> *Watt Matthews, 9-6-95.*

I nodded humbly in appreciation and he wrote the same thing in my books. How I wish I had asked for that yellow sheet of paper.

I saw his open journal and his bench in the corner that he called his office and asked if I could take a look. Found this entry:

> *Beautiful starlit morning. Hope the wind doesn't come up with the sun. We got the cows in, separated, vaccinated and dipped in time to get started with the branding at ten.*

Later, I got to see some of the buildings he had restored, the civic work he led and funded. Watt died a year later. There was a car wreck on the ranch, followed by a stroke and pneumonia. He asked to be brought home from the hospital and died the next morning.

They laid him in a plain pine box dressed in jeans and boots and denim jacket, put the box in the bed of a faded yellow buckboard, and surrounded it with bales of hay. Two cowboys in white shirts and black hats sat in the seat and handled the horses. More walked behind and alongside to the family cemetery on the ranch. They laid him to rest on the ranch he loved. Over 700 mourners attended and the burial was covered by news outlets nationwide.

They sang "America the Beautiful" and Watt's favorite song, "Prairie Land."

> *A prairie plain, a bright blue sky,*
> *A now white cloud a sailin' high,*
> *A wanton wind, a blowin' free,*
> *This is the land for men like me.*

Yes it is.

---

AUTHOR'S NOTE: Seventeen years after his death and a year after the above article was written, Watt was the subject of a feature article in the August/September issue of *American Cowboy* magazine. The article written by Jill J. Dunkel is titled: "Watt Matthews: Dean of Texas Cattlemen." Jill relates the story told by neighbor rancher Billy Green. Watt took a phone call one day, spoke to the caller for twenty minutes or so. When he hung up, someone asked, "Who was that, Watt?"

Watt replied, "Well, it was a wrong number, but they're coming for supper."

That describes the man I met.

# A Voice from the Past
## Tales from the Quien Sabe, Part I

WHEN I TOOK A SABBATICAL FROM THE financial services field, I never imagined it would be permanent. Walking away from knowledge and skills I had spent most of my adult life honing and accumulating seemed, well, dumb, even incomprehensible. But my list of *things to do before I die* included a few things I might be too old to do before long. So I rationalized my *sabbatical* as a chance to check off a few things on that list while I still had the physical stamina and desire to do them. I'm glad I checked off those things, because I don't think I have the energy now.

Shortly after I extricated myself from most of the entanglements of my profession, I got a call at home one night from cousin Shep challenging me to retrace our grandparents' and parents' journey across Texas in a covered wagon in 1918. To his surprise, I accepted. That trip changed my life for the better. I chronicled the trip in *Biscuits Across the Brazos*. It gave me the confidence to pursue a few other dreams that had seemed a little less plausible. After that, anything seemed possible.

It's not too hard to figure that a lot of my dreams had to do with fulfilling the cowboy life I had imagined for myself as a boy, but had put aside for more sensible endeavors I had to do to make a living and support a family. With newfound freedom, it was not unusual for me to make a decision one day and leave to fulfill it the next. In other words, I was having the time of my life. On a whim, I drove to Alpine for the Cowboy Poetry Gathering in cold February. At a chuckwagon breakfast the next morning, legendary author and storyteller Paul Patterson brushed away snow on a bench and sat down beside me. I didn't recognize him. Paul told me he was a good friend of Elmer Kelton's and that Kelton had illustrated and written the foreword to one of Paul's books. At that time, Kelton was the most prolific and beloved writer of westerns alive, but I had not known that he was also a talented artist.

Before leaving the Big Bend area, I dropped in on Ft. Davis, Marfa, Marathon and the Gage Motel, and Terlingua, home of the Chili Cook Off. I still marvel at the carefree freedom I felt as neither distance nor obstacles seemed to matter. I was hungry for different experiences after being tied to schedules, desks and telephones for thirty years.

I became a regular at the Abilene Western Heritage Classic. I enjoyed sitting alone in the stands for hours watching ranch cowboys show their ranch horses. I marveled not only at their horsemanship, but their style, the tall-topped boots, big spurs, colorful wild rags, and big hats. Always a lover of tack, I relished watching what they put on their horses' backs and heads and in their mouths. I was fascinated by romel reins, bosals, mecates, and the little grass ropes that the cowboys tucked under their belts. I was intrigued by the pull harnesses that replaced breast harnesses. Many years earlier, my fascination with tack and love for good boots had inspired me to open a western wear store called Chute I.

On my second trip to the Abilene Classic, I was sitting in the stands watching ranch team roping when I heard a deep voice holler, "Yeah!" as a roping team made a clean run with two feet caught. The voice seemed like an echo from my past. I looked around for the source, but could not find him. As the competition drew to a close and the winning team was announced, I heard the voice again. It was a distinctive voice, one I knew I had heard before, but I just could not put a name to it. It came from a mouth that seemed to be full of something like bubble gum or chewing tobacco. A throaty, bass sound, almost slurred.

On the final cheer, I saw a large man stand with a clenched fist, a sign of approval for the ranch team in the arena. He wore a hat that matched his size. When he walked past me, the large hat kept his face shadowed, but I now knew who he was. The voice was older, mellower, like it was emerging from the long, dark, tunnel of my past and just waking up from a long sleep. I followed him and another cowboy out of the arena, waiting for a break in a conversation that seemed very serious, but they entered a room open only to ranch rodeo contestants before I could approach.

I waited almost an hour for him to reappear, still engaged in deep conversation with the same cowboy. I followed behind them, enjoying myself, taking my time to observe everything he wore from the tall riding heels on his boots, the large spur rowels, and the huge palm leaf hat, looking for a sign of the seventy-pounds-lighter boy I once knew. Finally, the other cowboy peeled off and I stepped beside my old friend, matching him stride for stride, looking straight ahead. He glanced in my direction, nodded and kept walking.

For a second, I thought I had made a mistake. I had not seen him or spoken to him in almost forty years. But no, this had to be Calvin. But he did not recognize me. I purposely bumped him enough to take him off stride. He turned again. I smiled and he stuck out his hand. "Well, damn, Jimmy Ainsworth, you got old, didn't you?"

"Tried to stop it, but it just took hold."

He patted his stomach. "Guess I've changed a little myself."

"You have, but I recognized your voice."

We talked a few minutes, trying to cover forty years, recalling raucous tales from our teen years, but he had a team of ranch cowboys and stock to look after and had to prepare for the ranch rodeo that night. He introduced me to his ranch hands from the Quien Sabe Ranch. I stood out of the way and watched as they took care of their horses and checked their tack for the events to come. Calvin had been ranch manager at Quien Sabe Ranch for more than twenty years. I was surprised. I had always thought of my old friend as a wheat and milo farmer. But when I thought back, he had a black horse he called "Old Stud" and hired out to do daywork as a cowboy when his family could spare him from the farm.

I watched him and his team compete that night and saw how the years had made him into a genuine ranch cowboy, an occupation I had aspired to during our years of roaming the Panhandle countryside and playing sports together. I thought I could best him team roping, but he had me beat in all the other events. He had both horse sense and cattle sense, and was clearly the leader of the team in that arena. The other cowboys, mostly younger, obviously looked up to him. I left the next day, expecting I would never see him again.

# A Visit to the Who Knows Ranch
## Tales from the Quien Sabe, Part II

ABOUT TWO YEARS AFTER MEETING Calvin in Abilene, I completed the manuscript of my first novel. I had read a lot of books about writing and decided to attend my first writers' conference and try to connect with real authors. My expectations were low, but I hoped to discover if what I had written was anything close to worthwhile. An article in *Writers Digest* magazine drew me to the Panhandle Professional Writers Conference in Amarillo. I was impressed by the line-up of speakers, especially Elmer Kelton, but I also wanted to drive out to the stomping grounds of my youth and maybe visit Calvin on the Quien Sabe.

If the conference turned out to be a waste of time and money, at least I could rekindle a few old memories. Daddy had been gone for more than thirty years and Mother almost two. I felt a need to reconnect to the Panhandle farm we had left forty years earlier.

When I traveled on business, I planned trips down to the last detail; every minute accounted for. Now, I had the freedom to be spontaneous. I had some vague ideas about what I might do in the Panhandle, but I left a couple of days early and decided to just let things happen. I was surprised at my own boldness when I blew past Amarillo without stopping at a motel. I found myself in Channing (north and west of Amarillo) on a June day about quitting time. The town had not changed much since I played high school sports there. Calvin and I attended school in Adrian (about an hour south). I found a small grocery store and asked if anyone knew Calvin. The owner and all the patrons did, of course. I got directions to the Quien Sabe. I asked the proprietor where the ranch name came from. He told me about a Mexican who drove the first herd of cattle to Texas. When asked the name of the brand on the cattle, the Mexican replied, "*Quien Sabe?*" (Who knows?).

The ranch entrance was only a few miles out of Channing and not far from Old Tascosa, the home of Boys Ranch. I was tentative as I stopped at the desolate railroad crossing a few yards from the ranch entrance. When our family moved to the Panhandle, I was just a boy. As I explored the country, I often felt a strange feeling of *déjà vu* at certain places. The Matador Ranch was one such place, Old Tascosa was another.

From *Rivers Ebb*:

> *Jake climbed the arena fence, sat on the top rail, and let that been-here-before feeling wash over him.*

I felt that been-here-before feeling as I stopped at the railroad crossing. From high school, I remembered that the railway was The Fort Worth and Denver and was called the Denver Road. It ran from Fort Worth through Wichita Falls, Childress, Amarillo, Dalhart, to Texline (another *déjà vu* place), where it connected with the Colorado and Southern. My friends and I had often talked of hopping the train to Texline to see girlfriends when the train slowed in Channing.

Here's Jake in Texline in *Rivers Ebb*:

> *He stopped at the sidewalk and looked down the street. A row of cottonwoods had been planted to separate the field crops on the east side of the street from the houses on the west. A few scattered trees that looked distressed from lack of water dotted some yards, but the snow was falling on hard dirt, not grass lawns. A horse bowed-up against the blowing snow stood beside a small tin barn in the middle of the mostly-small, mostly-stucco houses.*

I guess I expected to see an impressive entrance of some sort merely because I knew the ranch was big. But just north of the dirt road, only some letters on stone announced the Quien Sabe. But as whirls of dust followed me down the road, I saw a more impressive sight.

Big evergreen shrubs lined the drive toward what looked like an oasis in the desert. Live oaks, poplars, and other trees surrounded a compound sitting on a high spot. There was a huge native stone house on the left with a stone fence around it. I later learned this was the abode of ranch owner Joe Kirk Fulton, who inherited the ranch from his father. Joe Kirk chose to live in more hospitable Hill Country, but stayed in the big house when he visited the ranch.

A smaller, but more than adequate brick house was on the right. Calvin was filling a cattle spray tank when I drove up. I am not the type to be a surprise guest, but my excuse for dropping in was just to find the ranch, maybe wangle an invitation to come back after the conference for a tour. A three-month-old colt kicked up his heels in the yard fenced with horse wire as I stepped out of my pickup. Calvin nodded toward the colt as he finished filling the spray tank. "His mama didn't have any milk, so we're bottle feeding him." It had been two years since we met in Abilene for the first time in forty years, but Calvin showed no surprise at seeing me again, acted as if I dropped in frequently.

I nodded toward the frisky colt. "Got a name?"

"We named him Iffy, because he had such a rough start we didn't think he'd make it."

I apologized for just dropping by, explained my reason for coming to Amarillo, and asked if I might come back for a tour the next day or the day after the conference.

"You had your supper yet?"

Less than an hour later, I found myself sitting at a table covered with plates of fried buffalo (grown on the ranch) steaks, garden salad, fruit salad, cornbread, navy beans and ham, fried okra, corn, cake, Jell-O, and iced tea—all prepared by Calvin's wife, Linda.

Three grandchildren at the table were friendly and polite to this intruder, and I got the definite feeling guests for supper were not uncommon. As we dug into the buffalo steaks, Calvin told me that he had lost thirty pounds on the Atkins Diet. After supper, he took me on a tour of his home. Tastefully furnished in Panhandle style, the walls were covered with photos and artwork by famous photographers and artists who had come to the ranch to capture a ranching lifestyle they feel is rare and disappearing.

Famous photographer Jay Dusard (more about him in a later story) had been to the ranch for a photo shoot and his work was on the wall. There were also photos that had appeared in *Western Horseman* and other well-known magazines. I recognized R. W. Hampton, famous singer and poet, in lots of the pictures. I was recently gifted with one of his CDs and he mentions the Quien Sabe, calling it the "Kin Sabby." I thought it was pronounced "Cane Sabby." He had worked for Calvin several times. There was also one of Sam Brown, cowboy poet and author and a schoolmate of Calvin's and mine.

I stopped at a photo of a huge rock with this crude carving—*William Bonney—1881*. Calvin told me the rock was only a few miles from where we stood. Billy the Kid is known to have frequented nearby Tascosa, bringing in herds of stolen horses to sell. He also frequented the bawdy houses. It is likely that someone carved his name there shortly after his death in 1881, but nobody knows for sure. Of course, it is possible that Billy was there that year before he died and did the carving himself.

On the mantle, Calvin's own trophy buckle had a prominent spot. He had won all around cowboy at the Coors Ranch Rodeo the previous year. Beside the buckle was a framed, moving tribute written to him by a woman who had observed him at the rodeo. She had not known him, but wanted to recognize his leadership of his rodeo team and the way he interacted with his wife, children and grandchildren. Calvin was easy-going in high school and his charm and wit had mellowed him into a father and grandfather who displays gentle firmness in his interactions with all his family members. I had noticed it at the supper table, but the tribute confirmed it.

Beside the woman's tribute stood a framed essay written by a grandson about the most influential person in his life. The essay about Calvin won them a trip to the famous Big Texan Steakhouse in Amarillo.

# A Panhandle Test of Mettle and Murder on the High Plains

*Tales from the Quien Sabe, Part III*

A FLOOR LAMP MADE FROM THE SKULLS and racks of two large bucks locked in mortal combat served as a reading lamp by Calvin's easy chair. The bucks could not disentangle themselves and died together. Calvin found them on the ranch. He said their last words were, "You can have her."

Family photos lined the walls of the hall. Calvin pointed and named each, pausing to clear a catch in his throat when he pointed toward Billy, the son he lost to cancer at twenty-eight. Billy was movie-star-handsome. Calvin told me he had won all-around cowboy in the Amarillo Ranch Rodeo several times. As I looked at Billy's picture, I thought of the poem I had recently read about mettle. Calvin's mettle had been tested as mine never had. And he had passed. Instead of using crutches like alcohol to deal with a tragedy, he had propelled himself to be a better father, grandfather, husband, and manager of men.

Billy's children, Zack and Zane, were still riding their father's trophy saddles. Billy had his own string of horses and started branding them with a cross during the years he battled cancer. His sons now jointly own his string of horses. They have a ZZ brand of their own, but also kept the cross in honor of their father. The boys live in the ranch bunkhouse and make cowhands during the summer. I learned one younger grandson had recently won a trophy buckle at a dummy roping in Amarillo. As we walked outside in the pre-dusk cool, the kids all carried chicken ropes (short ropes used for roping everything that moves and everything that doesn't).

As we watched Grandson Zack, sixteen and already six-four, work colts in a round pen, the subject of another classmate came up. I think there were only about twelve in our class at Adrian High School and half were girls. One of the boys we'll call Joe (not his real name). When he was just a sophomore in high school, Joe took charge of the family farm for his mother when his father died. I remember that Joe was a big guy even at sixteen with huge hands. The story of Joe and his wife Mary (not her real name) that Calvin told is complex and almost unbelievable, so bear with me.

I had heard Joe had been shot and killed by a ranch hand a few years before and his wife Mary was in prison for being involved, but I was not sure of the details. Thinking of our old friend meeting a violent death and the shy girl we knew in high school in prison was incredible to me. Joe's wife, Mary, was in the class below us. Joe and Mary went steady all the time I knew them. They were model students and seemed mature beyond their years. Several years after they were married and had a family of their own, Joe and Mary took in a problem teenager, grandson of a friend in Adrian. Joe put him to work on the farm and was a pretty tough taskmaster.

But Mary and her eldest daughter admittedly allowed the boy to seduce them. The assumption is that the boy grew afraid Joe would kill him if he found out. Most of Joe's friends agreed that was a distinct possibility. One evening while Joe was reading the newspaper at his kitchen table, the troubled teen approached from behind and shot him in the back of the head. Joe was later pronounced dead at the scene.

When the teen killer was arrested, he implicated Mary in the planning of the murder. She was accused of delaying her call to the police after the shooting, allowing the killer time to get away and possibly delaying life saving measures for Joe. Mary and her teen lover were each sentenced to 35 years in prison.

Calvin's stepson Troy (Linda's son by a previous marriage), married Joe and Mary's daughter (let's call her Jane). Jane subsequently divorced

Troy but maintained a relationship with ex-in-laws Calvin and Linda. In fact, Troy and Jane's daughter was employed at the ranch doing housework. More complications: The granddaughter's son from a second husband was staying in the bunkhouse at the ranch—a testament, it seems to me, of the depth of Calvin's and Linda's kindness, forgiveness, and hospitality.

I had heard the teen killer had recanted his assertion that Mary was involved. I leaned on the round pen and asked if Mary was still in prison. Calvin answered, "Joe's still dead, ain't he?"

# A Breakfast I Will Never Forget
## Tales from the Quien Sabe, Part IV

I LEARNED THAT THE QUIEN SABE RANCH is home to about a hundred registered quarter horses including about ten that belong to Calvin and Linda. The ranch horses are all named Quien Sabe with successive numbers. When Calvin started work there, they were at 79. Now they are at 501. He told me he got started in ranching after attending West Texas State University. He worked for Earl Brown (father of Sam Brown, another schoolmate from Adrian mentioned earlier) on the Matador. Then he worked for another classmate's dad, Louis Spinks. He liked ranch work and studied what old timers did, learned what to do and what not to do. He was recommended for the Quien Sabe job by a man who had turned it down.

We watched Zack and Zane work colts until dark. I was enjoying myself so much I let time slip away. I apologized again and headed for my pickup, intending to spend the night in Adrian or Vega so that I could go out to our old farmhouse the next day.

Calvin saw my luggage in the front seat of my pickup and picked it up. "Follow me."

I lamely protested and told him my plans. I didn't want to intrude.

"We'll be starting branding in the morning. I'll loan you a horse and saddle if you want to go along."

Well, this was a dream come true. I had secretly hoped I might get to see a branding and had brought along spurs and chinks just in case. I followed him to a very nice guest house across from their house. Calvin set the alarm clock. "Come over to the house when that goes off." He left me alone to peruse the Fulton book collection—everything from classics to westerns to investing. I chose a western novel and read till about eleven.

The alarm went off at 3:45. I dressed and walked over to Calvin's house for coffee, feeling good physically and mentally. I wondered about breakfast, but was not hungry yet. We drained our cups and I stopped to retrieve my chinks and spurs on the way to the horse barn about 4:30. Calvin smiled when he saw I had brought them.

He pointed to a Quien Sabe palomino and a saddle and bridle on a stand. We had our horses saddled and in a trailer in less than a half hour. We drove by moonlight for about twenty minutes along ranch roads that looked more like gully washes. On the way, Calvin explained how the branding took about two weeks. The 117,000-acre ranch was divided into sub-ranches, each with its own foreman or manager. The managers lived on their sub-ranches in small, but sturdy cabins.

Calvin parked beside several other pickup-trailer rigs in front of a small house with a few trees in the yard and a barn to the side. Inside, I met Rooster Falcon again. I had seen him at the Abilene Ranch Rodeo. Rooster's wife was friendly, country-girl pretty and looked to be in her late twenties. There was a screened-in overhang porch to my right where I saw a sea of big hats, all brim-up, crown-down on the floor beside four freezers that Calvin said were full of beef. I added my Panama to the mix, though it looked like the runt of the litter beside the five-inch-brimmed palm leafs and black felts. Nobody wore a hat inside.

Calvin told me the branding was a community endeavor as I watched twenty-one cowboys crowd into the small house. Neighbors join the Quien Sabe at branding time, and the favor is returned on the other ranches. Most probably drove an hour or more to arrive predawn.

I had immediate respect and gratitude for Rooster's young wife as she organized the flow of hungry men through her tiny kitchen. She crowded orange juice, coffee, platters of toast, omelets and gravy, beef strips, jelly and preserves along her kitchen counter tops.

My appetite had returned, but I was more interested in the cowboys. They ranged in age from pre-teen to men in their sixties. Wrangler jean legs were tucked into tall, slanted-heeled boots with thirteen and fourteen inch tops of green, yellow, red, white, and blue. Big spurs with big rowels adorned every pair. I was pleased that I had brought my spurs, though they were smaller than anyone else's. There were no t-shirts, no short sleeves, and no caps.

After breakfast, chinks and batwing leggings were taken off the fences, tree limbs and pickup mirrors where they had been left, pulled on, and buckled up. I didn't see any shotgun chaps, but there might have been a pair or two. My chinks and Wranglers were about the only thing that made me fit into this group. We drove another five minutes to a pasture gate. As we unloaded our horses, I noticed that some cowboys had tapaderos (a leather covered hood) on their stirrups and some did not. I wondered if we were going to work in heavy brush or mesquite thorns. I also wondered how long it would take me to adjust my own stirrups on the loaner saddle. I was surprised when they were exactly the right length. I wondered if Calvin or his sons had set them the night before after judging my height.

# Roundup on the Quien Sabe and a Sad Goodbye
## Tales from the Quien Sabe, Part V

AS WE RODE THROUGH THE FENCE that surrounded Rooster Falcon's home, Calvin told me we would be rounding up cattle in a 3600-acre pasture. The cattle were mostly Charolais and Herefords, purebred and crossbred. We all broke into a long trot with Calvin leading. My horse knew the drill.

Cholla (pronounced Choya), other plants that looked like Yucca cactus, gramma grass, and purple sage were prominent. We paused at regular intervals to drop off one or two riders to start sweeping the pasture. I stayed with Calvin. As we passed pastures with sixteen-foot fences, Calvin said they called that area the zoo. The ranch owner had wanted to raise exotic animals for hunting, but they eventually became coyote bait. Calvin spotted a lone cow off to our right on a tall ridge and rode almost out of sight to move it in the right direction. Lightning streaked the sky on the horizon and the weather turned cool. Wind gusted to about forty miles per hour. I was pleased when my Panama with the self adjusting band stayed on. Calvin's big palm leaf brim bent with the wind, but didn't blow off.

I was humbled, almost awed as I stayed put and watched Calvin ride his horse to a rock ridge for a better look at the roundup progress. I was unsure how the pasture lay or where the fences were, since none were in sight and the cattle did not seem to naturally herd. I was surprised at how scattered they were.

I finally got a sense of how things were going to work as the cowboys

# ROUNDUP ON THE QUIEN SABE AND A SAD GOODBYE

drove the cattle together against a north fence and pushed them toward the corrals. When the cattle were penned, the cowboys separated seven bulls first (one bull for 14 cows or 7 to 100) then about thirty dry cows. I helped a little with this, but most of it was handled by cowboys who wanted to get their horses work in the herd as well as test their own skills. Each man politely asked Calvin's permission to work a new horse.

Calvin pulled a new Chevy three-quarter-ton truck into an adjoining corral. Pairs (70) were then herded into this smaller pen. The pickup rocked as the cows pushed against it. Two cowboys rode into the pen and started pushing them toward the gate. Rooster flagged off the calves using his chinks. If he missed one, two cowboys on horseback stopped the calves and pushed them back inside.

With the calves separated, Rooster fired up a propane blower and dropped five branding irons into an iron bucket. He heated them with propane flame. When the irons were ready, two cowboys started roping calves by their back feet and dragging them to the fire. All the cattle were branded, ear-notched, dehorned (if required), and vaccinated for blackleg under their left shoulder. Bulls were castrated and given a penicillin shot. Testicles were dropped into a bucket for later cooking—about twenty pairs. Then all cattle were sprayed using the rig Calvin had been filling when I drove up the previous day.

We were done by 11 A.M. Back at Rooster's house, his valiant wife was ready with buffalo steak strips, garden salad, mashed potatoes, toast, gravy, iced tea and gelatin dessert. Incredible.

After lunch, we unhooked from the sprayer and headed back to headquarters with three horses in an old open-topped trailer. I was filled with gratitude for the experience afforded me and gushed with admiration for the life Calvin had made for himself and his family.

I asked more questions about the ranch and its history. Calvin said the ranch real estate alone was worth about $250 per acre at the time of the elder Fulton's death. The ranch was about 150,000 acres back then ($37.5 million), but the son had sold it down to 117,000 acres.

R. H., the father, had been a pipeline installer and installed a lot of Alaska pipeline. Calvin said the board of directors of Texaco had visited for weekends of hunting "back in the day." The ranch had plentiful pheasant, deer, and quail back then. The son, Joe Kirk, once raised game animals as conservation measures, but did not allow anything shot on the ranch now except coyotes. R. H. had also owned a lot of the works of Remington and Russell, as well as first edition books that were sold at auction by Christie's in New York when he died.

Calvin stopped the pickup and rolled down a window. "This has been a good life, but the problem is that I don't own a single thing you see. Not that house, not this pickup. Not even most of the furniture. I lose this job, I'll be leaving here empty-handed after giving this ranch the better part of my life."

I sensed a sadness I had not seen and asked if he got along well with Joe Kirk. Calvin told me that Joe Kirk was the first Texas Tech Red Raider (mascot). He had recently mortgaged ranch property to purchase a 600-acre ranch in the Hill Country with a villa for six million. He also owns homes in New Mexico and Colorado as well as race horses.

Without directly answering my question, he started the truck again and headed back toward headquarters. We had gone less than a mile when Calvin lifted a finger and pointed at an approaching ranch truck. "Speak of the devil."

Joe Kirk Fulton visits the Quien Sabe about five or six times a year, and chose this day to arrive. He pulled alongside us, rolled down his window and asked Calvin to show him the current crop of yearling horse prospects. Calvin asked if I could drive the truck back and unload the horses. We said our goodbyes.

I unloaded and unsaddled the horses and left the ranch about mid-afternoon without seeing Calvin again. A few months later, I heard Calvin was working for a feedlot in Dalhart. I haven't seen him since.

# Old Tascosa, the Mother Road, the Bent Door

## Tales from the Quien Sabe, Part VI

I LEFT THE QUIEN SABE ABOUT MID-AFTERNOON and headed south toward my high school stomping grounds, but could not pass Boys Ranch and old Tascosa without stopping. I toured the old Tascosa courthouse donated by Julian Bivins. Tascosa is an aberration of Otascoso (means boggy–for a nearby creek). Western legends abound here and the town has been the subject of many books and movies.

Bivins also donated land to form Boys Ranch. Cal Farley and his wife then established a home for wayward boys and orphans. They ran the place for many years and are buried in front. Cal was a semi-pro baseball player and a professional wrestler before he came to Amarillo to open a tire shop. Mr. and Mrs. Farley were there when I came with the Adrian boys to play the ranch high school boys many years ago.

I left the town and the homes where boys stay with foster parents and drove up to Old Tascosa Boot Hill. It was serene to sit on top of the hill with so much history laid out before me. I always feel a deep connection to Tascosa—as if I have lived there in another life.

I drove south to Adrian and roamed around the town full of high school memories. Route 66, what Steinbeck called the Mother Road, runs straight through the town. When I went to school there as a boy, the Mother Road was lined with service stations and cafes, a grain elevator and one of the best general, hardware, mercantile and clothing stores I have ever seen. It was two-story and had once been the Giles Hotel. But traffic has been rerouted to Interstate 40, and it bypasses the tiny town.

Adrian has almost become a ghost town, but my old school was still there. I drove across the cattle guard and onto the Matador Ranch, then out to find the old abandoned corral that used to be the southern loading pen when this land was part of the XIT. The ranch is said to have done spring works here, then shipping in the fall. The Matador once reached all the way to South Dakota. Not connected, of course.

From *Rivers Ebb:*

> *Something about the place stirred him. Maybe his great-grandfather or even his grandfather had worked cattle here. Maybe he had been a ranch cowboy in another life.*

I drove back to Adrian and rode around reading caution signs that had been painted with all sorts of weird proclamations I can't recall. It looked like an artists' colony of sorts. I stopped in at Mid-Point Cafe, the Route 66 halfway point between Chicago and Los Angeles (1139 miles). Inside, I found copies of Sam Brown's (the high school friend who became a cowboy poet and author) books and I learned the post office had cancelled a commemorative stamp with Sam's image a few months earlier.

As I headed out toward our old home place, I saw the Bent Door Cafe and stopped to look through its abandoned windows. What a waste of a unique old building with bent doors and windows. Looking at the booth where I sat so many times inspired me somehow. I wanted to take a few notes. I had left this country unwillingly, my cowboy dreams abandoned. Now, I had come back with dreams of becoming a writer. Suddenly tired, I realized I wanted to stay in Adrian a while longer.

The Fabulous Forty Motel seemed my only choice. The old woman who had me sign the register was really gruff and unwelcoming. The room was clean enough, but austere. I pulled a metal chair outside, leaned against the building and listened to traffic going by on I-40. Still inspired, I wrote about my time on the Quien Sabe and the visit with Calvin on a tablet.

I had brought along a copy of *Hold Autumn in Your Hand*, a book Dr. Fred Tarpley had suggested was similar to my manuscript. I finished it before bedtime.

On Friday morning, I drove out to our old house and farm. We leased the place back then and cousin Arliss had farmed it for another forty years after we left. But Arliss had died the previous Christmas and the farm and outbuildings seemed doubly sad. His old farm truck was in the shop garage with a lot more dings and dents. The shop building seemed in better shape than when we left, but our house was falling down.

I shoved open the back door and walked in. The house was hardly recognizable because it had been used as storage for farm castoffs. I could see through the ceiling, the roof and holes in the sides. The place was falling in. I worried a little about rattlers because Arliss had told me they liked hanging around in the living room. I spooked a little when a white owl fluttered its feathers and flew out through a hole in the side wall. I have returned to this site of so many memories about three times in forty years, and a white owl has flown each time. I wondered if it was a sign I am not perceptive enough to decipher.

I was dressed for conference registration later in the day, so I decided not to climb over the junk blocking the doorways. I stood still for a while, trying to reconnect to the three people who had lived here for only a brief period in our lives. I always felt the presence of my parents here, though we spent most of our lives five hundred miles southeast. Maybe it's because it was only the three of us then, alone in new country. Looking back, I now realize how frightened my parents must have been in this unfamiliar life. I grew to love it, but they never did.

# Getting Ready for the Last Roundup
## The Moorhouse Ranch, Part I

COUSIN MARION SHEPHERD (SHEP) AND I thought of ourselves as experienced trail riders after our 325-mile horseback-and-covered-wagon trip to recreate our ancestors' covered-wagon migration from Ranger in Central West Texas to Delta County in Northeast Texas. Six years later, Shep was itching for another adventure. And, unlike the Brazos trip, he had a horse gentle-broke to ride this time. We were excited by a once-in-a-lifetime chance to ride with genuine cowboys doing real ranch work. Ain't no place like Texas to get that done.

Danny Pickering, a Delta County boy who was superintendent of Guthrie ISD, offered us the chance we would not otherwise have had. He knew the famous Moorhouse brothers (Tom and Bob) and said he could arrange for us to ride along on Tom's spring roundup. Tom had said we could come along if we brought our own horses and could manage to stay aboard them. He didn't want to mess with a couple of dudes who might spoil good ranch horses or get in the way or get hurt.

I have always been fascinated with big ranches and the cowboys that make them hum. I have read a lot about them and have visited several. My fascination may have begun when I went to high school in the Panhandle only a half mile from one of the entrances to the famous Matador Ranch. I had some experiences with real ranch roundups, but mostly as a spectator rather than working cowboy. But I had also spent five years doing competitive team roping. I knew that didn't make me a real cowboy, but I felt ready for just about any cowboy experience. And I didn't think any horse could have been subjected to more diverse experiences than my horse Rowdy. Given the chance, I figured I could rope-and-drag-to-the-fire with real ranch cowboys.

I had watched Tom and Bob Moorhouse show their ranch horses in competition a few years back at the Abilene Western Heritage Classic. Friend Larry Mitchell, now a cowboy pastor at Rimrock Cowboy Church, drove a matched pair of horses and carried dignitaries in his restored buckboard during the grand entry each night of the rodeo for many years. He filled me in on the Moorhouse brothers and other ranches involved in this historic and entertaining event.

During the time of our planned trip to Guthrie, Bob Moorhouse was running the Pitchfork Ranch and his brother Tom was running the family's Moorhouse Ranch. Both have been featured in just about every cowboy and ranching magazine known to man and Bob was also garnering national acclaim for his photography.

Tom was known for running his roundups the way they did a hundred years ago, complete with chuckwagon. The prospect of participating in such an event was right up there with heaven for a couple of wannabe cowboys born a hundred years too late.

Shep and I felt so experienced from our Brazos trip that planning for this one seemed like a piece of cake. So we didn't do much planning. My horse and I had taken a few months break from roping, but I spent several days getting Rowdy legged up for the trip and felt he was ready. Unlike the Brazos trip, we didn't have to worry about two mules and four horses, sixteen days of provisions for four men and the many guests who joined us. There was no wagon to transport and drive, no detailed trail to plan, no cars or trucks to bother our stock. All we had to worry about was ourselves and two horses. Piece of cake.

# Heading for the Last Roundup and a Horse Love Affair
### *The Moorhouse Ranch, Part II*

ON SUNDAY MORNING, APRIL 11, 2004, we threw our gear in a pickup and trailer, loaded our horses and left for Guthrie. We had no idea where we would be camping, no idea whether we would have access to our pickup and trailer while we helped work cattle. No matter, we had it covered. Spend one or more nights out in the brush country without access to our stuff? We could carry all the necessities horseback.

We were about an hour away from home when Shep got a call from wife Pat saying he forgot some pills he needed. Not sure what kind they were, but they were necessary. No problem. We sat in a small cafe, told old stories, and waited for Shep's daughter Trish and husband Tommy to bring them. The horses were fine. We weren't in a hurry.

At Stoney, Texas, we stopped to visit with Morgan Hull, named one of the fifty best chefs in America. We had met Morgan and his parents during our Brazos trip. He wanted to cook for us, but we had stayed too long at the small cafe and had to be on our way.

We pulled up in Dan and Jennie Pickering's yard in Guthrie about five that afternoon. Danny had left word for us to leave our horses in a small corral across the street from his house. When we unloaded the horses, I examined Shep's gelding closely for the first time. TT was a very light sorrel, almost blond, with four white stocking feet and a blaze face—a horse that stood out in a herd. But the thing I noticed most was his feminine features. I would swear he had long eyelashes and was wearing makeup. The prettiest horse face I had ever seen. A mare's face, not a gelding's.

Rowdy, my red sorrel, dwarfed his trailer companion and seemed to have taken a proprietary interest in TT during their six hours together in the trailer. He even stood aside to let pretty TT have the first serving of feed and water. That was so unusual I started to wonder if my gelding was suffering from a little gender confusion. I figured he would know better by morning.

Gary Garrett, stud manager for the Four Sixes (6666) and the Pickering's neighbor, came over to introduce himself. He invited us to watch semen collection at the stallion barn the following morning on the historical ranch. As I recall, both Jennie and Dan were attending an event with son Welton and had asked Sandy Burkett, their neighbor, to play host until their return. Either Jennie or Sandy (not sure which) had fixed wonderful chicken enchiladas. Now that's hospitality.

After the meal, we rode out to the Moorhouse Ranch to get our bearings and to see if we could find Tom. No luck. My recollection is that the Pickerings were trusting and hospitable enough to let us spend the night in their house alone. We flipped a coin for bed or couch and I got the couch. Slept like a baby.

Next morning, we drove out to the Sixes and Gary allowed us to take a self-directed tour of ranch headquarters. Describing this ranch and its history would take another whole article (make that a book). I recalled looking at a pictorial display done by Skeeter Hagler as part of a magazine article a few years earlier. Meeting Skeeter Hagler, who won a Pulitzer for those photos, was on my bucket list. Little did I know he would show up about three miles from my front door a short time later. But that's another story.

Gary found us a spot to stand where we would not be in the way and we watched as veterinary students (all women) from A&M handled teaser mares and studs during the semen collection process. I had witnessed controlled horse breeding in Kentucky a few years earlier and semen collection on a ranch near Commerce, but this was indescribably different and even more remarkable. We marveled at the efficiency and cool composure of the young female college students engaged in what can be a very dangerous procedure. Guess further description of the process is best left to the imagination.

We drove out to the 6666 Supply Store and wandered through the little no-frills store full of tack and basics. We stopped at the small museum at Pitchfork headquarters and Shep bought one of Bob Moorhouse's photography books. We also visited the Tongue River Ranch (Tom now runs that ranch) headquarters before going on to Aspermont to buy horse feed, some trail snacks and ice.

We spent another night with the Pickerings, then back out to the Moorhouse early Tuesday morning. Not a soul in sight. Just as we were starting to believe Tom was only a legend, we saw a few horses headed for headquarters, leaving behind a cloud of dust. Tom and his horse emerged from the cloud as the horses ran across the headquarters yard into a waiting catch pen. A photographer could have made the scene into another magazine cover.

As he stepped off to greet us, I couldn't help but put myself in his boots and wonder why he had offered hospitality to two complete strangers who had the audacity to actually show up and get in his way. But he was gracious. "First, let's go inside and get some coffee."

I don't remember many details about the house. Only that it seemed all Texan, solid as a rock, and there was a lot of native rock. There was little evidence of Tom's fame in evidence, just one photo of him on a magazine cover hanging near the kitchen. As we moved to a small nook off the kitchen, I noticed a copy of Rick Warren's *The Purpose Driven Life* on an end table. I was in the middle of reading it at home, so we discussed it a little while he put coffee on to boil.

We wanted to show our gratitude for his allowing us to participate and to assure him we would not get in the way. But he seemed relaxed about the whole thing and peppered us with questions faster than we could interrogate him. He poured our cups to the brim and I sipped cowboy coffee like Daddy used to make. I like coffee in the mornings and occasionally on a cold night, but I can spot an all-day coffee drinker and Tom was one of those. Just like Uncle Arch (Shep's dad) and Teadon (my dad). The coffee was not as bitter as I expected. In fact, it was really good if you didn't mind chewing a stray ground or two.

He shared a little history of the ranch and showed us the dugout his ancestors had built as their first home. We could see the entrance from where we were having coffee. We could tell Tom was proud of his father Togo and his deep connections to historic Texas ranching, but he had that Texas cowboy brand of humility about everything. He told us roundup preparations would begin in the afternoon on the Parramore Ranch. I knew large ranches are often made up of smaller ranches run by different managers. I assumed the area where we were going was part of the Moorhouse, but was not for sure. I now think they leased the Parramore. The roundup mattered—working with Tom Moorhouse mattered—not the ranch. Shep and I followed Tom's directions to the Parramore (between Guthrie and Aspermont) and unloaded our horses a few minutes after noon. We saddled them and gave them some needed exercise.

We were relieved when the chuckwagon arrived (towed behind a pickup). That assured us we were in the right place. We offered to help, but the young cowboys who erected a canvas cover over the wagon had obviously done it many times. The horse remuda, along with extra saddles and tack, arrived in a deuce-and-a-half truck soon after. About twenty head were unloaded in a corral a few yards from where our trailer was parked and our horses were tied.

Usually unperturbed by such things, Rowdy seemed disturbed by the invasion of new horses on turf he had already claimed as his own. It was not like him. He worked at his lead rope until he got enough slack to stand closer to TT.

The cook arrived in a small sedan (not the usual cowboy transportation) just as the wagon cover was finished. A dozen or so cowboys were not far behind. We were surprised to learn the cook was a traveler who cooked for several outfits. He was affable and full of conversation as we helped him unload some of his utensils from the trunk of the car. He went right to work with the fire and cast-iron cookware.

Tom Moorhouse arrived soon after, carrying a fairly large mattress rolled into a bedroll. I was surprised at the size of all the cowboy bedrolls. Made for comfort, but too big to tie behind a saddle. In what seemed like only minutes, we sat down to sourdough biscuits, beans, stew, and peach cobbler. Coffee made with gyp water was the only liquid.

The cowboys eyed us with friendly wariness. One could almost read the question in their eyes as they wondered how much extra trouble we were going to be. They were polite, but short on helpful information. We knew there was a pecking order and a cowboy code of sorts that we did not want to break.

We always hobbled our horses on the Brazos trip, but figured they would be just fine tied to the trailer all night. I knew that Rowdy had learned how to roam with hobbles and worried about him getting into something he shouldn't. Tom's head wrangler (we'll call him Jackson because I can't recall his name) finally told us to throw them in with the rest of the horses. "They'll stomp around all night and keep you awake tied to that trailer." Relieved to have approval, we led them into the big corral. The rest of the evening was just about perfect. When I asked Jackson about my old friends Calvin Peters and Sam Brown, he knew both. Seems the cowboy community is close knit, though hundreds of miles apart. We sat around the campfire until close to bedtime, then watched another small group of cowboys arrive from Oklahoma. Like us, they wanted to do a roundup with Tom. I heard one of the ranch cowboys tell the newcomers to be cocked and ready if they wanted to help with a Moorhouse roundup.

Shep slept in the trailer on a cot and I unrolled my bedroll outside. I had learned my lesson on the Brazos trip and had added a small cot mattress that could be rolled up in the bedroll and still be small enough to tie behind a saddle. As I drifted off to sleep, we still did not know what the next day would bring. We had a lot of simple questions that we were embarrassed to ask for fear of sounding like greenhorns. Would we be away from camp the next night? What would we eat the next day and did we need to carry our own food? Did we need to take provisions to last for more than a day? Should I put my bedroll and saddlebags on the horse in the morning?

# Cowboy Rituals at Dawn

## *The Moorhouse Ranch, Part III*

I WAS ALREADY AWAKE AND VERY COLD just before dawn when I heard a young cowboy approach my bedroll. His words were stiff and formal. He gently nudged my foot inside the bedroll with his boot. "Mr. Ainsworth, sir, Mr. Moorhouse asked me to tell you that breakfast would be ready in about a half hour."

I thanked him and got up. The bracing cold hit me. By the cook fire, I learned the temperature had plunged to just below freezing overnight. No wonder I was stiff and sore. We had fried eggs and bacon, more biscuits, and prickly pear jelly made by Tommy Sprayberry, a friendly young cowboy who took great pride in his jelly and deservedly so.

A burly young cowboy skipped his breakfast to ride a horse in a narrow lane between the corrals, making repeated rollbacks against the fences at full speed. The others laughed and told us the horse had thrown him the day before. They said he had something to prove. "That is, if Tom allows him to ride the horse again today." I wondered about that "allowed" part.

As we finished our breakfast, the cowboys mentioned, "horses by 6:15" as if speaking in code that we were meant to hear, but not understand. Sure enough, at six, the young men dropped their plates and utensils in the cook's dishwater and trotted toward their saddles and tack. Feeling unprepared, we gathered up our halters and rushed to the corral. Tom and Jackson were already in the corral, ropes in hand, frowning at a spectacle that made my heart jump into my throat.

Ears pinned and teeth bared, Rowdy was circling TT in the middle of the herd, occasionally kicking up his heels as a warning to any horse that approached TT. "Whose horse is that?" Tom asked.

I fessed up. "He's mine." Head ducked and face warm, I walked over to Rowdy, haltered him and led him out of the corral. He protested, but only until my jerk of the lead rope told him I meant business. Shep followed with TT. I felt like a parent does when a normally well-behaved child makes a spectacle in a restaurant.

We stayed to watch the cowboy tradition of "choosing and catching up" the daily mounts. Each cowboy approached Tom in a pecking order we did not understand, pointed to a horse and described him (the gray roan with one back sock). Tom could either decline or consent to his requested mount. I saw no declines, including the cowboy who was thrown. He got his second chance. When the selection was made, Tom and Jackson took turns throwing houlihan loops (a loop designed to be delivered in only one swing, usually from the ground, and meant to sort of float from high to settle around a horse's neck).

Although the loops are meant to cause minimal disturbance, the horses still ran to the corners. I wondered why each cowboy did not just walk up and catch his mount, but this was tradition and what did I know? One has to consider the danger of being bitten or kicked if you walk into a corral full of horses that are bunched up and feeling early morning friskiness.

Mesmerized at the almost mythical dawn ceremony, we were late getting our own mounts ready. Saddles, blankets, and other tack lay haphazardly on the ground as we headed toward our horses. There was no grooming of horses. The cowboys ran their hands over their horses' backs and under their bellies to clean off any dirt or mud before slinging pads and saddles across them.

I dispensed with my usual brushing of Rowdy. I took pride in getting my horse saddled quickly and efficiently, but when I saw a few cowboys mount, I knew I was over-tacked. I quickly unbuckled my breast harness, my neck rope, and my saddlebags and threw them in the trailer along with my bedroll. As Tom and the others rode up to our trailer, Shep and I were scrambling to get ready. One cowboy told me, "Might want to leave that tie-down here. Saw a horse break his neck once when a limb got under one and he fell down the side of a hill." I complied. I have never been a fan of tie-downs, but almost all roping horses wear them. And once a horse gets used to one, they don't know how to behave without it.

We mounted and quickly broke into the same long trot that the other horses were in. Now, a long trot is not the most comfortable for the rider, but you get used to it and it is a good way to "untrack" a horse and get him limbered up. It's good for their legs. Riders in the long trot do what I call a West Texas Post (not the same as the English style of posting). We stayed in a long trot for about four miles. Rowdy tested the new freedom he had without the tie-down by slinging his head as he tried to get closer to TT. I was irritated when he seemed to think he was in charge instead of me.

# Riding the Breaks
## *The Moorhouse Ranch, Part IV*

WE SLOWED TO A WALK AS WE REACHED the cedar breaks (sometimes called a mott), and I had time to really observe the country we were in. Rugged is probably overused, but it fits. Beautiful but harsh. I had seen cedar breaks from a distance, but had never ridden in them. Again, there were few instructions. I saw no cattle as we entered the breaks. The terrain was hilly and rocky and a man riding horseback can only see a few feet. The trees are just tall enough to block your vision. A horseback man disappears in a matter of seconds.

I did not realize until six years later that it was country like this that allowed my great-grandfather to remain a fugitive for almost five years, always seeing his *Home Light Burning*, but unable go home.

> *Mary Ann was surprised when Alfred came out of the barn and ran after his father. She caught him and held his arms as Lev rode into the cedars, disappearing a little with each step. In two of little Alfred's deep breaths, his father was gone, a ghost once again.*

Jackson told Shep and me to stay with him until we reached the top of the hill. I was pleased when Rowdy straddled the smaller cedar trees and plowed over them like he had worked in them all his life. Little did I know he would have run through a barn wall to get close to TT. I was starting to relax when he stopped. I looked down and a tree limb had managed to get inside the girth strap that I had left too loose.

We weren't exactly on the side of a mountain, but there was a steep incline on the side where the limb was caught and it was loose, rocky ground. As I dismounted, Rowdy was highly anxious because TT was leaving his sight—along with all the other riders. I slid backward on the loose rock a few times as I tried to hold him still long enough to loosen the flank girth. They were all out of sight by the time I freed the limb. I could hear the stories in my head as I remounted: *Ainsworth lost in cedar breaks, never seen again.* I couldn't believe they were out of sight and sound in such a short time. I rode straight ahead and finally caught up to them as they stopped at a small stream to let their horses water. The horses had to climb at a sharp angle as we left the stream. The higher we climbed, the rougher the ground, until it seemed we were traveling on solid rock.

When TT and Shep and Jackson and his mount emerged and stood in a small clearing on solid rock, Rowdy clawed his way to his buddy, literally making sparks fly from his shoes. I worried about setting the woods on fire. We entered the small clearing and made the two-horse opening accommodate three. Jackson shook his head, probably wondering why Tom had allowed us to come.

As I write this, I realize it sounds like I was just a passenger holding onto the saddle horn with both hands—the dude that Tom was concerned about. Let me try to redeem myself. I may not be a great horseman, but I have ridden all my life. And I had ridden Rowdy for over ten years in almost every situation. His infatuation with TT and the few months he had rested from team roping seemed to have erased the memory of all that training. And there was neither room nor time for any retraining to take place. I was embarrassed and more than a little disappointed in my old friend.

From our high vantage point, we finally heard the yelps and whoops of the other cowboys. I still saw no cattle, but we did see trees moving, indicating that there was a herd. About sixty head finally left the cedar breaks and entered a mesquite thicket. We went from cedars to mesquite thorns, but at least we could see where we and the cattle were going. When the cattle were penned, we trotted back about three miles to the chuckwagon for a meal of fried steak, beans, corn and blackberry cobbler. The sheriff was waiting.

It cast a pall over the camp when one of the cowboys was taken into custody for rustling. But it didn't stop us from trotting back more miles to work that herd and gather another one. Shep and I more or less stood guard and handled stragglers as Tom built a fire for branding (no blow

torches here). They branded and vaccinated all the calves and castrated the bull calves. Then we gathered a second herd in a small corner of the pasture (not a corral or holding pen), built a second fire, and did the same. The cattle were held on two sides by fence, the other two by mounted cowboys. For the first time, I felt moderately useful. Tom actually signaled me to bring back in a straggler. Rowdy performed well. As we started to gather a third herd, Tom pointed toward a fuel tank on a hill to the northwest and spoke to Shep and me. "You two head over to that tank. If they try to go past it, point 'em north. That's the only hole they can get through."

As we started to climb the hill where the tank was, a cowboy rode up, hat waving. "Jackson says you're supposed to go over to the other side of that tank."

I nodded. "That's where we're going."

He pointed a little south of the fuel tank to a body of water. "There's the tank." I had forgotten that pools are called tanks in West Texas. Tom had been pointing to the pool, not the fuel tank. I felt foolish again.

# The Last of the Last Roundup
## The Moorhouse Ranch, Part V

WE GATHERED A THIRD HERD AND drove them back to camp. The temperature had risen from thirty-one to about ninety-one and I had one of the worst headaches of my life by the time we reached camp. Fortunately, Rowdy had settled down and was behaving like a gentleman, even without the tie-down. I stood guard for stragglers and runaways and waited for Tom to build another fire, but we only sorted this herd—no branding. We finished by about seven-thirty and had beef covered with cornbread, English peas and blackberry cobbler by the chuckwagon.

My headache left after the meal, but Shep looked a little pale when he revealed that he had forgotten to take his medicine that morning. We sat around the campfire for a while, but were soon ready for bed. We agreed this had been one of the hardest days ever spent horseback. I can't be sure, but I think we trotted close to twenty miles. Not as bad as pulling bolls, but we were sore and so were our horses.

I was unrolling my bedroll when I saw two of the young cowboys from Oklahoma bent over losing their supper. I felt for them, but it made me feel not quite so old. One of their companions came over and pointed to our pickup bed. "Sir, if you have any cold beer in that cooler, I would happily pay you ten dollars for one."

I laughed. "I'd give you one if I had it, but I don't. Sorry."

"I would give the same amount for a cold Coke."

"So would I."

Gyp water and coffee were still the only liquids.

Though tired and sore, we rested well that night. The next day, our horses were sore to the point of lameness and so were we. We rode out and watched another branding and captured it on a borrowed video camera. Over dinner of roast beef, beans and corn, we visited more with Tom and Charlie the cook. Both were forthcoming about their lives, even personal matters, and we did get to meet Tom's wife.

We left shortly after the noon meal and stopped at Guthrie ISD to thank Danny for his hospitality and for helping us to have the experience of a lifetime. We were not sure we had measured up, but we had something we could mark off our bucket lists. We had arrived with a healthy respect for cowboys, cattlemen, and horsemen. We had dreamed of becoming all three, but circumstances and necessity had taken us in different directions. This adventure proved that Tom Moorhouse was all three, and allowed us to vividly imagine what might have been.

In the middle of chronicling our trip, I heard a sniveling, pompous, vain, ignorant politician use the term cowboy in a disparaging way, referring to a series of stupid blunders by bureaucrats as "cowboy." Nothing could be further from the truth. I wanted to take him through the cedar breaks and come back alone. I often hear "Cowboy" bandied about in derogatory fashion. Soon after the trip I read the book *Cowboy Ethics: What Wall Street Can Learn from the Code of the West*. With a little experience on both sides of that equation, I heartily agree with the book.

Six years after our ride with Tom, I did a lot of research about my ancestors' coming through that part of the country as fugitives and our trip took on added meaning. This scene is from *Home Light Burning*:

> *Butter hit the cedars like a buffalo bull, creating a din of cracking and popping. Lev felt his shirtsleeves being torn and was grateful for the loan of his father's leggings as the cedar limbs scratched along both legs. He could almost see over the tops of the cedars, but not quite—just enough to make a man feel trapped and blind.*

Sound familiar? After all was said and done, I never threw my rope, never dragged a calf to the fire. It was not offered and I did not ask. But I am still grateful for the experience. Rowdy and TT? They never saw each other again.

# A Saddle with a Story

SATISFIED THAT WE HAD CHOSEN THE RIGHT hotel in the right town for our broker-dealer conference, I drove out to a peaceful middle class suburb of Fort Worth. I knew where I was going, but did not know why, and I was going unannounced. I stopped in the driveway of a nice, but non-pretentious house. Nobody answered the doorbell, so I knocked on the door of a small building in the backyard. I knew it was an artist's studio because I had seen pictures of it in *Yippy Yi Yea*. I had a copy of the magazine with me along with some of the other magazines that had feature stories on Bob Moline.

When he opened the door, I apologized for intruding, told him I knew his friend Don Edwards, and invited him to our conference. He invited me inside. A beautiful saddle almost exactly like the one I had seen being crafted in the magazine article sat on a wooden stand, surrounded by Native American artifacts including Bob's personal medicine wheel (Bob's heritage is Comanche-Pawnee) and a white buffalo head.

The studio was bright and immaculately clean. Many of Bob's paintings hung on the walls, some just leaned against in what some might see as haphazard fashion, but I suspected an artist's sense of order prevailed. One painting in progress seemed to take center stage.

I learned Bob Moline had been named official artist of the Texas Bicentennial Wagon Train (friends Charles Horchem and Larry Mitchell were part of that train). He showed me some of the greeting cards he had designed and I asked him to sign a few for me. He also signed the magazines where his paintings and saddles had been featured.

I also knew his work graced the walls of the Cowboy Hall of Fame because I had seen them there. I did not know his work had appeared on the covers of The Cattleman and Paint Horse Journal magazines. I saw awards naming him an outstanding artist from Texas Professional Artists, The American Indian and Cowboy Artist's Society and the Texas Ranger Hall of Fame.

Moline had worked for Ryon's Saddle Shop for twelve years and painted as a hobby. His Ryon saddles were purchased by folks like cutting horse legend Buster Welch, singer Loretta Lynn and movie cowboy Guy Madison. When he left there and turned to painting, his success as an artist surprised him. Now, he said, he paints for a living and makes saddles as a hobby. He also does four or five sculptures a year.

I was surprised when he said making saddles was his first love. His trademark is a single eagle feather, which symbolizes his personal vision of the West. In Indian culture, it stands for strength, wisdom and courage.

All the time we were talking, my eyes kept going back to the saddle on the stand. It had the type of stamping and tooling I prefer, oxbow stirrups, was the right color of leather and I loved the feather symbol. I guess nobody will be surprised when I say that I now own that saddle, along with a matching buffalo head nickel belt that Bob made for me. I wanted a sculpture of the saddle, but he seemed reluctant to take an order for a sculpture. I suppose a sculpture is best when inspired, not made to order.

I rode it on our trip across Texas and in many team roping events. I still ride it today.

# The Old Roper

## The Lost Thumb

*The following story is true but names have been changed*

BLOOD FROM HIS SEVERED RIGHT THUMB ran through the fingers of his left hand, dripped on his boots from the stump where the thumb used to be. As the barrel-chested man made his way through the riders in the waiting pen, his eyes downcast as if praying for the clock to roll back so he could have a do-over. The smell of blood and fear overpowered the thick haze of dust and the sweat of horses and nervous riders. A sense of foreboding traveled through the waiting ropers and their horses like molten lava.

Asa Mackie stood in his stirrups to see inside the arena, deciphering reasons for the accident, assuring himself that such a wreck could never happen to him. A flagman led the horse of the thumbless rider close enough for Asa to touch. Asa and his horse Gambler were crammed into a too-small waiting pen outside the arena at Glen Rose, Texas, waiting to rope in the short go—the final round of competition in a four-header, roping for a shot at a saddle or trophy buckle and part of six-thousand dollars in prize money. The high-point roper would also win a new Dodge dualie. Asa and his partner were fourteenth after three runs, in a good slot for some cash and a saddle. Asa had no chance at the pickup, but his partner was sitting pretty to win it, too. Asa wanted the saddle more than the money or even the truck–something to pass on to his grandchildren as eternal evidence that their grandfather could handle a horse and rope.

Asa's partner, the heeler, was a stranger, drawn by lot. Asa liked it that way, and stayed far away to avoid last minute coaching from a man good enough to rope for a Dodge truck. Last minute coaching made him nervous. They would soon be able to count heads in the chute and see which steer would be theirs, and Asa did not want to know if he was fast, ducked, went left or set up. He roped better not knowing. Cattle sometimes did not follow routine, and Asa did not want to fall victim to expectations that the steer would behave a certain way. Sometimes they did as expected, sometimes not.

But when they were third in line, he couldn't help himself. He counted heads until he came to their steer. He recognized him—a pup that always ran straight, not too fast, not too slow, horns not too big, not too little. He always followed the head horse like he wanted to nurse and lifted his heels to be roped like an obedient puppy.

The heeler grinned when he saw him. "We got this thing won."

Gambler still didn't like roping much, especially in front of big crowds, but he surprised Asa by backing into the head box like a gentleman. Asa wasted no time in nodding for the steer. The steer left, but Gambler leaned back and stayed put. Asa spurred and the horse exploded out of the box well behind the steer. Asa spanked him with his loop to catch up. Still a little off balance, Asa lifted his loop to swing, but it would not come up. He had hung a spur with his loop when he slapped Gambler.

By the time he straightened his loop, it was too late to even swing. The heeler roped the steer's back feet anyway, just to show his contempt. The compliant little steer seemed to mock Asa as it trotted past him and entered the stripping chute. The heeler rode by as Asa recoiled his unused rope. He looked in the man's eyes and said, "I'm sorry."

The heeler nodded. "That's all right. I didn't need no Dodge truck, no cash and no saddle, anyway." He was not smiling. It wasn't the first time Asa had come close and failed. He rode out of the arena and tried to console himself that at least he still had both thumbs.

Asa had always owned a horse, even when he held suit-and-tie jobs. Scar, Charlie, Badger, Jubilee, Dixie, Sugar, Shortcut, May, Yellow Dog, Cutter Boy, Snicker, Rowdy, and Shooter. He even tried a few broncs in real rodeos to prove his mettle, but kept his lack of roping skills a secret. Every cowboy worth his salt knew that roping was the measure of a real cowboy.

At fifty-one, Asa bought a colt already named Gambler. He team-penned on the sorrel, used him in ranch roundups and on long trail rides.

Gambler did it all well. But when Asa decided to learn to rope, real cowboys warned that a rider new to roping needed a horse that was an old hand. That went double for an old roper.

Asa insisted they could learn together. But Gambler did not like roping. He refused to go in the head box, then refused to leave, rearing back on his hind legs to the point of tipping over. Cowboys shook their heads at a green cowboy trying to rope on a green horse. Gambler dumped Asa when a rope got hung under his tail. He let roped steers run around him to drag Asa out of the saddle and through the dirt. Asa's wrist was caught and his hand swelled to bursting when a roped steer stopped and Gambler kept going. He lost the end of a finger. Asa looked so bad that cowboys assumed he was not only a beginning roper, but also a novice rider—after five decades of riding.

The worst happened in front of a large gathering of friends and family. Chasing a steer at full speed, Gambler suddenly made a hard left, leaving Asa in the arena dirt. On his feet and dusting off, he felt his face warm when he realized he had lost a boot. He made two circles in the dirt before he saw it, sitting upright, spur intact, laughing along with the crowd, in the saddle seat. Asa could not have duplicated such a stunt in a thousand tries.

People assumed he would give up after that, and he did consider it. But the proper excuses would not come. Soon after, Asa and Gambler helped to herd escaped cattle off a highway in the dark. Gambler worked with focused calm despite speeding traffic, bright lights, and horns. Job done, Asa stepped off and praised the horse. "Why can't you do that when we're roping?"

Gambler looked at him as if to say, "Because you don't expect it."

Asa's father's voice spoke from the past. "You get what you expect from a horse." How could he have forgotten? Gambler read his mind—through his hands, seat, legs and feet.

After that night, Asa took deep breaths, visualized and expected good performance. Gambler delivered. They won a fifth in a big roping, a first in a small jackpot. On a cold November night, a Twister saddle was on the line for high-point roper. Asa wanted it so bad his teeth hurt. He caught all of his steers, including three in the finals, but the runs were slow. Brisk winds buffeted him as he led Gambler out of the arena, wondering if third place money would cover his entry fees.

A voice called from the dark. "Better get back in there, Asa. You're up for the saddle."

Asa felt his leg being pulled. "Can't be. Too slow."

The heeler's reply made smoke in the cool night air. "Yeah, but you caught 'em all."

Asa led Gambler back in stunned silence, skin tingling, ears ringing, ashamed to acknowledge how much he wanted that saddle. He kept his back to the officials' box, made small talk, acted unconcerned, tried to find a graceful way to go back into the dark, but he knew, at worst, he had at least some money to collect. He couldn't just go home. Minutes that seemed like hours passed with no word from the officials.

He barely noticed the quiet until a tinkle of laughter stirred behind him. Gambler nudged him forward a step. Asa turned at the laughter. Gambler wore two saddles, the beautiful trophy Twister on top. Friends slapped his back, shook his hand, and went home, leaving Asa alone in the arena with his horse. Gambler looked tired, silly with two saddles on his back. He looked in Asa's eyes as if to say. "Are you finally satisfied? Can we quit now?"

Asa put a palm between Gambler's eyes. "Good job, old son, but this is number one. I've got seven grandkids."

# Checking Off
# the Bucket List

I had a bucket list long before Jack Nicholson starred in the movie. I titled mine "Things to do Before I Die." The following stories are about the remarkable people I met and places I visited while checking off that list.

# Falling Down a Mountain
## The Magnificent Seven—Minus Six
## Part I

A HORSE PACKING TRIP IN THE MOUNTAINS had been on my bucket list for a long time when I read an article about a Wyoming outfitter in a cowboy magazine. Three months later, I was driving down the Chief Joseph Scenic Trail, alongside the Yellowstone River, then through the park. In Cody, Wyoming, I saw a sign that made me stop for a meal at the Proud Cut Saloon. The name made me chuckle (look it up if you don't know the term). A sign over the bar read, "Some people are alive only because it's against the law to kill 'em." My kind of place. A place where folks have a sense of humor.

Spent the night in a small cabin in Jackson. A driver in a small van picked me up the next morning. I was the first passenger, but expected at least six more to join me. I had been promised a full excursion into high-elevations in the Gros Ventre wilderness area with a group of experienced horsemen from New Mexico and Colorado. Two were even hunting guides.

I had been riding all my life, but had little experience riding in the mountains. I expected to learn from a group of rough and tough hunters and horsemen. The brochure described treacherous switchbacks, perilous canyons, rock slides, mountain vistas. But it was the picture on the brochure of six grizzled horseback veterans that brought to mind *The Magnificent Seven* (I saw myself as the seventh) that really got my attention. It was described as *"A Real Man's Ride."*

I frowned a little when the van stopped to pick up a couple from Minnesota. The small green rabbit felt hat worn by the wife with a stampede string tucked tightly under her chin and the way the husband stumbled along in boots two sizes too large gave me an uh-oh feeling. I figured they were going with another group.

By the time we picked up the remaining passengers, I had a real sense of trepidation. When we unloaded at the trailhead, I approached head outfitter Phil, nodded my head toward my riding companions, and asked what happened to the tough guys he had told me about. I was disappointed and angry enough to ask for my money back. Phil stepped off a big red roan, put his hand on my shoulder and guided me away from the others. He explained in whispers the six other gentlemen scheduled to ride with me had cancelled at the last minute and these riders were on a waiting list. Said I had already left home before he could notify me.

That was possible, because I had left a few days early to conduct some business. But I still wanted a refund. Phil told me he had no choice but to take these folks to the same places he had planned to take the magnificent seven. He said I could have my pick of the horses; could ride alone if I wanted to; would be treated as a member of the crew, not a guest; guaranteed me the experience of a lifetime. If I did not have it, he promised a refund at the end of the trip.

I didn't believe him. "You're really gonna take these folks on the same ride you promised me? The ride for experienced horsemen only?"

His face held a pained expression. "Got no choice. Plans already been made. Camps already set up. That's why I may need your help."

I felt my leg being pulled. Phil was one of those people who had an obvious knack for fooling you and making you smile at his effort. I looked up to the mountains for a few minutes, walked over to the van, got my saddlebags, tied them behind the red roan's saddle, and mounted. Phil patted the roan's hip. "That's my horse."

I nodded. "You said I could have my pick. Did you mean what you said, or not?"

He removed his hat, ran his finger around the sweatband, and grinned. "My friends call me Buck. I'm short a hand since both of my brothers are staying behind to pack the food, cookstove and other supplies. You mind bringing up the rear in case one of these dudes falls off?"

I called after him as he ambled away. "Mind if I adjust the stirrups?"

He never turned. "You a cowboy. Do what you think's right."

I thought Buck was pulling my leg about dudes falling off, but we had traveled less than a quarter of the way up the mountain to our first campsite before one did fall. Six horses jumped across a spruce that had fallen across a stream without losing a passenger, but the seventh drug a hoof and stirred up a hornet's nest. Hornet stings on a horse's belly will cause him to buck.

The man in front of me had talked non-stop to his horse since leaving the trailhead. "Okay, can we leave now?" evolved into things like, "Would you mind catching up to the others?"

His legs, feet and arms were useless appendages and the horn was his only means of steering. He had no idea what to do with the reins. He seemed to believe he could make friends and negotiate with his mount in human speak.

I shouted a warning when I saw the hornets, but he could not hear me over his ceaseless prattle. Soft mud in the stream broke his fall. I helped him up and he bravely remounted, whispering to his horse, "I know you didn't mean to do that."

An hour later, the dude (Will) and I were becoming friends, I learned the man in the too-big boots was called Joe, and I was enjoying some of the most beautiful, pristine scenery I had ever seen. The temperature had dropped twenty degrees and I could see snow in the Grand Tetons in the distance (this was August). I could also hear, see and feel the mist off a waterfall.

The narrow trail sloped off steeply on our right so that we were eye-level with the tops of gigantic whitebark pines. The serenity and quiet had really enveloped me when I heard a squeal from the woman in the green hat and saw her husband tumble down the deep slope. Joe tumbled for what seemed like a long time. The base of a lodgepole pine about fifty yards down finally stopped his descent. I saw a solo boot against a tree trunk about halfway down.

Buck wrapped a rope around a big tree limb, tied the other end around his waist, and put a second rope he plucked from one of the pack-horses over his neck and under one arm. He yelled for me to try and keep the horses calm as he semi-rappelled down to his customer. He wrapped the extra rope under Joe's arms, and then climbed back up. Buck's stock

went up as I watched his calm and skillful descent and ascent. He led the big roan I was riding forward a few feet and dallied the rope around the horn. I pulled the rope about chest high against a tree and he gently eased the roan (and Joe) forward.

Joe tried to keep his feet, but fell several times on the way up. He suffered more from scratches when the rope dragged him along the ground than he had from the fall. Bruised-but-not-broken, Joe reluctantly remounted less than an hour later (with both boots on). He had panicked as he stared down the deep slope, pulled a rein hard enough to cause his horse to fall and dump him down the mountain.

# The Old Hag Arrives

## *The Magnificent Seven—Minus Six Part II*

AT THE MAIN CAMPSITE, BUCK KEPT HIS promise and assigned me to a private tent several yards up the mountain and close to the cook tent. I liked the location, but the tent sagged with the weight of accumulated water. When his two brothers and Patty, the cook, did not arrive with food and the wood cookstove, he sent me back down a different trail to see if they were in trouble. Alone in that pristine wilderness, I was in cowboy and mountain heaven. I found the stragglers and discovered they were behind schedule because the owner of the packhorses and mules (an experienced rider) had been thrown. They had to take him back to the trailhead to be treated for a sprained ankle. It was well past dark when we rode into camp, but the brothers installed the cookstove and Patty had steak and potatoes ready in less than two hours. We ate together in the cook tent. The stove warmth felt good.

I learned Phil was called Buck because he had broken his back and both knees riding broncs (I had a great deal more respect for his rapelling down a mountain when I heard this), his brother Randy was called Rangey, and brother George was called Stanley (no reason was given). They had children with names like Snow Ann, Wolf and Whiz. Patty told me the brothers always took turns drinking on trips like this. One brother stayed sober each night in order to handle any emergency that might arise while the others got roaring drunk.

# THE OLD HAG ARRIVES

The next morning, Buck awakened me well before daylight to help wrangle the horses. My bedroll was cozy and the water on top of my tent had turned to ice. I started to rethink my desire to be treated as a member of the crew. They tied bells on the horses each night and turned them loose to forage for themselves because they could not pack enough feed up the mountain. We found them by listening for the bells (every morning except one).

At sunrise, Buck pointed toward a herd of elks in the distance, said he would be back during season with hunters. I asked about hunting for bears and he said he could get away with shooting me easier than he could a grizzly.

Unshaved and unbathed after four days of riding and camping, I was beginning to feel like Jeremiah Johnson. I was sleeping like a baby in the wee hours when two mounted riders leading two packhorses complete with banging pans rode by my tent and stopped at the cook tent. I rolled out of my bedroll in my longhandles, pulled back the tent flap, and watched. A dying campfire by the cook tent revealed Buck and Stanley asleep on bare ground with only a light blanket for cover and their hats for pillows in freezing temps. It had been their turn to drink that night.

I had come to like and enjoy the brothers, but one could never accuse them of proper cowboy etiquette or attire like most ranch cowboys adhere to in Texas. Their hats were bent out of shape, their boots worn over on the heels, their shirts and jeans torn. By starlight, the two new arrivals looked like something out of a Gary Cooper western when compared to the brothers.

Lights came on in the cook tent and Patty shouted loud enough to wake us all that "The Old Hag" had finally arrived. Laughter filled the mountain air as Patty hugged one of the riders and Rangey shook the hand of the other.

When we gathered for breakfast, we all knew Julie Hagen (the Old Hag) and her companion Jimmy before we took our first bite. Both made the rounds and introduced themselves. Julie was a ranch manager who had worked on ranches in Arizona, Colorado and Montana, and the Little Jennie in Wyoming. Jimmy was an outfitter who led safaris in Wyoming, Montana, Alaska and Africa. She and Jimmy had been friends since high school and possessed that kind of free spirit most of us long for but rarely achieve.

Jimmy and I were close to the same size. As we rode together the next few days, I tried to buy his chaps, his hunting knife, his pistol, even his boots. He wouldn't sell a thing. They all looked like something the first People might have used before Columbus discovered America. I had never seen any like them, before or since. Everything he wore was handmade.

Jimmy and Buck told me Julie was also a painter and poet, that her brother was an Olympic skier, her father a biologist, her mother a professional flutist. Not your usual resumé for a ranch manager or horsepacker. I also learned she had met famous photographer Jay Dusard in college and they had remained close friends. Years later, I would cross paths with Dusard. One of his photos of her when she had been ranch manager for Wagstaff Land and Cattle Co. had become famous and had been included in his book, *The North American Cowboy: A Portrait*. She was definitely more than an old hag.

# The Stranger in the Mirror

## *The Magnificent Seven—Minus Six Part III*

THE TRIP DOWN THE MOUNTAIN ON THE final day was not as pleasant as the one going up. It was warm and dusty; the horses knew we were near the end and fought their bits, finally taking off with the inexperienced riders, drowning us in a sea of dust. We had started to sweat, so the dust formed a dark cover on our faces. I held the big roan back and stayed with the brothers. I glanced at Jimmy and Julie as Buck and Rangey calmly watched their string of horses run full speed down the mountain, the riders (their responsibility) hanging on for dear life. Jimmy and Julie had apparently watched the spectacle before.

Rangey pointed at the riders. "We did these folks a lot of good in a short time. Not a single one fell off. Last week at this time, we woulda lost at least three or four."

Buck asked me if I still wanted my money back as he reached for a billfold I knew was empty ("I never carry money in the mountains. Ain't no place to spend it.") I laughed and said no. It had not been the Magnificent Seven, but it still ranked as a great experience.

As we said goodbye at the trailhead, The Old Hag told me where I could buy some of her greeting cards in Jackson. When I walked into the lobby of the little cabin court back in Jackson, I saw a reflection of a stranger in a full-length mirror and briefly wondered who he was. The bearded, dust-covered man's face was about three shades darker than my own—he wore spurs with saddlebags over his shoulder and appeared to have stepped out of a time capsule from a century earlier. Then I knew that, for a second or two, he was the man a certain boy had dreamed of becoming long, long ago.

I dropped by the store Julie told me about and bought some of her greeting cards and the framed photograph I later learned had appeared not only in Dusard's book but in *American Cowboy, Cowboys and Indians*, and many other magazines. I have seen it in publications many times since. The store promised to get it signed before shipping to me. Julie signed it, *"To Jim, till our trails cross again."* It hangs in my office today.

# Meeting the Marlboro Man

## An Evening at the Cowboy Hall of Fame, Part I

IT WAS ONE OF THOSE SPUR-OF-THE-MOMENT, I-can't-believe-I-did-that types of decisions when I look back on it. I had occasion to visit Oklahoma City on business several times during the early nineties and one of those visits included a tour of the Cowboy Hall of Fame, now called The National Cowboy and Western Heritage Museum. Fascinated, of course, by all things cowboy my entire life, I felt a connection, so I joined the organization. My membership included a subscription to their magazine, *Persimmon Hill* (that's the name of the site where the building that houses the museum stands). I eagerly devoured the magazine every month.

I don't recall how much later it was, but I received an invitation to attend their annual Western Heritage Awards banquet. I also don't remember how much the tickets were, but they were more than I was used to paying for a night out on the town. Not exorbitant, but not a paltry sum. So I put the invitation aside. There was, after all, not only the tickets, but travel costs and time to consider.

Then business called me to Oklahoma City again. I am not making that up. It really did. The trip was necessary. Really. It so happened that I had to be in Oke City (that's what Okies call it—or just plain The City) on the night of the banquet. The coincidence was just too much—and I had already stopped believing in coincidences, anyway. I felt as if I was being *called* to attend this banquet. I made reservations without a minute to spare.

Jan and I felt right at home in the sea of black ties and boots, black hats, and friendly, welcoming, down-home folks during the reception. When it was time for the banquet to begin, we were ushered to a front table only a few feet from the stage. We felt fortunate, but had no idea just how fortunate we were (and uninformed).

I don't recall everyone who sat at our table, but a humble man to my left looked very familiar. He certainly looked very comfortable in his cowboy hat. I knew I should know him but was reluctant to ask. A classic, handsome, chiseled-face cowboy that I guessed to be in his early sixties. He introduced himself as Bob Norris, a rancher from Colorado. Someone else at the table had to add that he was the original Marlboro Man (there is a lot of confusion as to who was the original guy in print ads, but Bob is the cowboy who first appeared in TV commercials).

An ad agency had rented use privileges for part of Bob's T-Cross ranch to shoot cigarette commercials back in the sixties. They brought along a model to be the Marlboro man. But as Bob rode out horseback to offer assistance and expertise, the contrast between the model and Bob became so obvious they fired the model and hired Bob. He was under contract to Marlboro for twelve years, but he told us his conscious about the links between smoking and cancer led him to finally give up the gig that made his face famous.

I was certainly impressed enough that he was the owner of a large ranch in Colorado (130,000 acres) and was the Marlboro Man, but Bob failed to mention he was the grand-nephew of a guy named Gates who owned a little oil operation called Spindletop that later became Texaco. I found out much later that Bob was chairman of the stockholders' committee that locked horns with corporate raider Carl Icahn that led to a three-billion-dollar settlement with Pennzoil. He also has his own charitable foundation. In his eighties now (and still looks in his sixties), Bob spends his winters in Arizona, but still does a little cowboy work on the T-Cross during the other seasons. What we still don't know is why Jan and I were at the table with him and his wife. I expect there was a last minute cancellation by someone else.

Jan and I glanced at each other in astonishment as we saw the folks who surrounded us. Far from being star-struck types, we nonetheless recognized we were in for a unique experience. I was surprised as I watched usually shy Jan walk two tables over and start a conversation with Michael Martin Murphy, one of our favorite cowboy singers. I can't recall if wine had anything to do with her bold move. I looked behind me and saw Barry Corbin, pretty fresh from his great performance as Roscoe Brown in the best western of all time, *Lonesome Dove*. Then I saw Bill Wittliff, who wrote the teleplay for *Lonesome Dove*. Jan and I have part of his *Lonesome Dove* photo collection in our home.

Richard Farnsworth (maybe my favorite actor of all time) and Ernest Borgnine were also at the next table over along with William Devane. Two tables away from that, I saw a favorite western villain, Jack Elam. Elam had been inducted in the hall of fame of Great Western Performers the previous year. He lost sight in one eye when he was stabbed with a pencil in high school at a Boy Scouts meeting. Few know that he began his career as an accountant.

# The Sunrise Side of the Mountain

## An Evening at the Cowboy Hall of Fame, Part II

ANOTHER COUPLE SAT ACROSS FROM us at our table. They were quiet and I had no idea who they were until Richard Farnsworth began the program as emcee. When Tom Lea was announced as an inductee in the Hall of Great Westerners, I was shocked to see all eyes turn to the elderly gentleman across the table from me as he stood to receive the award. I don't have the space here to list Tom's lengthy list of accomplishments. The best summation would be from an award-winning article in *Roundup*, the official magazine of the Western Writers of America, titled "Tom Lea: The Eyes of an Artist and the Ears of a Writer." He had previously received the Owen Wister Award (a lifetime achievement award in western history and literature) from the Cowboy Hall of Fame.

Five years later, he would be quoted in George W. Bush's acceptance speech at the Republican National Convention.

> *My friend, the artist Tom Lea of El Paso, Texas, captured the way I feel about our great land, a land I love. He and his wife, he said, "live on the east side of the mountain. It's the sunrise side, not the sunset side. It is the side to see the day that is coming, not the day that has gone. The best day is the day coming."*

Tom was weak and blind when the President later requested the loan of his painting *Rio Grande* to hang in the oval office.

During the Great Depression, Tom produced paintings that still hang in post offices from Washington, DC, to Odessa, Texas. He illustrated some of the books of the great J. Frank Dobie. Tom was a war correspondent for *Life* magazine during WWII and accompanied Allied Forces into both theaters of war, documenting the horrific reality and raw emotion of war in a way that had rarely been seen before. He was aboard the USS Hornet with Jimmy Dolittle. He watched a Japanese sub sink the USS Wasp and later did several paintings of that event. While in China, he painted portraits of Chiang Kai-shek and the head of the Flying Tigers, General Claire Lee Chennault (who hails from our hometown of Commerce, Texas).

Lea produced six books over the next twenty years, fiction and nonfiction, winning numerous awards, including two from the Texas Institute of Letters. Two of his novels were made into movies. He also authored two volumes on the King Ranch. His paintings hang in private and prestigious public places all over the world, including the Smithsonian. Yet the man was unassuming and accepted his induction into the Hall of Great Westerners with deep humility and appreciation.

# True Unity

## An Evening at the Cowboy Hall of Fame, Part III

JUST AS WE THOUGHT OUR EVENING at the Western Heritage Awards could not get any better, I heard Michael Martin Murphy (who had earlier received an award for Outstanding Original Western Music) announce the winner of the Chester A. Reynolds (founder of the Cowboy Hall of Fame) award. This award is given to folks whose lifestyles best represent the ideals of the American West. Tom Dorrance, eighty-two at the time, stepped on the stage to accept the award, flanked by Red Steagall.

I had read Tom's book, *True Unity*, and was amazed to find myself in the same room with the man who (along with his brother Bill) is widely recognized as the founder of the modern horsemanship movement. The brothers were buckaroos raised on a ranch in the Great Basin. Tom and Bill had a particularly strong influence on Ray Hunt and Hunt's disciple Buck Brannaman, who coached Robert Redford in *The Horse Whisperer*. These guys were practicing the gentling craft long before Monty Roberts wrote *The Man Who Listens to Horses*.

And let's not forget the presence of the spirit of William Boyd (Hopalong Cassidy) who was posthumously inducted into the Hall of Great Western Performers. And we'll always remember the Sons of the Pioneers and their performance that night. Their founding members were also inducted into the Hall of Great Western Performers. I imagined Roy Rogers looking on and being well pleased.

Looking back on the evening, I still marvel at how fortunate we were to be in a room so full of positive energy and accomplishment. The mood in the room was ebullient. All the folks seemed to like each other and everyone else. I don't think it is too much of a stretch to say we felt in the presence of greatness.

# The Straight Story

## An Evening at the Cowboy Hall of Fame, Part IV

BUT THE EVENING WAS NOT OVER, NOT by a long shot. After the banquet, Jan and I were touring the museum when we saw Richard Farnsworth and Ernest Borgnine walking toward us, engaged in jovial conversation and storytelling. As an aficionado of the Western lifestyle and Western movies, I tried not to gush as I asked Farnsworth to sign my program. He obliged with a smile. I still have it, of course. Someone called Borgnine away before I could get his autograph.

Consider Farnsworth's accomplishments: He left home at fifteen during the Depression and found work as a stable hand in a polo barn owned by Walt Disney. Soon after, he began riding broncs in the Southwestern rodeo circuit. Then he worked as a stuntman for thirty years doing stunts for the likes of Gary Cooper and Kirk Douglas and doubling for Henry Fonda, John Ireland and Joel McCrea.

Remember the great riding done by tenderfoot Montgomery Clift in *Red River?* That was due to Farnsworth's coaching. If you want to see the difference Farnsworth training made, watch Clift mount and dismount in *Red River,* then watch Matt Damon jump down from his horse in the remake of *True Grit.*

Shy, unassuming and dyslexic, Farnsworth was reluctant to take his first speaking role in 1976. Two years later, he got his first Academy Award nomination as supporting actor for another great Western with

James Caan, *Comes a Horseman* (Jane Fonda notwithstanding). Then he starred in another of the greatest Westerns of all time starring Steve McQueen as *Tom Horn*. Folks who have visited our Across the Creek barn know that the movie poster hung there. It hangs in my office now.

Farnsworth played real life train robber Bill Miner in another great flick, *The Grey Fox,* and garnered a Golden Globe nomination. And he wasn't only great in westerns. He played a baseball coach with Robert Redford in *The Natural,* starred with Colleen Dewhurst in *Anne of Green Gables* on PBS, with Redford again in *Havana,* in *The Two Jakes* with Jack Nicholson, and teamed with James Caan again in *Misery.*

In 1999, at age 79, he earned his second Academy Award nomination, this time not for supporting actor, but for a leading role in *The Straight Story.*

I have thought about that evening many times, especially when I learned that Farnsworth had cut short his battle with terminal cancer by taking his own life in 2000. I wish I had a "do-over," knowing what I know now.

The lesson learned? Probably to pay better attention, absorb life's "moments," and not believe in coincidences. God must have been tired from winking so much that night. Or maybe not.

# Writing, Reading, Readers, and Why Fiction Matters

The stories that follow are mostly about why we read, why we write. They're personal, but I think everyone can learn from the lessons I had. In *We Read to Know We Are Not Alone*, you will read several stories of people I have met because they read. Why do we need to know we are not alone? Reading helps us see that other people have the same or similar tragedies and triumphs, struggle with similar issues. We also get to see how they deal with them. Maybe we learn from them.

I have several friends and relatives that can recite vital statistics of as many as four professional sports teams, yet they have not read a book in decades. Their excuses usually boil down to low comprehension and low reading speed. To them I say, "Reading is a sport, possibly the greatest sport of all. And it's a sport most of us can participate in our entire lives. And yes, I said participate as a player, not a spectator. How do you get good at sports? Practice. Same goes for reading. Even reading a cheap novel will help you get better at enjoying the sport."

I am a great advocate of team and individual sport participation and watching sports can be a good escapist hobby, but who wins or loses a professional game is of real consequence only to rich owners and spoiled players. Losing skill in reading and comprehension, however, can have an enormous negative impact on our lives.

> *How many a man has dated an era*
> *in his life from the reading of a book?*
> —Henry David Thoreau

> *Why can we experience the same story a thousand different*
> *ways and never get tired of it? Perhaps it's because the story*
> *line appeals to a deep-seated need we all share: a desire to be*
> *rescued from a world we know is deeply flawed... something*
> *elusive and ineffable that dances just beyond our grasp... we*
> *get to experience it vicariously through a story.*
> —Jamie Hughes

# We Read to Know We Are Not Alone

I MADE A NEW FRIEND SEVERAL MONTHS back—one of those rare occasions when you seem to "connect" with someone you have just met. Bill had that look-you-in-the-eye, do-what-I-say-I-will, when-I-say-I-will kind of demeanor that is so rare these days. He was a former police chief in places as far away as Alaska who abandoned his career to shoe horses for a living.

Bill and wife Penny came to the launch party for my novel, *Go Down Looking,* though we had only been friends for a short time. We were soon on the fast track to becoming great friends. A few days later, I was at the funeral of another old friend and reader when I saw that a second grave was being prepared at Shiloh Cemetery. I was shocked to learn the grave was for Bill. The death of two friends, a few setbacks in writing, frustration with social media and technology in general had me pretty discouraged.

Then I got this e-mail from a cousin I seldom see.

> *Teresa and I were at Bill McClendon's funeral and I guess I wasn't too surprised to look up and see you sitting two rows in front of us. When it came to friends and friendly acquaintances, Bill threw a pretty wide loop. I worked with him for over two decades and counted it a sad day when he told me he was retiring from the department. He was my training officer when I hired on and good friend thereafter. The people that fit the latter category, I can count on one hand.*
>
> *As I sat there wondering how Bill might be remembered by all the different folks in that funeral parlor that I didn't know, Arliss Edwards' "High Plains Tribute" came to mind.*

> *I don't know how long you knew Bill, but I do know it wasn't long enough. I tried to get over to you after the service but people got between us and you escaped. We will talk one day.*

That probably doesn't sound like much to you, but *High Plains Tribute* is the title of a piece I wrote more than ten years ago about a cousin who had died. I consider it a high honor that my other cousin Jay thought of it as he mourned the loss of his good friend.

When I told my daughter Shelly about meeting Kathleen, the 95-year-old voracious reader and Biblical scholar I write about later in this book, she told me a story about my mother's Bible. On a day when she was having doubts about her own business (she is an artist who transforms guitars and other objects into works of art), she picked up Mother's tattered old Bible and a faded, ragged piece of paper dropped to the floor.

She picked it up and read.

> *In the "parable of the talents," we get an idea of what God expects us to do here on earth. We're all given talents, some great and some small—but whether your talent is epic or miniscule, we glorify God when we use it to further His kingdom. God isn't rating His followers based on the number of converts they win over or the number of church pews they fill; He's interested in the passion with which we use whatever gifts He has given us.*

I occasionally express to wife Jan my frustration, not so much with writing itself, but in getting a larger audience to read and enjoy what I write. Jan selects fabrics in various colors, designs, and texture; cuts her chosen fabric into tiny pieces; sews them together like a complicated puzzle; then quilts them into color coordinated, beautifully symmetric works of art.

One of her quilts might be called my own tapestry of life. I watched with some wonder as the pieces came together with pictures, logos, symbols, even business cards converted to fabric that tell a lot of my life story. She suggested calling it *I Did It My Way*. I hope a better title might be *He Guided me to do it His Way*. I could not conceptualize a beautiful work of art coming from mere stacks of fabric, old photos, assorted t-shirts, and keepsakes. Sort of like writing a book.

In the movie *Shadowlands* about C. S. Lewis (one of my favorite writers), a character says, "We read to know that we are not alone." Professor and writer John Dufresne says, "A book should offer hope. It should lift up the reader. It should give the reader a reason to live—should he need one. Life is not easy for any of us, but the pain of loneliness is often unbearable. The writer is saying, among other things, *You're not alone*." I hope my books make readers feel that they are not alone and that they are *lifted up* by my writing.

In an article about finding one's purpose in life, the author describes the difference between a gift and a calling.

> *A calling forces us beyond our own abilities into utter dependence on God. A true calling commands our complete humility.*

Writing demands my complete humility, so maybe it is my calling.

# Buyers, Readers, Fans, and Evangelists

MY SINCERE GRATITUDE TO THE FOLKS who filled the large room at the Alumni Center to capacity and waited patiently in line to buy and get copies of *Go Down Looking* autographed. I tried to acknowledge all the folks who came from long distances, showed up with gifts or special memories, but I know I missed some.

Larry and Elaine Whitlock brought me a framed photo of the Delta County Champion Indians in the charter year for Little League. Geral Dewitt of the Giants was also there. Dr. Stephen Turner came from Plainview with his latest book *On the Western Trail*. And poet Wanda Myers Glawson, ninety, came from San Antonio. She's one of those people I knew, but didn't know that I did before *Rivers Flow*.

My attempts to chronicle the past through fiction brought about more connections than I can list here. Wife Jan said I should write about them all. When I saw the faces of people that I would never have known if not for the books, saw old friends reuniting for the first time in decades, I discovered an answer to a question I have been asked many times.

Some of my friends seem incredulous about my now twelve-year venture into writing novels (many are guys who might buy a book, but never crack the cover). Their questions range from a simple "Why?" to, "How many novels are you going to write before you give up? Have you had a best-seller yet? Why don't you write a thriller so it at least has a chance of selling big?"

I now have an answer, but they still may not understand. Someone said writers write to explain the world we live in to ourselves. But during this signing event, I learned I also write because of the people in that room, people who send orders, all the people who read my books, people who read my articles, and people who reconnect because of the books.

And writing has given me a whole new appreciation for songwriters. One of my favorites is Tom T. Hall. A particular line in one song often pops into my head when I hear those comments and questions. You remember how the young boy follows Clayton Delaney around because he is *"the best guitar-picker in our town"*? The young boy asks Clayton why he doesn't *"pick up his guitar and head on down to Tennessee."* Clayton's reply, *"Son, you better put that old guitar away. There ain't no money in it; it'll lead you to an early grave."*

That part about the money could certainly be said about writing. And writing non-genre novels could lead to an early grave, I suppose. Publishing and marketing those babies is tough.

But writing allows me to be more introspective and reflective. I hope it helps readers to do the same as they identify with my stories.

The few early readers of *Go Down Looking* want to know if any of the stuff I wrote about happened. Again, I turn to a song. Remember when George Burns recorded "I Wish I was Eighteen Again" when he was in his final years? I always thought one of the lines was *"Going where I've already been."* Turns out it was *"Going where I've never been."* Well, both lines apply to this book and me. Writing allows me to be eighteen again, going where I've already been *and* where I've never been (but maybe always wanted to go).

Ken Ryan, who came to the signing from Lufkin, had already read the book and sent me his comments. We were both astonished to learn he was an eyewitness to at least one critical scene in the book. I can't share all that he said without giving away too much, but suffice it to say the connections are uncanny. And he is a guy I never met before the signing.

It is said writers have buyers, readers, fans, and evangelists. I appreciate every single person who fits into any of those categories. I know a few folks buy the books, never intending to open them. I still appreciate them because they want to support my efforts. I also recognize the tendency to think someone we know can't be a *real* writer. That's even truer if you are related to the writer. Some readers read to see if they recognize the characters.

I know there are readers who are indifferent or just don't care for my books. I even appreciate them. At least they gave me a chance. Fans are the good folks who read them and take the time to let me know they liked them and why. I need more of them. They encourage me to keep going. Then there are the evangelists. They hold a special place in my heart because they like the books enough to make their reviews public and to spread the word. They are the biggest sellers of my books. I need many more of them. They may keep me away from that early grave.

The publisher wanted to know if I wanted a catchphrase on promotional items for *Go Down Looking. Find the Flow, Hear the Music*, sort of tumbled out in a split second. Those six words underscore an underlying theme in all my books. Did I know that when I started writing? No.

# A Sign...
# a Whisper...
# a Nudge

### *Meeting a Remarkable Woman*

ONE OF MY FAVORITE QUOTES IS, *"The unexamined life is not worth living,"* usually attributed to Socrates. I probably read that in some assignment in college or even high school. As a youth, I likely found it sort of depressing and fatalistic. Years later, I rediscovered the quote and found it comforting. Why? Because I have had a tendency most of my adult life to question the direction of my life. I thought of this as a weakness, a symptom of unhappiness, dissatisfaction, and indecisiveness.

I think most of us start looking at where we have been and where we are going at midlife if not sooner. That examination can be brought about by unhappiness or discontent with the direction our lives are taking, or just our first recognition that we really are mortal. One of my earliest deep self-examinations led to a risky job change and a move. I thought the move and job change would fix things and this examination thing would be done. It was not to be. Examinations, I think, will be with me until the end of my days. They have led me toward major changes in my life many times.

Through the voice of an older Jake Rivers in *Go Down Looking*, I tried to explain:

> *It didn't come with thunder and lightning or as an immediate epiphany. It took hard work, lots of mentoring, lots of reading, lots*

> *of listening, and a lot of blind alleys, disappointments and confusion. Mostly it took commitment. Lights finally began to come on. And I knew I was being guided.*

Several people who read the book have asked me "how" Jake was being guided (more about that in the last part of this book).

Trial and error has me convinced that nobody really knows how an unknown author markets mainstream, southern (Texas) or family saga fiction. There are many books and articles on how to market nonfiction, but I have never seen any proven methods for marketing fiction (at least the type that I write). For example, I love signings at launch parties, book clubs, and at almost all other venues, but bookstores are another matter. I am grateful when a bookstore hosts me, but the process can be grueling and is usually disappointing. One source says the average number of books sold at such events is six—another says fifteen (yes, that includes best-sellers). And the paperwork is atrocious. At a recent bookstore signing, I was assaulted for hours with nerve-wracking sounds that I assumed might be music. However, I did sell a few books and was grateful when friends came some distance to connect and pick up a few copies of my books.

The paperwork, loading and unloading, and a day spent watching people shop for videos rather than books, however, can bring questions to one's mind. Like, "What the heck am I doing and why am I doing it?"

This wasn't the first time I had asked myself this, but the event sort of brought the question front and center again. Trying to answer the question was anything but illuminating and invigorating. Was it time to hang it up and make another change? Writing has been fun and rewarding, but maybe it has run its course. On the other hand, I have told a lot of stories that I thought needed to be told and many readers have connected their lives to those of the Rivers. I have made hundreds of connections and good friends with readers all over Texas and in a few other states as a result of writing the novels. Still, maybe I am done, finished. There is a certain virtue in knowing when it is time to move on to something else. Could I do this without thinking of it as giving up?

I did learn something from those previous life examinations. I learned to ask for help. This time, I was bold enough to ask God to send a sign—maybe whisper in my ear—give me a nudge in the right direction. Some would say that is both a brash and a weak request and shows a lack of faith. Maybe, but I believe my request was answered.

The Monday morning after the less than stellar bookstore signing experience, I used my riding time on my horse Shooter for contemplation and requests for guidance on my next move. When I unsaddled and passed her quilt house, Jan shouted that she had a message for me. She said the caller was one of the most pleasant strangers she had ever spoken to.

When I called, the lady (Gela) told me that her mother was approaching her ninety-fifth birthday and she had kept a notice of my book signing event in her eyeglass case in the hope that someone would take her. Family emergencies prevented that, however. The family had called the store to obtain copies of my books for the mother, but to no avail. Gela asked about getting all six of my books for her mom's birthday. She offered to pick up the books, but I wanted to deliver them.

Let me correct that. I felt the *need* to deliver them. Gela said she would fix me a sandwich if I came to her mother's home. It's not all that unusual for me to deliver books, especially to the homebound, but I felt a definite need to meet Kathleen at ninety-five. I could not explain, even to myself, how much I was looking forward to it. I was not to be disappointed.

I signed all six books and left my house with a sense of urgency, not the least bit bothered that I was going to meet strangers dressed in faded jeans about to tear at the knee and a faded t-shirt. I don't know what I was expecting when I arrived at the small rural home. I just knew I was looking forward to it. And that's not like my introverted self at all.

Looking back on my visit and the unnatural "pull" I felt to meet Kathleen, I drove without any preconceived notions, uncharacteristically looking forward to meeting strangers. I felt this family's welcome long before I got out of my car. The house was more than a century old and the place had once been a dairy farm. I saw tender loving care burnished with years of weather on the porch. The house had painted siding that had faded with time.

Kathleen, daughter Gela and granddaughter Jody, were waiting as I entered the small living room that doubled as a bedroom. I felt the familiar unsteadiness of the floor and heard bottles rattle on a nearby dresser with my steps. I suspect the house is supported by bois d'arc stumps, just as ours was. But the home did not have the musty smell that some older homes have. It smelled of warm food and hospitality—a fragrance that cannot be defined, only experienced.

I did not know what they had told Kathleen about my visit. Was it a surprise? Did she know I was bringing books? And why had she wanted my books? Had she read one of my books before? Gela introduced me to her mother and daughter. Kathleen stood and walked toward me with the energy and grace of a much younger woman, both eyes twinkling. She took both of my elbows, told me how wonderful it was to get to meet me. I hugged this lovely lady I had never seen before, feeling as if I was getting a long-wished-for last hug from my mother, gone more than a decade now.

It's a worn-out phrase and a cop-out for a writer to say this, but words cannot describe the feeling she gave me. I wondered if she had confused me with someone else, possibly a long-lost son or nephew. No. We connected at that first moment on some higher plane. She seemed much younger than her years and her face was full of youthful joy, curiosity, and love.

Looking back, it seems as if we were all talking at once, recounting the sequence of events that had led me to their doorstep, but Kathleen's eyes seemed never to leave mine. I told Jan later that it was one of the warmest feelings I had ever felt and one of the most astonishing encounters I had ever experienced. Nobody ever fully explained how it was that Kathleen cut out that tiny notice of my book signing. I never even saw it myself. We think maybe she had read one of my first books and wanted to read the new one. But none of my books were in her large collection. Maybe it had been loaned to someone else.

At her advanced age, she remains an avid reader, though her hearing is almost completely gone. Jody feverishly wrote on a whiteboard so we could communicate, but I prattled on, absolutely positive that Kathleen understood everything I was saying. I seemed not in control of the situation. Kathleen was in charge.

I have examined and re-examined this visit. I have asked myself if I am I "making too much" of a pleasant encounter. Am I being overly sentimental? Was I caught up in a vulnerable moment and susceptible to suggestion? Maybe, but I don't think so. I do regret that I may have gushed as I talked to these three ladies, spilling out my life history because it seemed to parallel much of their own and because they were all so easy to talk to.

Through it all, Kathleen looked deeply into my eyes as if I had her rapt attention. More than that, I felt her communicating with me on another level. She asked Jody to go into another room and bring in a small container of books she had left on a table. Kathleen pulled a book from the box and showed it to me. I was taken aback when I saw the title. *The Bootlegger's Other Daughter* by Mary Cimarolli. Mary and I are friends and colleagues and she had just ordered a copy of my most recent book two days before. Kathleen did not know this. She pulled a second book from the box—*The Glass House* by William Thompson. Bill Thompson and I have been good friends for many years. My old publishing company published his book. I turned to the acknowledgments page in the book and showed Kathleen my name. She had not known.

A preacher told me after my visit that Kathleen is one of the most learned biblical scholars he has ever known and that she has an extensive library of religious books. Some of you skeptics (I used to be among you) are probably saying this is only a group of coincidences. Maybe, but I cannot escape one thing—the warm feeling I had when this lovely lady took me into her arms and looked into my eyes.

When I rose to leave, she walked me to the door and grabbed both of my arms and squeezed them. "Now you go on home and get to writing."

Tell me that's not a sign.

# The Blurry Line Between Fiction and Truth

## Bob Lee = Arliss Lee

THOSE OF YOU WHO READ MY NOVELS (thank you) will recognize the name Bob Lee Boggs. There is a hint of him in the first two novels and much more about him in *Rivers Ebb*.

> Bob Lee waved once as he danced his way through the snow toward Jake and String. Jake's cousin had always carried twenty or thirty extra pounds, but it was evenly distributed.

His character is even more important in *Go Down Looking*.

> Damn, Jake. I babysat you for six months and you didn't get thrown in jail once. Let you out of my sight for a little bit and here you are in the hoosegow.

I've never tried to hide the fact that the character named Bob Lee was inspired by my cousin, Arliss Lee Edwards. Arliss was one of those "bigger than life" characters who seemed more suited to fiction than real life. There are hundreds of stories about him. He was eight years older than me and lived five hundred miles away in the Texas Panhandle. The stories, however, traveled the distance back to my home in Northeast Texas regularly and Arliss became a sort of legend in my boyhood mind. He wasn't a bad boy in the traditional sense; he just did things that inspired laughter and more than a little tongue-wagging.

We moved to the Panhandle when I was fourteen and the distance between Arliss and me was reduced from five-hundred miles to about thirty miles. Our house was literally in the middle of nowhere (twenty miles from a paved road) and you could not distinguish the front from the back. You could see one small shack from our farmhouse if you knew where to look and the sand wasn't blowing. It seemed to me that we had moved to the moon. The only people I knew out there were Arliss and his family.

Arliss sensed my fear and misery and would sometimes take me for a ride in his '57 black Chevy. I will never forget the rooster tail of dust that Chevy left on the dirt road that led to our house; or watching Arliss "peg" the Chevy's speedometer and take the needle around to the other side; or watching him land a small plane on a farm-to-market road just for kicks. Irresponsible for a man twenty-two to take a boy fourteen on such a wild ride? Even reckless? Yep. But Arliss sensed that lifting my spirits was worth the risk. Most men that age have little time or patience for a boy as immature as I was.

Panhandle distances and my parents' sympathy gave me a lot of latitude when I began dating. I remember stopping at an all night cafe on Route 66 on the outskirts of Vega late one night. Arliss sat alone in a booth, having a piece of pie and a glass of tea. We had both been out courting, and it gave me a sense of camaraderie with my older cousin. He regaled me with rapid fire jokes until my sides hurt from laughing. I still repeat at least one of those jokes (my all-time favorite), but I can never match his storytelling skills.

I grew to love my new home and enjoyed the growing relationship I had with my cousin. But my parents were never really happy out there and we moved back in less than three years. I was bitter again. I found myself afoot on the last night before we moved, and Arliss tossed me the keys to his new Chevy (or was it the '57?). In my mind, it will always be the '57, but what matters is that he loaned a very nice car to an unhappy, angry kid not quite seventeen so he could have one last fling before leaving the life he loved behind.

I also can't remember if I actually heard the argument he had with his father when he bought a new car or if I have been told the story so many times it has become a visual image to me. I do remember his famous words after being severely dressed down by my uncle. "Don't know what to tell you, Dad. Just work hard and save all your money." That still makes me laugh.

I saw him only at funerals and rare reunions after I left the Panhandle until I began occasionally traveling to Amarillo on business more than three decades later. I always made it a point to look him up. The visits were invariably entertaining. I got to know him man to man and found him to be a very complex character. He, like a lot of us, struggled with balancing discipline and praise when raising children. He had trouble showing affection or expressing his deepest emotions to those he loved most. We shared a tendency to speak our minds and to see things in black and white and not in shades of gray. We were both stubborn when our minds were made up. Our tendencies often led to words best left unspoken. Talking about our shared weaknesses helped.

During one of my business trips, Arliss and I parked near a grain elevator between where he grew up and the farm where I lived during my Panhandle years. It was an overcast, cold, and of course, windy day—a good time to reminisce. I recalled memorizing the exact miles from the main highway to the turnoff that led to my house because it was easy for a boy used to using corner posts and big trees as landmarks in Northeast Texas to get lost on the plains. Out there, all roads look pretty much the same.

We talked about how the grain facility office served double duty as a community center back in the day and the time I saw my parents dance there for the first and last time. And about how I grew to love the big sky, arid air, and wide open spaces carved up into square and rectangle giant farms and ranches with little distinguishable features to the unpracticed eye. I even grew to be comfortable with the more or less constant wind.

But my parents never adapted. They missed giant shade trees, landmarks, creeks, and bois d'arc fences. They wanted a farm measured in acres instead of sections—one they could farm with one tractor—one you could "get your arms around." Maybe a few cows. The roots of their youth called them home.

On the day of our talk, I had recently had a business book published and Arliss knew about it. He said he wanted to buy one for himself and one for each of his "bull barn" buddies. I appreciated that, but told him this was a business type of book written for a target market. I doubted he or his friends who farmed would find it useful or interesting. Besides, the publisher had not provided any copies for me to sell.

He turned to me as if I had insulted him. "You wrote it, didn't you?"

I nodded and he pulled out a roll of bills, started counting twenties before he came across a hundred. He handed the hundred to me and said, "How many will that buy?" That gesture describes him about as well as anything could, I think. I made sure he got his books.

We kept in touch over the years until health problems that had plagued him a large part of his adult life overcame his indomitable spirit. I was honored when his wife and children asked me to serve as a pallbearer. More about the funeral later.

# Why I Write Fiction

"WRITING AND PUBLISHING MAKE HORSE-RACING seem like a stable, risk-free business." So said John Steinbeck. He was right, and writing novels is even worse.

Writing fiction is humbling. My first novel started as a memoir, a tribute of sorts to my parents and the hard struggles they faced in life. I had kept notes and scraps of paper that eventually turned into computer files for years without realizing why I felt a need to record memories. Maybe my subconscious told me I had better write these things down before they slipped away.

I started the book days after my mother died, because many memories had been rekindled with her passing. I wrote in a stream of consciousness for about a month, absolutely sure everything I wrote had happened exactly as I recalled. I even won an argument or two with relatives about specific events. Then one day, while searching through pictures, newspaper clippings, and family memorabilia, I discovered a mistake or two. I had been wrong about the time frame, the people involved or the sequence of events on more than one occasion. That's when I decided to change the manuscript to a novel.

If novels are so much harder to sell than nonfiction, why do I write novels? No answer seems adequate. I recently watched a scene in a movie where a man played the violin in a private home for two people. He had been hired to make this couple's celebration more romantic. It struck me that his beautiful performance had taken more than talent; it had taken years of practice. Yet, there he was, playing for two—probably for a pittance.

Why? Because playing provided something more—not only for himself, but for others. Most musicians never play for huge audiences—never become famous—most never play professionally at all. Yet, they practice and they play. I would never compare myself to an accomplished musician, but I think the same things spur me to write. Music calms, inspires, motivates, excites. So does writing. So does reading.

Alexander McCall (Smith) said,

> *The whole world is a process that is slipping away from us. Writing is often an attempt to respond to that, to capture the moment, to help to heal that sense of separation and loss.*

In his book, *Myself and Other Important Matters*, Charles Handy wrote,

> *Few took notice when John Jerome died, though he was the author of eleven books. Jerome's brother-in-law wrote for* New Yorker *magazine. He said that Jerome had once been bothered by his lack of financial and critical success, until he realized that the purpose of his writing was the pleasure he derived from the act itself.*

I do derive deep pleasure from writing, but it seems hollow to say I just write to please myself. Jerome's revelation, however, was liberating for Handy and freed him to turn his writing to the purest purpose of all: to explain the world he lived in to himself. I do write to explain the world to myself. Still, that's not enough. I want readers to be interested enough to *read* what I write and I want them to do their own exploring through my writing.

Henry David Thoreau said, "How many men's lives have been changed by the reading of a book?" I discovered, quite by accident, that two books had a special impact on my life that I had not realized at the time. How did I discover that? I revisited the text of an interview I gave a year before making the biggest career decision of my life. The books? *Goodbye to a River* by John Graves inspired me (though I did not get the connection until I crossed the Brazos River) to retrace the journey made by my father as a boy (a boy who carried two biscuits). At the same time I was reading Graves' book, I was also reading *Flow* by Michael Csikszentmihalyi and that book provided the theme for three books. Only years later did I see the trail I was unwittingly traveling.

So, if I write about family and memories, why fiction? Many people say they don't have time for fiction, thinking incorrectly that one cannot learn anything from a novel. But nonfiction books, especially biographies, have gained new life from David McCullough's ability to write them like novels. My mentor, friend, and colleague Dr. Fred Tarpley told me talking about novels is different than talking about my nonfiction books. "You must make your audiences laugh and you must make them cry."

"And if that does not work?" I asked.

"Then you must really bare your soul."

Abraham Verghese, MD and medical school professor, said,

> Good fiction can achieve a higher kind of truth than nonfiction. Good stories are instructions for living...a great novel transports you to another planet, lets you vicariously live a full life, and when you come back it's still Tuesday, and yet you've learned the lessons of a lifetime. That's what everyone, doctors included, could get from fiction....and God is in the details.

Stephen Crane (*Red Badge of Courage*) escaped a sinking ship on a lifeboat. When he wrote the account of his and other passengers' survival, not much attention was paid. But when he wrote the fictional account *The Open Boat*, it became one of the most famous stories in American Literature. Why? Because he could flesh out the characters, give them motivations, get inside their heads, thus making them more intriguing than a mere recitation of facts and events, even in a life-threatening situation.

Willard Spiegelman's book, *Seven Pleasures: Essays on Ordinary Happiness*, lists reading and writing as two of the seven. Listening, dancing, looking, walking, swimming, are the other five. A good novelist pours his entire life experiences and knowledge into each manuscript. Then he goes to the trouble of sending his readers only the best parts. Hopefully, the best parts are sewn together like an intricate, beautiful quilt. A story, though not exactly true, is still knowledge—knowledge that can be useful.

Fiction is a reader's ticket to unfettered access to characters' lives. We get to walk invisibly through their homes, even their bedrooms. We explore the depths of characters' personalities; examine events; experience sensations; and travel to places we might not otherwise go. Best of all, we get to walk undeterred and unashamed through their minds. When we tire of them, we just close the book.

Many novels have changed society, the economy, or even altered the course of history. Tom Spanbauer said, "Fiction is the lie that makes the truth truer. Nonfiction is about a series of events, fiction is about the meaning of events." Ah, now we are onto something. Meaning? I get meaning from many of the novels I read. I get inspiration. And...I get information. I get myself into a thoughtful, contemplative mood. All these things, plus escape and entertainment. Novels do have value, after all.

So I wrote and I continue to write....

# The Healing Power of Family Stories

From the earliest days of my writing, I wondered why anyone would be interested in my own family stories. But readers soon taught me that they saw their own families reflected in mine. And, of course, I want the stories to be passed down to future generations.

# A Christmas Star and Scar

*A true story with fictional names*

NORTH WIND WHISTLED THROUGH THE warped pine boards of the old farm house. Shredded strips of stubbornly clinging wallpaper shivered as if feeling the biting wind. Icicles bought from the five-and-dime trembled on the cedar Christmas tree that had been placed dangerously close to the woodstove. Outside by the dairy barn, twelve-year-old Gray Boy helped Rance and the driver load cans into the back of the milk truck. Jake, six, finished with his work in the dairy parlor, stood with his hands inside his coat pockets, too small to lift the milk cans, but too big to go inside before his brother and father did. He shuddered not only from the cold, but with the excitement of opening Christmas presents after supper. The milk truck driver thanked them, wished them a Merry Christmas, and drove away.

Using bowls of water warmed on the woodstove, the men took sponge baths and dressed in clean clothes while Trish, fourteen, and her mother Mattie put strips of fresh tenderloin between biscuits and boiled coffee on the kerosene kitchen stove. In the living room, Rance and his sons scooted the worn couch and chairs closer to the fire. Everyone wrapped in quilts, ate their sandwiches and stared at the presents under the tree. Jake finished his cobbler first and waited for a signal from his father that it was time to open the presents.

A knock came at the front door. Jake and his brother followed their father out into the open dogtrot and saw a blurred image of the milk truck driver through the milky glass in the door. Rance sent the boys back to the living room and stepped out on the porch. The brothers knew something was wrong, so they eavesdropped through a crack. The milkman's voice quivered with cold and sadness, but the boys understood enough. A wreck on Jernigan Creek Bridge, a horse lying by the creek with a white star under its forelock. The little black horse we called Star, who could take a bow, be ridden without a bridle, rear on command, and untie knots, must have learned to open the lot gate.

Eyes filled with tears, Gray Boy threw on a coat and wool cap and headed out the back door, intent on running to the creek. Rance caught him in the yard, pulled him to his chest, let him have his cry. The horse was really Gray's, but both boys claimed him, rode him and cared for him, so Rance relented when they begged to go with him. The sight of the little horse, eyes full of surprise and pain, milk cans floating in Jernigan Creek, was forever etched into their memories. Jake thought there could never be another merry Christmas. Gray Boy said he would never own another horse.

Jake had never played with cars and trucks. He preferred his cowboy hat, six-shooter, boots and spurs, and the stick horse he called Chocolate. When Star came along, he stood Chocolate in the corner, never to be ridden again. When Star was killed, he felt guilty, but he soon began to dream of having his own horse. As another Christmas approached, times were really tough, so a horse was out of the question. Temperatures in the seventies and fears of another ominous knock on the door ruined that Christmas.

The year Jake turned eight, he feared there would be no money for Christmas presents at all. Rance had been sick for months. They had lost half their dairy herd to a devastating drought. On Christmas Eve, a cold mist seemed to tease that more rain might be coming. Opening presents came and went. Jake struggled to keep from crying when he only got warm socks. Rance and Gray went outside and Rance returned with a hissing lantern and Jake's coat. Mattie and Trish rose and followed Rance without a word being spoken. Jake reluctantly left the warmth of the fire and followed them into the mist, across the muddy dairy barn lot, and into the dark hall of the hay barn.

A mousy little bay filly with ribs showing seemed to be leaning against the barn wall for support. Gray held her lead rope. Bite and kick marks scarred her dull, mangled coat. Her forelock, mane and tail were tangled and full of straw.

Mattie propped her elbow with her hand, dabbed at her eyes. Gray Boy handed Jake the rope and whispered into his ear, "If that horse dies tonight, and it looks like she will, don't you cry, cause it'll ruin another Christmas."

Rance put a hand on Jake's shoulder. "Haven't had her more than an hour or two. No time to clean her up. Figured you'd want to do that, anyway."

Jake barely heard. He did not see a wormy little filly. He saw Koko, Champion and Trigger in the sparse light provided by that lantern. He named her Scar, not for the bites and kick marks, but for his favorite horse on a radio program called Dr. Sixgun.

# Under the Porch

DADDY WAS SICK A LOT WHEN WE were kids and doctors could not determine the problem. He spent the better part of four years going in and out of hospitals and Mother almost always stayed with him when he was hospitalized. I was the youngest child, so she usually took me with her. I went so often that I still get a little nauseous when I enter a hospital waiting room. I remember sitting in the one at Janes Clinic in Cooper, watching the door that led to the stairs, afraid every footstep was someone coming to tell me Daddy had died.

That scene was repeated so many times I had nightmares about it. He lost about a quarter of his body weight during one particularly bad time, but only missed work when hospitalized. His face stayed contorted with pain a lot. He could not keep any food in his stomach long enough to gain nutrition. Desperate, he and Mother decided to go through an extensive diagnostic program at a hospital in Dallas. They sold virtually everything we owned to pay the cost.

The day he was scheduled to leave, I hid in my usual spot underneath our tall front porch. The dirt was cool there and it was a good place to shoot outlaws through the cracks in the boards. I watched through those cracks as our driveway filled with cars. Nobody gave me details; I just sensed something ominous was happening.

When the time came for Daddy and Mother to leave for Dallas, (which seemed like a foreign country to me), he asked all the relatives and well-wishers to give him a few minutes alone with his kids. They left the house and stood by their cars in the driveway, reminding me of a funeral procession. I know now (and suspected then) that most thought he would never return.

Mother sent Eddy, my brother (six years older) to find me. Even when his calls became impatient, then threatening, I did not come out from under the porch. But my hideout was well known. He crawled under the porch and dragged me out. Everything I had dreaded waited for me in that old, drafty, leaking farm house we lived in. My whole family stood in the living room. Mother's eyes were red and held a look of desperation I had seen in hospitals before as she stood beside Daddy's bed.

My sister Trish was sobbing. Daddy's copper-colored skin could never look pale, but it looked faded. He seemed less powerful in his best khakis and shirt than he did in his usual overalls and brogans. The man I had depended on all my life for protection, a bastion of strength and authority, the man I wanted most to please in my short life, was afraid.

Mother lined us up and I was sure this was the end. I bolted to return to the porch, but Eddy caught my shirt and held me. The line was oldest to youngest and Daddy hugged Trish first and told her he loved her. I should pause here to say we were not a hugging family, nor did we express our love much in words. Somehow, however, our parents made sure it was never doubted. Not for a minute.

Hearing love expressed by my tough-as-nails daddy, the hug, were ominous signs for a small boy. I lost it when he hugged my brother. I blubbered against his shoulder as he dropped to one knee to hug me. He put a hand on each of my cheeks and told me he would be back. Things changed then. I believed him. He told me not to stay under the porch so much and to help my mother and my brother and sister. As I recall, he went through a list of my daily chores and told me he was counting on me to keep them done.

I had seen Daddy cry only a few days before when he came out of a doctor's office. He waited until we were in the car and then whispered to Mother that the doctor said he probably had stomach cancer. His voice broke when he gave her the bad news. I wasn't supposed to hear, but I did. But on the day he left for Dallas, his were the only dry eyes on the place, the only smile.

Time has claimed many of the details of that day, but I will never forget the smell of him, the feel of his rough hands on my cheeks, the sound of his words, believing him when he said he would return. It was better that we did not know what heartaches were in our future that day, how much more suffering Daddy would have to endure. There was a lot.

The best doctors in Dallas could not diagnose what was wrong, but a few months later, Dr. Olen Janes in small-town Cooper did. He performed surgery and Daddy's pain and suffering appeared to be over. It was not cancer, just an abnormality in his digestive organs.

I was at a ballgame in the West Delta gym the day he came home after the surgery. I think Trish found me in the crowd and Aunt Hildred took us home. I was almost embarrassed as I walked into my own house. In the kitchen, I saw something I had not seen in a very long time—Daddy seated at the head of the table (though my memory says he was on the wrong end). He was eating a breakfast-supper, eggs and ham and homemade biscuits, food he had not been able to digest in years.

Daddy left us before he was sixty. More than three decades after his death, he returned as Rance Rivers in *Rivers Flow*.

> *Jake saw Rance leaning against a cattle trailer, arms folded against his chest. When Jake looked at him, he unfolded his arms, put a finger and thumb on the brim of his hat, and tugged slightly. Jake took a deep breath. The Rivers' Flow was back.*

Rance returned in *Rivers Crossing*, *Rivers Ebb*, and *Go Down Looking*. I think he would smile and tug on his hat brim at that.

# The Chance He Never Had

I OVERHEARD MOTHER AND DADDY fretting about how to pay for my college tuition. Only a few weeks away from high school graduation, I was angry that they were taking away my euphoria before I had a chance to enjoy it—before I walked across the stage. I had never said I was going to college, anyway. I sure didn't want to.

Problem was—I didn't know what to do if I didn't go to college. It was time to go out in the world, and I had no marketable skills, no natural abilities. East Texas State College was only eight miles from our front porch, but it seemed like a foreign country. My parents expected me to go, even though nobody else in the family had.

I knew money would be tight, knew about the medical expenses and the drought that had wiped us out. How could I add college expenses to their burdens? I searched through the college catalog of courses and majors. Nothing there for me. Why waste hard-earned money? When I told them of my decision, Daddy stared at the floor for a long time. He always had a habit of drifting off, staring into space. I hadn't inherited his ability with his hands, but I did inherit that drifting off thing. He stood and motioned for me to follow him outside.

I was surprised by the tone of the discussion that followed—no longer man-to-boy, but man-to-man. "Sounds like you're backing out on college because of money."

"I know we can't afford it. I don't know what good a degree would do me, anyway. I got no idea what to do with one."

"That's the point of going, Jim. They put that college over there in

Commerce for kids just like you. Go a year. Give it a chance. You'll find something that suits."

"How are we gonna come up with tuition and books?"

"You always had a job of some sort. You help out with gas and spending money, your mama and me will take care of the rest." He started back to the house, then turned and came back. He put a calloused hand on my arm and looked at me. "You make the grades, keep out of trouble, do your part, money won't ever be mentioned again."

I was surprised at the intensity of his expression and his words. A little tenderness crept into a selfish boy's heart. But I did not answer.

He focused his one good eye on me. "Take the chance I never had."

I nodded. Daddy has been gone for more than forty years now, and that last sentence returns to my mind often.

I found a job at City Pharmacy in downtown Commerce jerking sodas, mopping floors, and delivering prescriptions. No skills required. Mother cosigned a note for a '54 Ford so I could get back and forth to school and work. I delayed college for the summer, dreading it every day. In the fall, I stood in the college Field House, staring at a sea of tables, kids and professors spread out on the basketball court. Everybody in that gym looked smarter, more experienced, and worldlier. Some well-dressed young man asked if I was a freshman. I said I guessed I was about to be and he handed me a beanie. I stuck it in the back pocket of my Levis, hoping that wearing it was not mandatory.

I had dog-eared the pages of my catalog, devising a plan to get through one semester. I decided on the general studies courses and an easy elective. Dr. Arnspiger, they said, was nationally known as the father of general studies and he required everyone to attend Forum Arts and to take Personality Foundations.

My job started at one, so I had to get all my courses in before noon. I was making progress before I stopped at Dr. Elton Johnson's table. The morning session of Business Math was full, he said, and I would just have to take it in the afternoon. I meekly protested that I had to work in the afternoon. He removed his cigar and pointed it in my direction. "Work or school. You need to decide, boy." I hid behind the bleachers and waited until he left for lunch break. The graduate assistant who replaced him took pity on me. Little did I know that I was destined to cross paths with Dr. Johnson many more times. I even grew to like him.

In freshman English, Dr. Fred Tarpley wrote a nice note on one of my first college papers. He asked me to consider English as a major. He doesn't remember either of these events, but his words made me think I might just be able to do this college thing. I learned more about literature from Bill Jack and Bob Dowell and was privileged to meet and listen in on a discussion with Flannery O'Connor, though I am ashamed to admit I did not appreciate the significance of the event and the effort it must have taken to bring a legend of literature to Commerce.

Dr. Lawrence McNamee joked with me in German class and made me feel collegiate. E. W. Roland seated us alphabetically and separated the boys from the girls. He made showing up late a humiliating experience, but he and Dr. Joe Saylor taught me things about politics and government that I still use today. Hugh I. Shott asked me to join the honors program, but I declined, still not sure how I would ever make it to graduation, much less with honors.

When Accounting and Finance chose me (I did not choose them), I started to feel a part of a small circle of new friends. I met Carroll Kennemer, another small-town boy, and we have remained friends for more than five decades. Ken McCord and Emmett McAnally convinced me that I could actually get a degree. In Office Machines class, Weldon King told me I had excellent hand-eye coordination. Too bad it had to be with a ten-key adding machine instead of a baseball bat or the reins of a good cow horse.

Some students went to SMU in the summer to avoid Dr. Carroll Adams' classes in economics, but that was impossible for me. He made me sweat, but taught me lessons that continue to serve me well. Dr. Perry Broom's statistics class featured tiny mechanical calculators with knobs that had to be rung backward and forward with ears pressed close until a bell sounded. Distinguishing my bell from twenty others was impossible. He taught from a book he had written instead of the text listed in the catalog. His book was long out of print, but I managed to procure a worn copy. A tennis player in the class challenged the three-hundred-pound-plus Dr. Broom to a tennis match. The whole class watched as Broom beat him three sets without moving more than ten feet.

When graduation moved from dream to reality, and ET changed from college to university, the school arranged interviews for prospective graduates. The economy was booming, and prospective employers came to campus to interview seniors. Dr. Graham Johnson took me aside and counseled against a job I wanted. "You'll be bored in a month."

I told him it paid twenty bucks more per month than the second best offer. He looked down at the shoes I had bought for job interviews and asked how much they cost. I said seven bucks. He looked down at his. "These cost twenty. You'll get used to quality." With that analogy, he tried to convey the naïveté of a career decision based on the price of a pair of good shoes. I missed his point and accepted the job anyway. What matters is that he cared enough to take the time.

ET provided an opportunity that changed my life for the better. I have one of the last ETSC rings and one of the first ETSU diplomas. I was a student when the first doctoral programs were added and when the Memorial Student Center was constructed. I parked on campus and watched when they tore it down forty years later.

The Four Lads performed on campus when I was a student, singing "Moments to Remember," the chosen song of my high school class. I was so disassociated with campus social life and so short of funds that I did not attend. I regret missing that event and many others like it, but in retrospect, I appreciate the university more because the institution, the professors and fellow students pulled a green country kid along paths for his own good, even when he resisted. The student center of my day may be gone and the campus changed forever, but I can still walk across it, imagine President Gee carrying his swagger stick, and have those "moments to remember."

# For Eddy Boy

### *He blazed the trail, took the blows, so that I wouldn't have to.*

*From* Go Down Looking: An *excerpt from a novel, but true except for names*

I FOUND NO TANGIBLE MEMORY AT THE crash site. The scorched grass grew green again; the black hole was long gone. I took the burned buckle from my pocket and held it in the air as if it might recognize the place, maybe conjure up memories or messages that it could pass on to me. I had started polishing the soot off years ago, but the blackened metal seemed to take on a life of its own and resisted my efforts as if the burning were a posthumous badge of honor, always to be worn with pride. Sunlight danced across the polished part, laughing at my foolish efforts to go back in time, to connect with the dead, to see my departed brother's reflection in a piece of metal. The buckle was inanimate, but it had been made by him, had been on his belt consumed by flames when he died. And it had found its way to me after being discovered in the terrible wreckage. Was there a message in that? Was my brother trying to speak from afar?

In the years after his death, I often had the feeling that he was looking over my shoulder, whispering in my ear. Time lessened that feeling until it finally disappeared, but it has returned of late. When the feeling returned, I was surprised to see that he has grown old with me. Is there something he wants me to know about the way he died? About the way he lived? Does he want me to learn something from a tragedy that seemed senseless then and now?

Did he have a premonition? A death wish? If he knew, how did he

know? And had he known how he was going to die? Or did he just keep doing dangerous things, pushing the envelope, sure that his luck would run out? I don't believe any of that. He had his deep mood swings, but he loved life too much to end it voluntarily. And life loved him back.

He certainly hastened death by taking chances, but he was defying it, not inviting it. He challenged death, wanted to defeat it, to triumph over it, to reconnect with his son, to forever stamp him with his memory so that he could seek forgiveness and continue to live through him.

His death undeniably changed my life, almost as much as his living. Mortality slapped me in the face that day and every day for months afterward. The slaps were sharp and stinging. Then Mortality became a distinct personage and regular traveler on my shoulder. He was heavy at first but then grew lighter with time, even lifting me up on those occasions when I wanted to bend with the weight of living. Having Mortality there caused me to make better decisions, to take chances I might not have taken without his constant reminders that life is often short and always fragile.

# George Clooney, Johnny Cash, Jimmie Rodgers, and Daddy

DO THINGS ALWAYS HAPPEN FOR A REASON? Can we cause coincidences to happen? Can we bring the powers of the universe into our particular lives? Can something we did long ago cause an event (intended or unintended) today—many years later? Instead of just wishing for a desired event or outcome, can we do something to bring it about?

Most people who know much about me know that I have two biscuits left by my father when he died more than forty years ago. They are sealed in a small malted milk jar and are now over ninety-six years old. Obviously, they had special meaning for Daddy and thus, to me. Every Fathers' Day brings back the biscuits story.

Those biscuits made a journey across Texas in 1918 in a covered wagon with Daddy and his parents and siblings. He kept them because they were made by his beloved Aunt Minnie. I carried them on a repeat journey (in a different covered wagon) in 1998. It was symbolic, for sure. Sentimental? You bet. My way of apologizing to my father for not paying more attention to the stories he told me about what the biscuits meant to him, why he had kept them all those years.

They say when a man dies, a library burns down. And I had let part of my daddy's library burn down. So I chronicled that return trip in *Biscuits Across the Brazos*. The trip was more Marion Shepherd's (my cousin) idea than mine, but we both wanted to honor our departed fathers, our grandparents, our aunts and uncles, and our heritage.

If I had known then what I know now, I would probably have written more sentiment into the little book, more of the feelings I had as I tried to bring back something that could not be seen with the physical eye. I made a stab at it in a few places, but I didn't want to risk being too sappy or causing readers to roll their eyes. After all, who cares about somebody else's old biscuits? People have their own stories to tell.

I was wrong, of course, people do care. And not just because they have their own similar stories, but they really do care about yours. It was heartening to discover that.

A few years after the book was released, Jan and I went to see *O' Brother Where Art Thou* with George Clooney. I was skeptical and not a huge fan of Clooney's (sorry, ladies). But Clooney was brilliant in this movie. Laugh-out-loud funny, too. He plays a vainglorious fellow whose primary purpose in life seems to be finding a ready supply of pomade for his hair. He has an inflated sense of his intelligence and is possessed of a vocabulary of words he can't string together in coherent sentences. Yet, he is profuse in advice for those he views as lacking in all the wonderful qualities he possesses in abundance. It's not that the character doesn't know anything, it's just that most of what he knows is not true.

As I look back on it now, I am reminded of what self-effacing Richard Farnsworth, one of my favorite actors, said about his role when he was nominated as best actor for *The Straight Story*. Richard said something like this, "It's pretty easy to do well when you're playing yourself." Maybe that's why Clooney was so good in his role.

What does this have to do with coincidences? We made the trip across the Brazos in 1998. *O' Brother* was released in 2000. When I saw the movie, I was surprised (make that shocked) by how much I enjoyed it. Yet, I could not explain exactly why. When I bought the soundtrack, I discovered that it had a lot to do with the music. I played the CD repeatedly. I loved "Man of Constant Sorrow," "O' Death" and all the songs. But one song in particular almost always made the hair stand on the back of my neck and chill bumps come up on my arms. More than once, it brought unexplained tears to my eyes. I memorized the words to "In the Jailhouse

Now" from hearing it so often, but there was nothing in the lyrics to explain the feelings it brought.

> *I had a friend named Ramblin' Bob,*
> *He liked to steal, gamble and rob*

Not all that inspiring, and it doesn't improve much in later verses. So I attributed my abnormal reaction to the plaintive, pure sound of the old-time instruments and the voices of the Soggy Bottom Boys and Ralph Stanley.

In 2005, Jan and I went to see *Walk the Line*. I boasted on the way home that I had one of (and maybe the first) Johnny Cash album, a 33 RPM vinyl record. When we reached home, I searched through my collection and found it. When I picked up the album, showing young Cash in a straw farm hat, I noticed another album just beneath it—Daddy's copy of a reproduced Jimmie Rodgers album. We had given it to him for Christmas more than fifty years earlier.

I sat in the floor and looked at the list of songs on the cover. My eyes went directly to it—"In the Jailhouse Now." Daddy loved to hear Jimmie Rodgers sing. Call me sentimental, but I like to think those moist eyes, chill bumps and hair-standing episodes were Daddy saying he approved of our trip across Texas carrying his biscuits.

About four years after that, I came across a relatively obscure book (*Provinces of Night*) written by William Gay that led me to visit the author in Tennessee. There, I saw an old poster of Jimmie Rodgers. Gay uses Jimmie Rodgers tunes in his books and short stories. One is featured in *Hate to See That Evening Sun Go Down*, later made into a movie. Gay's author photo has him sitting in front of that Jimmie Rodgers poster.

# Granny's Buttons

MY MOTHER, LIKE MANY WOMEN OF HER era, seldom disposed of any garment. When it was no longer suitable for wear, she found use for the fabric. Some pieces were used as rags; some might have been stuffed under a door to keep out the cold; some became quilt pieces. She also cut off the buttons and saved them. My wife, Jan, spent a great deal of time caring for Mother in her final years. She cherishes the small things Mother left, things valuable only to those who loved her. Jan is a quilter, and she especially loved Mother's collection of buttons. For Christmas one year, she decided others needed to share this legacy. This is the note she wrote to the women and girls in our immediate family. The button bags were given to Mother's granddaughters and great-granddaughters.

*"Granny" Button Bags*

*Granny was very frugal, as were most women of her era. As garments would wear out, Granny would cut off the buttons before disposing of the garment, saving them for future use. The buttons on your bag are some that she saved. She would have thought it very special that they were placed on a bag made just for you, her granddaughters and great-granddaughters, with special keepsakes inside. The recipes, in her handwriting, were in her recipe file box along with greeting cards she had received, receipts for various things, dates she purchased a TV (September 23, 1976), obituaries for family and friends and other important documents.*

*Such a special lady!*

When I looked through those buttons and notes and recipes written in Mother's distinctive hand, I noticed she titled her recipes not Key Lime Pie, or Mince Meat Pie, but with the name of the person who gave the recipe to her. Guess she figured the ingredients spoke for themselves. The names brought back sweet memories of some of the most important women in my life. Aunt Hildred, Aunt Jimmie Dee, Pauline Gervers, Stella Robnett, and many more. I was stunned at the number of truly remarkable women in our rural community—women who helped to raise me. And I do mean remarkable, resilient, kind, loving, strong women.

I wrote and presented eulogies for Mother and Aunt Hildred. Some of the other ladies left instructions for me to be a pallbearer at their funerals. Can there be a greater honor? I made myself a note to write more about them later. A short time before her death, Pauline got a message to me that she wanted one of my books. I was pleased to deliver it. The visit was short, and I don't think I can properly express how it made me feel. Pauline was the mother of my good friend Jake, and as we shared good memories, I felt my mother's presence. Pauline made me feel loved that day, just like she had when I was a little boy. What a gift.

# Reflection: The Art of Looking Back

## A Letter to My Children

*I love the man that can smile in trouble,
that can gather strength from distress,
and grow brave by reflection.*
—*Thomas Paine*

I DO SOME OF MY BEST WRITING AT NIGHT when I am half asleep. I have some great ideas just before I wake up on many mornings. Unfortunately, these ideas often leave before I can make notes. Two weeks ago, I thought of something each of you should do.

You are old enough now to engage in reflection. I know you do a lot of that without any prompting from me, but I just want to encourage you to take five minutes to sit down in a quiet place (yes, I know how hard it is to find the time or the place) and quietly think back on your lives thus far. You have heard me speak of the metaphorical tunnel of life where sometimes you look ahead and see only darkness. We all need to look back in the tunnel at those times and see the lights we have turned on and the ones we have had turned on for us.

Most times of reflection come unbidden to us, but you should learn to make them happen. Try to focus on where you are today vs. where you were when you began your adult life. You can't force it, of course, just let it come. I want to affirm that I think reflection is a good thing, though it can sometimes bring sadness, even disappointment.

Think about your spouse and the good times and bad you have had together. Reflect on how your spouse has made your life better and worse, and how you may have done the same to him or her. Think about the mistakes you have made that you wish you could take back; about the friends you have made and/or lost and how you could have handled those relationships better or how you handled them just right.

And think about the children you have raised and are raising and how they have turned out thus far; and about the good and bad things you have done as a parent.

Think about your careers and how far you have come and how far you want to go. And think a lot about how you have overcome adversity (I don't mean conquered—just handled) and how that adversity has made you stronger.

I just bet you will be pretty proud of what you find. I'll bet you will recognize you have made a lot of mistakes as a parent, but all in all, you have been pretty dang good. Same thing for being a spouse. We all make a lot of mistakes, especially in that department. I think focusing on the mistakes we have made helps us to accept the hurt (sometimes torture) our spouses inflict upon us. They probably don't mean to do that, either.

My guess is you may too hard on yourselves in this reflective process. Don't be. None of us is perfect. The purpose of this exercise is not to beat up on ourselves. Just the opposite. Reflection should be about forgiveness, not just of others, but of ourselves.

I think any realistic view will come out pretty positive for all of you. For me, it sometimes points the way for improvement on the next phase of my life. When the reflection starts to bring about a feeling of forgiveness, gratitude and warmth, deep sadness as well as sublime joy, effortless serenity, divine inspiration, then you are getting good at this reflection thing. And that will make you a calmer, more reflective person.

I don't know all the facts and foibles in your lives and that's how it should be. I do know one thing. In the "being good children" department, you have come as close to perfection as any father could possibly expect. In my own times of reflection, I think about the times when you filled in with strength when I was weak as a father, offering me a helping hand, forgiveness, and showing me how to be a better father. I wonder how I could have been so lucky. I pray your children will do that for you. When they do, be sure to thank them.

Most would agree it takes good parents to make good kids. However, I see bad kids with what appear to be good parents. Another thing—in my own case, I think it sometimes takes good kids to make good parents. That seems to be backward, but some things just are backward. Some kids just never forgive parenting mistakes. Thankfully, my children and stepchild did. When the ribbon of love (sometimes called the ties that bind) becomes frayed, untied, or even broken, it is usually the parent's responsibility to tie that ribbon back. In my case, you did a lot of that ribbon-tying. When I made mistakes or said or did the wrong thing as a father, you were very often the ones to repair the relationship. You took my hand (sometimes literally) and led me back into the proper parent-child relationship. Your forgiveness and love made me a much better father.

I am an expert on this one thing, and I mean this from the bottom of my heart. Any person who could be as good as you have been in the "being good kids" department just has to be pretty darn good in all the others. Thanks for that.

# Fiction, Truth, and Families

I HAVE A GRANDSON (GRAYSON RIDGE) who is named for two fictional brothers in my books. I should say they are real people with fictional names. I love the confusion. It inspires questions about our history. I even catch myself referring to my family members by their fictional names. I am surprised when readers recognize someone else in a character who is actually based on myself. I cannot decide if I should be flattered or disappointed when that happens. I do know that I enjoy getting to be child, father, grandfather, and even mother when I write. It was cathartic trying to get inside my parents' and grandparents' heads during times of crisis as well as in ordinary living.

Anton Chekhov said, "Any idiot can face a crisis—it is this day-to-day living that wears you out." I like to read about conflict and tension, but I also like to read about day-to-day living. I like a lot of that interspersed with my action and thrills.

This is a tranquil, day-to-day living excerpt from Chapter 5 of In the Rivers Flow.

> On the back porch, Jake drew water from the cistern and poured some into a wash pan and some into an empty Garrett's snuff glass.... He removed his toothbrush from the snuff glass and mixed baking soda and salt for toothpaste. As he brushed, Griffin Rivers and Buddy came through the pasture gate. Griffin rode Buddy all the way to the back porch and relaxed in the saddle while his grandson rinsed and spat over the shelf into the yard.

This scene, of course, is not filled with tension, but it shows a little slice of the characters' daily lives. Real characters and fictional ones definitely blur, but what about events? Same thing. Few who lived in Delta County during the fifties will fail to recognize a scene in *Rivers Crossing* in which a young girl drowns in a cistern. I first wrote the scene exactly as it happened because it occurred less than a mile from my childhood home, and I was at the scene that terrible day. However, the editing process required me to change it because the truth was so unbelievable. For those of you who have read *Rivers Crossing* and those of you who will, two people died in that cistern on that awful day—not one.

Have people challenged me about changing that? I expected many readers to help me out with the real facts. I have received many e-mails and letters about this part of the book—even several phone calls, but not one challenge. People who lived there during this time seem to intuitively know I am aware of what really happened. Other readers are left with a believable story. Many have written me about their own recollections of the day and night it happened, including a future physician who was on the scene with his physician father. I do not believe this event has been recorded for history anywhere other than in local newspapers at the time. Is it harmed because the story I wrote is not completely factual? You decide.

# Taking Down the Jellybean Jar

I LOOKED UP AT A LITTLE JAR I KEPT on a shelf in my home office. It used to be filled with Jelly-Belly brand jellybeans (they're the best kind). I opened the jar for the first time in years. The bottom was covered with an assortment of jellybeans in vivid colors, all much too old to eat. I had to sit down as I recalled the hundreds of times I had opened that jar to hand out jellybeans to my grandchildren. The rule was two jellybeans for one kiss (until they got old enough to negotiate for more). I had not been asked for jellybeans in years. Of course I knew my grandchildren were no longer babies, but the act of looking at those old jellybeans brought it home in a big way.

When I blew past fifty (yes, I blew past it), I started noticing short periods of time when I felt that a sea-change was taking place in my life. I know we gradually age, but I wonder if anyone else experiences these periodic "bumps" that, in my case, last from a few days to a few weeks. They have no definite beginning or end and are not usually triggered by any cause I can identify. During these transformations, I usually ponder things more deeply, reflect more often, become more introspective. I actually feel myself aging. These are some of the memories that came to mind during one of these periods.

## The Track Meet

Our oldest grandson Caden spent a few days with us about a dozen years ago. We were about finished burning a brush pile when son Damon called to say he had just learned that Caden was scheduled to run in a junior high track meet in Garland in a little over an hour. Garland is about an hour from my house. We hastily threw his clothes into the car and left.

I quizzed Caden about the track meet and why he had not mentioned it. He shrugged, giving me the distinct impression the meet held little interest for him. He wasn't even totally sure of the event he was to compete in, only that it was his first ever track meet. Dad was waiting at the stadium with Caden's track shoes and shorts when we arrived in Garland. Caden wordlessly changed out of jeans into his shorts in the back seat, casually laced up his shoes and started strolling toward the track. His gait made him look like he dreaded it.

I asked about warm-ups, stretching routines, at least a practice jog, etc. I knew Caden had done none of those things during the last two days. Heck, I didn't even know he was on a track team. When I saw his taller, older, and lean-muscled competitors, I was ready to pull him from the meet, but that was his dad's decision. Still, something seemed very wrong. I was worried not only about injury, but an embarrassment he might never live down. Damon said, "I know. I'm worried, too. I asked him if he was sure he wanted to run, and he just shrugged."

I learned he was going to run what we used to call the quarter-mile or four-forty, one lap around the track (now the 400 meter). As eight boys lined up in eight lanes, I started to get a headache and sweat. It was hot and humid, and I was hurting for my grandson.

When the gun went off, he seemed to start too strong and I feared he would run out of steam before the first fifty meters. It was hard to tell who was ahead because of the differing lane starts, but he seemed to be holding onto third or fourth as they entered the second fifty. Not too bad, but I admit I still expected him to drop back in the pack before the home stretch. As they entered the fourth and final fifty, it was clear he was in third—and he seemed to be moving up.

Damon and I were at the finish line, dumbstruck as he moved to second. When he passed the lead runner and won the race by three steps, we were too shocked to even high-five, did not realize we had been cheering at the top of our lungs for a hundred meters. Caden gave us a thrill that day we will never forget. And there were many more to come. As I looked at my son, I was reminded of similar thrills, other track meets, and another boy not so many years ago.

## *Flowers in a Jar*

I was beat, worn out, deep tired, looking forward to a good shower, maybe even a nap, when I came in from the garage. I had just returned from an almost three-hour round trip to return grandkids home after a very busy weekend.

The little fruit jar filled with water, wildflowers and colored weeds on the kitchen counter seemed to shout at me as I entered the house. Oldest granddaughter Peyton (about five at the time) had begged to take it home, but I had refused. "No. Absolutely not. In a car full of rowdy kids, you'd spill that before we got two miles down the road." I was tired and irritable and showed it.

As I returned from taking her home, guilt swept over me as I sat down at the kitchen table with that jar in my hand. What would it have hurt for her to take it home after she had carefully picked those flowers and weeds? So what if she spilled it? It probably sounds silly, but the guilt stayed with me the rest of the day and into the next. I finally called daughter Shelly (Pey-

ton's mother) and told her how bad I felt. She was surprised when my voice broke. "No big deal, not to worry," she said. But I did worry. That is, until Peyton called me that night to say, "That's okay, Papa Jim. I didn't need those old flowers, anyway."

## *The Best Message I Ever Sent*

My heart swelled as my granddaughter walked down the fifty-yard line on the arm of my son. His face and posture filled with pride, hers with joy and anticipation. I felt joy for both of them as I watched them walk toward me. Bailey was nominated for Homecoming Queen—quite an accomplishment for a student who had attended that school for less than a year. But I was pretty sure she had no chance of winning because of her short tenure.

When they announced she had won, I could barely see the field through clouded eyes. I was so surprised and proud, I did not rise from my seat to cheer until everyone else did. As she was carried around the track in a convertible, son Damon texted me. "R U here?"

I replied with one of the best texts of my life. "Yeehaw. On the fifty." I'll always be grateful I could answer that way. Years later, that little girl would write Jan and I a note at Christmas recalling all her memories of Jeep, horseback and bicycle rides, nighttime forays to haunted houses, fishing in our pond, sewing in the quilt quarters, and campfires at our place. We cherish that.

## *Gifts that Last Forever*

I was prowling through one of my many keepsake boxes when I ran across a homemade card (a folded piece of paper). Scrawled across the top of the paper was "Love you." Love was written twice, because the first one was in yellow and was too light to read. The second was written in green.

Inside the card, along with several hand-drawn hearts, I found two one-dollar bills and a quarter. Taylor, six, had given me her tooth fairy money, probably the sum total of her monetary resources at the time.

I remembered her little brother Landon, with no tooth fairy money, watched restlessly as I oohed and aahed over Taylor's gift. Always shy, he handed over a bundle wrapped in tissue by his own hands. "Wrapped it myself," he said. Inside the tissue I found two of his toys (a yoyo and a toy soldier). What generosity and sacrifice for ones so young. I held back the tears until later.

A few years later, their little sister Hannah gave me a Christmas gift. Inside a slightly used Christmas box with a picture of Santa going down a chimney, I found the following:

> A Reese's Peanut Butter Cup
> A Tootsie Roll Pop (orange flavor)
> A piece of grape Dubble Bubble gum
> A roll of Smarties candy
> One marble
> A used eyeglass case
> Three pieces of Now and Later candy
> One chocolate Kiss
> A regular Tootsie Roll
> A nice writing pen

A Quaker Chewy Granola Bar
Assorted fabric scraps from Gran Jan's quilting room
An envelope sealed with gray duct tape containing a small Christmas pocket note pad.

A second envelope (also sealed with duct tape) contained a Christmas card with a picture of Santa's sleigh and his reindeer. Inside the card was a child's drawing of a reindeer. Hannah wrote her name below the drawing. Best of all, she addressed both envelopes to Papa. I long to be worthy of such loving generosity.

## *Maybe Later*

The other grandchildren would agree our youngest grandson is the most resilient of them all. He's eleven as I write this, and he's already been through more than any of them as well as most adults, including his grandfather. Yet, he goes through life smiling with courage and aplomb, providing inspiration to us all.

I recall a Trades Day meeting when Grayson Ridge (I call him Gray Boy) Boles was about four. His mom was marketing her custom guitars and other Rockin' Vintage at one of the booths. Wife Jan and I went to see her wares and to see Grayson. I found a place to sit and he was leaning against my knee when he spotted a young man about six or seven playing with a toy rifle several yards away. He focused intently as the boy made shooting motions with the small gun and pantomimed the capture of outlaws (he was decked out in full cowboy gear).

Gray Boy was so enthralled that he stopped listening to what I was saying. Finally, without taking his eyes off the boy, he said, "I'm going to go over and ask that boy if he will let me play with his gun."

I knew it was probably not a good idea, but he seemed determined, so I watched him as he walked directly to the little boy. He was too far away for me to hear their conversation, but I could see the little boy was not about to turn over the gun. He held it away from Gray Boy with one hand and pushed him away with the other. I could see that he was angry, threatened and shouting, but could not hear what he was saying.

Gray Boy turned and walked back, his expression not one near tears,

just showing mild regret. He returned to my side and I waited expectantly for him to tell me what happened. He did not call the boy names, cry, pout or complain. When he was not forthcoming, I gave up and asked him, "What did the little boy say when you asked to play with his gun?"

He looked over at the boy and the coveted rifle wistfully, thought a few seconds, and then replied, "He said not now, maybe later."

I laughed until tears rolled down my cheeks and six years later, I still laugh about that reply. To me, the story says a lot about Grayson's boundless enthusiasm and unfailing courage and good humor. I wonder how one so young and precocious could somehow be so wise. I think he has an old soul in a young boy's body.

So now the jellybean jar is gone. Why did I choose these simple, maybe insignificant stories to mourn its departure? I can't really answer that, except they are what came to mind during one of these sea-changes.

# How Stories
Heal the Fear
of Public Speaking

I read and reviewed a book recently called *Quiet: The Power of Introverts in a World That Can't Stop Talking* by Susan Cain. The author's research solved what seemed to be a paradox in my life. People have often asked, but I had not been able to answer how a person who was quiet and shy his entire life could make so many public speeches and presentations. Cain's book explains how that could and often does happen to introverts. If I had read the book earlier, I might have understood sooner and better. But, as things happened, I can only say once again that I was guided and blessed when I had opportunities to speak to large and small groups hundreds of times during my career. I put everything I had into those presentations; trying to reveal things I did not know or did not have the courage to say when I was young. I learned a lot of what I know from reading the ancients, and have found wisdom often comes from surprising sources, but usually from experience. I almost always rely on those whose gifts, talents, and wisdom are much greater than mine.

A few of those presentations follow. I hope you find a gem or two to pass on to your children or grandchildren, maybe even something for yourself.

# There's Something about Old Country Graveyards

*Mt. Zion Church, 2006*
*Gafford Chapel Church, 2012*
Later published in Texas Folklore Society Anthology

MEMORIAL DAY—HOMECOMING—DECORATION DAY—or my personal favorite—All Day Singing and Dinner on the Ground. All the same? Not exactly, but close. The common thread—they bring people to churches and to cemeteries.

In the old days at Klondike, we would sing (maybe not all day)—and, of course, we would have dinner on the ground. When I was a boy, I always wondered if folks hadn't meant to say dinner on the *grounds*, because we mostly ate off of tables, under a tabernacle, on the *grounds* of the church or cemetery. Only a few threw down old quilts and actually ate on the ground—but, my folks said that was more common in the really-old days.

After dinner on the ground came the hard part. I marveled as men wearing ties mowed grass with real-push mowers (not self-propelled—but push mowers that only worked when you pushed them to make the blades turn). They righted stones, added sand to graves, repaired (even painted) fences, sweating through their Sunday best. My daddy sometimes wore a tie with his overalls—never a suit coat because he didn't own one. Many men did own suits and they wore them to keep people from seeing them sweat. It didn't work. Telltale signs would soon appear under their arms and down their backs—even through those coats. Women tried to stay fresh-looking in stockings, dresses, hats and bonnets as they hauled food and drinks, pulled weeds and placed flowers on graves.

For me—twilight was the best part—things had cooled down—the singing was better, somehow, and even cold fried chicken tasted good washed down with my mama's iced tea. Usually, there was homemade ice cream or watermelons. Folks went home at dark leaving the cemetery looking better than it did at any other time of the year. They went home full—full of wonderful southern cooking, of course—full of the sounds of music—prayer—church—memories—full of the spirit of having done something good and worthwhile.

What was the best part? In public, people would say it was the prayer or the church services, a memorable sermon, but in private, dinner on the ground usually won that contest. For some, it was the music.

In later years, *the ground* did give way to tables and tabernacles and air-conditioned fellowship halls. *Singing* moved inside where it seemed more formal, somehow. Decorating graves? It's still done, of course, but rarely on Decoration Day. Mowing and pulling weeds is often contracted out (thank goodness for that).

In the old days, like today, weeds grew back, real flowers wilted and died, plastic ones faded and curled up in the Texas heat. But what stayed behind? What's left when everybody goes home? So, why do we do it?

Why? Most would give the obvious answer. To honor the loved ones who have passed before us (and to provide a final resting place for ourselves). But with our spoiled selves today, we complain about the heat. We long for our recliners and our remotes—and especially for central air. Take-out has become food we bring home to eat in front of our televisions, not food we cook to take someplace else.

So, if we are decorating only a little, if we're not mowing or pulling weeds, if the heat is sometimes oppressive, if cooking is a chore rather than a delight... why do we continue?

Yes, I know that the business of managing, maintaining and financing of the final resting place must be done. It's a responsibility and we accept it. We gather once a year to report about last year and make important decisions about next year. I recognize and appreciate the importance of all that, those awesome responsibilities, and the volunteers who carry them out year after year. Those volunteers know why they do it. But what about the rest of us?

Several years ago, I heard a poem read at a funeral and fell in love with it. Most of you have probably heard "Do Not Stand." It was thought to be Indian in origin, because so many Native Americans used it. Actually, it was written by Mary Frye of Baltimore in 1932—about her mother. She wrote it on the back of a paper grocery sack (for you kids—grocery sacks used to be brown paper bags). John Wayne read this at director Howard Hawkes funeral.

> *Do not stand by my grave and weep*
> *I am not there, I do not sleep.*
> *I am the thousand winds that blow*
> *I am the diamond glint on snow.*
> *I am the sunlight on ripened grain*
> *I am the gentle autumn rain.*
> *As you awake with morning hush*
> *I am the swift uplifting rush,*
> *Of quiet birds in circling flight*
> *I am the day transcending night.*
> *So do not stand by my grave and cry*
> *I am not there—I did not die.*

I found those verses so comforting. Still do. It's comforting to think our loved ones are not there. But if they are *not there*, why do we continue to come—to decorate—to maintain?

If you asked members of this group or any of hundreds gathered across the nation in mostly rural areas why we continue to do this—why we have homecomings, memorial days, decoration days—you would get lots of answers. Many would be unable to clearly articulate the reasons why. It's just something they feel—maybe just an obligation to do the right thing. I think it's more than that.

In Klondike, there is the New Klondike Cemetery and the Old Klondike Cemetery. I remember as a small boy walking beside my maternal grandfather in the old one. He paused at the graves of two of his infant children who had died four decades earlier. He leaned down and brushed glass clippings and molded leaves from the small stones. When he rose, he scanned the graveyard and said, "There's just something about an old country graveyard."

What is that something? Especially if, as "Do Not Stand" proclaims, *they are not here.* That poem is correct, because Mary Frye knew her mother was not in that cold, often wet, sometimes cracked ground. She had gone to heaven. Yet, my grandfather, without waxing poetic, said something that seems to contradict that—something profound. Maybe it was because Mary's mother was buried in Baltimore and my grandfather was talking about an old cemetery in Klondike where he had buried his mother and several of his children.

Homecomings and Memorial days are mostly rural traditions now. Maybe there is just *something about* rural cemeteries, but I think it applies to all of them.

A little over ten years ago, I read my grandchildren a book titled *Last Innocent Summer* by Zenita Fowler. The novel revolves around the death of two little girls in Commerce almost seventy years ago. My grandchildren were enthralled—keeping the novel in their memories as we read it in parts over several months and several visits. When we finished, they wanted to find the graves of those two little girls—and we did—in *an old country graveyard.* Not too far from here, by the way.

When we visited, as much as children can, they calmed for a few minutes—they seemed to understand better—so much better that they wanted to read the novel again. As they stood at the children's graves, I thought about what my Papa Lee had said. There's *something about an old country graveyard.*

As part of research for writing my first novel, I read northeast Texas novels like William Humphrey's *The Ordways* and *Home from the Hill.* Many pivotal scenes in those books take place in old country graveyards. There are several scenes in my books in country graveyards. Not morbid scenes—but very important ones.

When I am writing a novel and need inspiration—when I am trying to get my children or grandchildren to understand and appreciate their heritage—when I am experiencing sad or hard times—when I just want to reflect and meditate—I find that *something about* my grandfather spoke of, at an old country graveyard—standing at the graves of my parents, grandparents, and two brothers.

Yesterday, as I was putting the final touches on this, I came across some old notes from years ago. I'm sorry I did not get a chance to give credit to the author of this poem. I'm not even sure of the title, but I think it is "Give What's Left of Me Away."

> *Now that I'm gone*
> *Remember me with a smile and laughter.*
> *And if you need to cry, cry with your brother or sister*
> *Who walks in grief beside you.*
> *And when you need me, put your arms around anyone*
> *And give them what you need to give to me.*
> *There are so many who need so much.*
> *I want to leave you something,*
> *Something much better than words or sounds.*
> *Look for me in the people I've known and loved*
> > *or helped in some special way.*
> *Let me live in your heart as well as your mind.*
> *You can love me most by letting your love reach out*
> > *to our loved ones,*
> *By embracing them and living in their love,*
> *Love does not die, people do.*
> *So, when all that's left of me is love,*
> *Give me away as best as you can.*

I, like you, now understand what my grandfather meant when he said *there's something about old country graveyards*. Yes, it is comforting to think *they are not here* as the poem says, but I find it comforting to think they are. I like to think they visit only when we do—they leave when we leave—return when we come again.

It's our meeting place—our place to reconnect and remember. It's not the *only* place where we hear their voices, feel their presence, but it's the *always* place—because they are always here.

As we visit—

> In the wind, we hear their whispers about the mistakes
> > they made and how we can avoid them.
> In the sun, we feel the warm touch of their embrace.
> In the rain, we feel cleansed and calmed

In the snow, we see the brightness of their smiles.
In the sounds of nature, the chirp of a cricket,
> the buzz of a locust, the song of a bird, we hear
> the healing stories of our childhood.

In the birds that fly around old country graveyards,
> we see our loved ones freedom from pain,
> and ourselves, flying away.

There *is* something about old country graveyards. And that...is why we do it.

# Going Home Again

## Mt. Zion Church, 2008

THOMAS WOLFE WROTE A NOVEL THAT SAID, *You Can't Go Home Again*. He was wrong. Ever notice how many people do go home again? An old proverb says *Home is Where the Heart Is*, meaning of course, that we are at home when we are with our loved ones. That's true. However, home is also where we grew up. For most of us, it is a *place*. For many, it's where we ran through the fields, heard Mama's call to supper; warmed our backsides by a woodstove or a Dearborn heater; warmed our feet on a wrapped hot brick or hot water bottle on cold nights—under quilts made during a quilting bee in our living rooms—on a frame hung from a tall ceiling—quilts made by our mothers, grandmothers and their friends. It's where we gathered around a Christmas tree that had been cut by our daddy (or maybe ourselves) and dragged to the house behind the family horse. A tree we got to decorate with whatever we made in the kitchen. Sometimes, we even had a few store-bought ornaments or tin foil cut to look like icicles. Home is where we placed cotton on windowsills to give the appearance of a white Christmas. I remember the first year Mother bought snow in a spray can. I went a little overboard—took me a whole day to scrape it off the windows after Christmas.

    I was grown when I first noticed that lots of people come home after they retire. I was fascinated by that at first—curious about the large number of people who lived their adult lives in urban areas, raised their children, completed their careers, and then came back home to complete their days. As for me, I came home early. Our farm was long gone when I finished college, so I felt there was nothing to hold me here. My world was *out there*—somewhere.

I took a job in what seemed like an exotic location to me at the time—Fort Worth. Later, I moved on to a really foreign place (called Tulsa) in a whole 'nother state. I was soon back in Texas, living near Dallas. I was ready to come back to Texas, but not quite ready to come home. When I lost my father at a young age, I began to see the community where I had grown up as being not so bad. In fact, it looked pretty good. *I realized that on a wind-swept day in Klondike*—standing at the foot of my daddy's grave. Just a few short years later, at the same Klondike cemetery, I stood there again, this time at the foot of my brother's grave. I was only twenty-eight at the time, but my mortality struck me that day...and home beckoned.

So, why do we do what Thomas Wolfe says we can't? Why do so many of us *go home again?* I wrote an article for the East Texas Historical Association a few years ago. In it I referred to the importance of *place*. Allow me to quote from that presentation.

> *I hope that place and his friend weather are characters in my books. I want readers to smell and feel the black gumbo soil, hear the tree frogs on spring nights in Texas, smell a rare thundershower on ground that has not felt rain in months. I tried to bring the mystery of East Texas creek and river bottoms and the merriment of Saturday nights on a small town square to the printed page. I hope my readers experience the economic, emotional, and physical hardships brought on by drought and by flood in the same way that my characters did back in the fifties. I have had comments and questions from readers about dogtrots versus dog-runs, galluses, saucered-and-blowed coffee, cisterns versus wells, Prince Albert tobacco, brogan shoes, lightning rods, coal-oil stoves, and what a real push mower is. Ever try to explain the difference between a slop bucket and a slop jar?*

Yes, *home is where the heart is*, but it is also where memories are, where a sense of place, a sense of belonging is. The feeling of place as described in the old *Cheers* theme song that says, "Where everybody knows your name." When I lost my brother and my daddy, some friends from my work attended their funerals. Their visits allowed me to see the places where

I had grown up, my family, and the people I grew up with through their urban eyes. I remember being pleased with the reflection.

In more recent times, I have had visits from old friends I worked with in big cities. I like to take them along on my daily sojourns—to a place where a few friends gather around a pot-bellied stove under half of a rusty grain silo in rainy or cold weather and under a big oak when it's warm and dry. I carry my visitors to coffee shops and barbecue joints where professors mingle with farmers and cowboys, local businessmen, writers and poets. I take them down a two-mile stretch of farm-to-market highway where authors of more than twenty books live. You only have to drive a mile or two to get your horse trained by one of the best trainers in Texas (that's on highway 11), a few miles more to get him shod by one of the best farriers. I know back roads where a cutting horse judge lives, where anything from a lawnmower to a shredder to an old Jeep can be repaired by a master craftsman—to places in the woods where one can find boiled shrimp and fried catfish if you know the right back roads and the right times to go. There are usually no signs, no advertisement for these places. You just know where to go, whom to see.

This is what I mean about a sense of place, a place where you can put down your roots, where you can charge purchases and be trusted to pay on time. Things are changing now, but you can still do like that old Merle Haggard song about the *"roots of his raising running deep"* and how his daddy could *"Borrow money at the bank simply on his word."* After running errands and riding in my Jeep around places like Campbell, Ladonia, Cumby, Miller Grove, Honey Grove, Enloe, Pecan Gap, and Cooper, grandchildren have asked more than once, "Papa Jim, do you know everybody?" Jan has been asked that many times at her work. We usually say, "Yes, and we're kin to most of 'em."

There were many drafts of my first novel. Most had a prologue about a man past middle age revisiting the house he grew up in and the haunts of his childhood. Someone he admired had asked him probing questions—questions that had intrigued him for years. "If you could talk to the *boy you were* at nine or ten, what would he say to you? What would you say to him? Would the boy be pleased?" The questions began a search that led the man to his boyhood home. The prologue was never published, and only a few trusted souls have read it. Allow me to read a portion of it for the first time in public. Remember, this is a man searching for himself by returning to the place where he grew up. It is a dream-like scene and the people are seen through the man's imagination. He finds a locked gate at the entrance to his old home place with *no trespassing* signs, but he knows more than one way to skin a cat. Here's the prologue:

---

Two miles down the dirt road, he stopped at a dead end. The familiar road from his past had been cut off like a cane pole over a fishing hole with no hook, no line, no sinker. The rest of the road had succumbed to progress in the form of a huge lake. He would never again be able to visit many of his favorite childhood haunts. He imagined how those places looked now: underwater, rusting, decomposing, shifting eerily with the movement of murky water.

He stepped out of his pickup and felt the soft sand under his boots. Many of the places of his childhood might be underwater, but his first home was not. It had been many years, but he felt sure he could still find it from the back—through the bottoms. The wind brought the pungent smell of leaves ready to fall, weeds giving up for another season, and the expectant aroma of green pecans. He remembered his father deftly peeling pecans with his pocketknife and handing the meat to him. The thought made his mouth water. The slope was steep, and bois d'arc and locust thorns scratched his face and hands as he headed deeper into the woods.

The bottoms were the stuff of legend, providing fertile ground for rich memories, folklore, and mystery. Hard to describe to an outsider, bottomland had to be experienced. Many areas never saw sunlight. Black gumbo soil stuck to itself and anything else that touched it. Parts of the bottoms flooded at least once during most years. When the land dried, great cracks formed that looked like the aftermath of tiny earthquakes. There were stories of small children and dogs falling into those cracks and never being seen again.

But along with danger and discomfort, the bottomlands offered solitude and quiet, a place to commune with nature. On some mornings and evenings, fog would roll along the creeks like a lost soul searching for its eternal home. His grandmother had told tales of red-eyed black panthers that screamed like a child in deep distress.

Fog rolled around his knees like an affectionate cat as he approached an old stock pool. He stopped and sat on the pool bank under a huge willow. Before the willow trees were here, when this pool was new, he remembered a boy who had bathed and swam here most summer days.

He leaned his head against the tree trunk and looked away from the pool toward the old cotton patch and wondered if it was true that the experiences one has in the first fourteen years of living set the course for the remainder of life. When he looked back, he was surprised to see a small boy—about nine or ten by the looks of him. He was wearing a pair of ragged cutoff jeans with no shoes, seeming not to notice the cool and cloudy day. An older boy in his mid-teens, dressed the same way, stood behind him. Their appearance said they were brothers, brown from the sun with that familiar rough-hewn look that country boys acquire.

As he headed north, the old buildings seemed to rise out of the fog. Their weathered gray color offered little contrast to the gray sky. He could see the house, the dairy barn, smoke house, hay barn, chicken house, and outhouse. A mound of dirt protecting the storm house was still there. He could hear the loose tin on the cellar door flopping in the breeze.

Elm and hackberry branches reached through the broken windows and over the roof of the old dairy barn, promising nature would soon reclaim it. The white paint on the barn wood was almost gone and the sheet metal was rusted. The old hay and cattle barn still stood as tall as the house, but it was listing to the north, slowly giving way to the prevalent southern winds. Approaching the wind-battered chicken house, he could hear the clucking, see the feathers, and smell the fine, choking dust chickens make when they scratch the ground and flap their wings.

A few feet away, a man clad in overalls was robbing a beehive. He wore a protective hood with a wire screen across his face. The man squeezed and released the bellows on a bee smoker as he removed the honey and honeycomb from the hives. The acrid smell of the smoke softened by the sweet smell of honey and honeycomb made him want to linger and talk to the beehive robber, but he felt compelled to go on.

He could see no livestock, but heard the lowing of cattle ready to be milked and fed. He could smell fresh milk and wild-onion cow-breath. Though it was late afternoon, he heard a rooster crow in the distance.

A young teenage girl was practicing basketball under a cow lot goal. Her movements were rhythmic and graceful in spite of the dirt court, as if she were dancing. When she saw him, she stopped, placed the ball under her arm as if it were part of her, and watched as he approached the back porch of the house.

The porch was the only part of the house that showed any signs of paint and most of it had cracked and peeled away, as if the porch wanted to blend with the unpainted, weathered gray of the rest of the house. A porch shelf held a water pitcher and wash pan, a small tin tray with bars of Lava and Ivory soap, and a Garrett snuff glass filled with toothbrushes. A woman was drawing water from a cistern. When the woman turned to face him, she smiled with expression, but spoke only with her eyes—eyes that were like the girl's; eyes that smiled, but held a deep sadness and a little fear. Dressed in a plain, faded blue sundress, she wore no jewelry or make-up, but was striking in her natural beauty. A small, white tea rose had been placed carefully in her hair. She watched him as he approached, their eyes meeting in silent communication. No words could be said… they could not touch.

A small boy stood beside her, leaning against her leg. The boy's arm draped gently around his mother's knee, as small boys are wont to do when they seek protection, but the boy seemed to be the comforter rather than his mother.

———⇒●⇐———

Thus ends the prologue.

Poet T. S. Eliot said, *"the end of all our exploring will be to arrive where we started—and to know the place for the first time."* So what brings us back to the place where we started? Memories, of course, family, friends and the place itself. But houses are bought, sold and torn down—roads rerouted, lakes built. What usually stays constant? The most dependable sense of place we can come home to is found where? Churches and cemeteries. They are often the threads that pull us back home.

And, of course, there are those who had sense enough not to leave at all. We owe them a debt for keeping these churches and cemeteries in tact so the rest of us can have a place to come home to. *Home **is** where the heart is,* and a lot of the hearts here today came home to this place, this church and this hallowed ground.

# Picking up the Fork and Spoon
## Texas A&M-Commerce (Old ET), 2009

WHEN I GOT THE CALL ABOUT THIS AWARD from the president of my alma mater, it was such a great surprise that I told my family to keep it quiet until I got something in writing. I didn't know the president well enough to recognize his voice and the man I talked to could have been an impostor.

I stand before you full of gratitude. I am honored and humbled to join the company of my fellow honorees tonight and those who came before. I cannot possibly name all the people who have carried me on this journey, but let me start with my family. My wife, Jan, who stood by me, never questioning when I changed careers and left good situations to pursue what must have seemed to be foolish quests. I strive to equal her as a partner.

My children, always consistent in their inspiration and support, made my life's road an easier one by respecting authority as children and by being responsible adults. They married well and are loving and attentive parents. I complained they did not listen to me when they were growing up. I learned almost too late that although they may not have heard all of my words, they *watched* everything I did. Had I realized this earlier, I think I would have been a better father.

And my sister, Patricia Ann White, another ET graduate, teacher, and matriarch of a family that includes many students and alumni of this university. I also have three double cousins here tonight. One met his future wife here as a student. All have graduates in their families. Double cousins are more akin to brothers and sisters than cousins. They understand my story in ways that only siblings can.

And then, my grandchildren. I was in the eye of a business hurricane that threatened to destroy everything I had worked for when my first grandson was born. Everything was going too fast, and I felt out of control. But that new set of innocent eyes looking up to me as one of his role models inspired me to remember what is most important in life, and those eyes made me better. The pure heart of a child, an uncluttered mind, brought inspiration to be the best I could be. And with the birth of each new grandchild, the tender feelings of love and the sense of what was important grew. We now have three boys and four girls. Each brought clarity and perspective to my life well beyond my highest expectations. I had just about given up on getting my first novel published when I learned my last grandson was to be named Grayson Ridge... for two characters in the manuscript. From that point forward, giving up was no longer an option.

I have one of the last rings from East Texas State College and one of the first diplomas from East Texas State University. Where do I begin to describe what this institution has meant to me? I came here in 1962 directly from the cotton patch and dairy barn. My parents were not depression-era children; they were depression-era adults. Both had to leave high school early to help support their families.

My father's name was Richard, but everyone knew him as Teadon. Teadon was a dairy farmer, dirt farmer, plumber, electrician, carpenter and mechanic. He drove heavy road equipment for the county. His last job for wages was as a janitor at this university. We attended basketball games in the old Field House together. Mother was Nadelle—homemaker, lunchroom cook, and seamstress who worked at many sewing factories. She had a knack for making a small boy feel good about himself.

Teadon and Nadelle sent me here with a firm set of values and five twenty-dollar bills to pay the $82 tuition and to buy a few books. I was paralyzed with fear—afraid of letting those two fine people down and afraid of what I might find here. They had taught me, by example and by words, the values of self-reliance and acceptance of personal responsibility. I don't know why, but I feared those values taught by two parents without high school educations might be challenged here. I was wrong.

This university, now and then, is about people, not just location and buildings. I can't thank them all, but the man who introduced me is a good place to start. Dr. Tarpley took the time to encourage me as a frightened freshman. To borrow from Robert Frost, his words made all the difference. I continue to be inspired by his boundless enthusiasm, unfailing good humor, his innovative ideas, his sharp instincts and his deep desire and ability to help others.

Dr. Carroll Adams is also here tonight. Dr. Adams' reputation as a stern professor was so well known that many students went to SMU in the summers to avoid his classes. I couldn't afford to go to SMU, and my only path to a diploma traveled through Dr. Adams' classroom. So I traveled—frightened or not. He never gave me anything, but he did inspire me to learn something. An A or B from him was a badge of honor because everyone knew you had earned it. He also, by the way, taught me basic economics... and that has made all the difference.

Then there was Dr. Graham Johnson. When I was a senior, the economy was good and I had three job offers. I told him I was taking a job with an oil company in Tulsa because it paid $20 more per month than the other offers. He smiled and pointed at my shoes. "How much did you pay for those loafers?"

I knew exactly. "Seven bucks."

He pointed at his shoes. "These cost twenty bucks."

I thought, but did not say, "Dr. Johnson may be a great accounting teacher, but he sure overpays for his shoes."

"These are more comfortable," he said. "You'll soon develop a taste for quality."

He was trying to tell me why $20 should not be the basis for my decision, but when I did not connect the dots, he told me I would be bored with the job I had selected.

With the typical wisdom of a twenty-year-old, I told him that my prospective employer had a good retirement plan. What I was really thinking however, was, *After more than three years of going to class every morning, working every afternoon and Saturdays, studying most nights, I wanted to be bored. Then there was the thing about the exotic location. Tulsa, Oklahoma. Most of my friends were taking jobs in plain old Dallas or Fort Worth. I was going to a whole 'nother state.*

So I did not take his advice. And I should have. I *was* bored with that job in a few months and never saw a penny from that retirement plan, of course. The fact that I did not accept his advice matters not, however. The important thing was, he took the time to make me feel worthy of his time... and that has made all the difference.

It's a real shame many of today's business leaders and most of our politicians never had to travel through a Carroll Adams "Money and Banking" class or learn "International Economics," "Corporate Finance," or even the elementary principles of financial accounting from folks like Ken McCord and Graham Johnson.

Bill Jack, Bob Dowell, Joe Saylor and the irascible E. W. Roland and Lawrence McNamee also offered up the plate of knowledge and inspired me to pick up the fork and spoon. Often, their inspiration was less than subtle. They weren't much for hugging or coddling, but they did convey their attitude of, "I will accept nothing less than your best."

And thank you to Sam McCord, Bill King and Bobbie Purdy, who invited me to participate in alumni activities and made it a positive experience. And to Mary Smith who also placed her trust and faith in me for more than two decades as a partner and colleague.

I grew up in small-town Klondike, graduated from small-town Cooper High School at a time when every faculty member had at least one degree from this university. I started and built a small-town financial services firm from scratch. I learned a lot from traveling most of our great country, but I got my most valuable knowledge and experience within a thirty-mile radius of where I stand now. So there is one other group I have to thank.

I returned here eight years after graduation to open a CPA firm and a Western Wear store, hoping one or the other might succeed. I made a lot of house calls, visiting clients and prospective clients, mostly at night. On one such evening call, I visited a home in a rural community about twenty miles northeast of here. The house was turn-of-the-century with a wraparound porch in need of paint. I noticed water had puddled in the dirt floor of the one-car shed. My potential client was in the kitchen, still in his overalls, helping his wife prepare supper. His wife fixed us iced tea and pushed us out of her small kitchen to the dining room table—a huge harvest table—one end piled high with dusty correspondence and paperwork. A phone sat at arm's length.

She set a plate in front of me filled with red beans, cornbread, corn-on-the-cob, and cantaloupe. I had already eaten, but was not about to be impolite. I felt right at home. These were folks like Teadon and Nadelle, and I judged them positively, but incompletely.

I placed a notepad beside my plate and tried to write and eat as the man regaled me with stories. I have read that a single conversation across the table with a wise man is worth a month's study of books. I began to write faster and listen closer as I realized that such a moment was at hand. Halfway through our meal, the phone rang. I could not help but overhear the conversation. He was talking to the Governor of Texas, offering advice on matters before the legislature. His wife noticed my surprise. She leaned forward and whispered, "He always calls at the most inconvenient times."

Why do I tell that story? Because that man was a 1936 graduate of this institution. He wore overalls but routinely advised people who held positions of great power. Because I later had the privilege of having many more people like him as clients—each unique and impressive in their own ways. Because this story illustrates the reach of Old ET and Texas A&M-Commerce, not just out into the nation and world, but right here at home, in ways most of us never think about. Farmers, entrepreneurs, teachers, ministers, artists, physicians, pharmacists, ordinary and extraordinary people from all walks of life became my clients. They continued my education in so many ways I cannot begin to describe them. Nor can I ever thank them enough. Most of them had one thing in common. They lived in small town, rural America and labored quietly, lived conservatively, accepted personal responsibility, and contributed greatly of themselves and their resources. Most would not want me to use their names, but the vast majority had some direct or indirect connection to this university.

From Teadon and Nadelle and the community where I grew up, I learned about truth, honesty, and forthrightness in dealing with others. This university and those clients enhanced and affirmed those beliefs—and that has made all the difference.

I never apologized for attending a small university and I never will. Our mission here has never been and never should be mediocrity. Excellence is not the exclusive province of the big and powerful. It is, and always has been...right here. You just have to want it—you have to pick up the fork and spoon. My deepest gratitude to my family, those clients and those professors, to this university, and to Nadelle and Teadon. Thank you.

# Formulas, Secrets, and Universal Truths

## For the Texas A&M-Commerce Graduating Class, Spring 2013

THOMAS SZANSZ SAID BOREDOM IS THE feeling that *everything* is a waste of time; serenity is the feeling that nothing is a waste of time. I hope you choose serenity for the next few minutes—*and it is a choice*. In return, I will try not to waste your time.

I dedicated my last book to the memory of my grandfather, saying "I wish I had known then what I know now." I don't mean I wish I had known life's secrets, nor do I wish that I already possessed the wisdom that can only come from success and failure, tragedy and triumph. What would be the point of living if we knew it all from the start?

What I mean is I wish I had known *better and sooner how to listen, how to pay respectful attention* in order to better build my own belief system.

Here are a few tidbits of the advice I received before I really paid attention:

- You have two ears and one mouth so you should listen twice as much as you talk.
- Spend less than you earn; save and invest the difference.
- The workplace is a hierarchy, not a democracy.
- Life is not fair; deal with it.
- Successful people make a habit of doing things other people don't want to do.
- Accept responsibility for all aspects of your life.

And the one I really did not want to hear on graduation day,

- Your education is just beginning.

With the great advances in technology since my graduation, especially during the last two decades, I am told I must say something about it. So here is my technology story.

I arrived at my first job after graduation and took my junior accountant seat at an old oak desk farthest from the seventh-floor windows of the oil and gas building in a big bullpen full of other bean counters. My first assignment was to go down into the basement and make copies of a report. You might think I was put off by such an assignment, what with my freshly minted degree. But I wasn't—I was afraid.

In the basement, I saw this giant machine that I knew must have cost thousands of dollars. I had seen a Xerox machine before, but had never used one. I walked around it a few times, afraid to touch the myriad of buttons for fear I would break it. I was about to panic when a lady about my mother's age walked in and stood behind me, waiting her turn to make copies. She saw my red face and asked if she could help. Oh, how I hated to admit I didn't know how to use that machine. I worried for days whether she would tell my new colleagues just how green I was.

If I can advance from that point to writing a weekly blog post and my own website, then I am not worried about a generation who grew up with computers being prepared to adapt to rapidly changing technology. Some of you are probably texting right now.

Here is what worries me. That in the rush to keep pace, we will forget or never learn basic principles that never change—timeless and universal truths that have been recognized by great men and women for centuries. These truths are more important than technology—*much more important*.

I learned this critical lesson, but I wish I had learned it sooner. I have told my wife, Jan, that I want these words on my tombstone.

> COULD HAVE DONE MORE,
> COULD HAVE DONE IT BETTER,
> WISH I HAD.
> IF I HAD ONLY KNOWN SOONER.

I had eight jobs in eight years after my graduation. Two companies went bankrupt while I worked for them, one more fell shortly after I left. I got justifiably fired from another. I felt like the cartoon character who walks around with a cloud over his head. I hope your first decade is better. But it is almost guaranteed that you will experience some missteps along the way, if not downright failures. I discovered later that each of those failures taught me invaluable lessons—lessons that led me to run a successful business of my own—even to advise others.

But in midlife, it seemed I had reached a plateau in my career and personal life, and that plateau was not very high. I opened branch offices in three other towns. Two failed, one struggled.

This was the era of learning leadership and business principles through books like *In Search of Excellence, Thriving on Chaos, Seven Habits of Highly Effective People,* and just about the time I jumped into shark-infested waters, *Swim With the Sharks Without Being Eaten Alive.* A year or so into reading and listening to these great trainers and writers, one of them told me to look in the mirror if I wanted to find the source of most of my problems. So I asked the image in my mirror, "How long before you start applying what you have learned to your own life?"

That look in the mirror led me to self-improvement and positive thinking folks like Zig Ziglar, Jim Rohn, Brian Tracy, and many others. They convinced me that certain truths applied to me, not just the successful and famous. And they taught me how to set goals. But I was still a skeptic, dismissive of rah-rah and platitudes. I wanted things to be proven by logic and empirical evidence. I sought the secret, the formula for success, while doubting that either existed.

W. Clement Stone, a poor boy who made good (very good), took Og Mandino, an alcoholic, under his wing. Og went on to write some of the most successful business books ever published, became editor of *Success Magazine,* and was one of the best motivational speakers I have ever heard. One of his books was called *The Greatest Secret in the World.* Mandino led me to Earl Nightingale and his recorded message called *The Strangest Secret.* The lights began to come on.

Stone also introduced me to a book that virtually every salesman (but few accountants) knew by heart in those days, *Think and Grow Rich,* written by Napoleon Hill and first published in 1937. Hill had been commissioned by steel magnate Andrew Carnegie to research and write a book about why successful people succeed. And Carnegie gave him access to some of the world's most accomplished people. It took Hill twenty years to complete his book. My skeptical ears perked up when I heard that. In twenty years, Hill had surely found that *elusive formula* I was seeking.

So now I had it—Hill's well-researched formula and Mandino's and Nightingale's secrets. They led me to Dr. Joseph Murphy's book, *The Power of the Subconscious Mind*, to Maxwell Maltz's *Psycho-Cybernetics*, and to Norman Vincent Peale's *The Power of Positive Thinking*. They proved to me the connection between mind and body.

My career went in a new direction as I weaved their ideas into the message I was conveying to the relatively new financial planning profession as part of my new company. One night in Canadian, Texas, the Oasis of the Panhandle, I had another awakening.

I did a presentation for local CPA Mike Gardiner. Mike invited all of his clients to the community room of his church to hear me. After the program, I discovered a set of my handouts had been left in a chair. They had been scribbled all over. Beside each of my formulas and secrets, someone had written a biblical verse. Mike's pastor had occupied that chair. Later at Mike's house, we started looking up the verses. The man had found biblical prose that espoused every principle in my handout. As my plane took flight out of Amarillo, I looked out the window at the desolate but beautiful Panhandle landscape and understood what Ralph Waldo Emerson meant when he said, "All my best ideas were stolen by the ancients."

Humility settled on me like a warm quilt on a cold night. Alexander Graham Bell (the Steve Jobs of his day) said,

> *What this power is I cannot say, all I know is that it exists and it becomes available only when a man is in that state of mind in which he knows exactly what he wants and is fully determined not to quit until he finds it.*

I now knew what that power was.

I told about my encounter with the preacher to one of the acclaimed trainers and authors I was following; about my discovery that his ideas and others were as old as time; about the *source* of the subconscious; about the connection between affirmations and prayer.

His response: "It took you long enough."

I asked, "Why didn't you just say so in the beginning?"

He replied, "Would you have believed me or would you have turned away? You were focused on results, not on principles. The *what* of things vs. the *why*. You wanted *proof* instead of *truth*."

That sent me back to the mirror and a serious look at whether their methods worked. I was surprised to find that many of my goals had already been achieved. Maybe not exactly when or how I had envisioned, but achieved nonetheless. I had just been going too fast, looking to the next goal, to see it. I now understood that life is lived forward, but understood backward.

As I looked back at some of the irrational and highly risky decisions I had made, I also discovered that *I had been guided*, that I had done many things that took me off the path I had chosen, but that guidance set me on the true path again. All I had to do was ask.

So what are these universal truths? I can't list them all, but here are a few:

1. Find folks who have been-there-done-that and emerged as successes on a personal and financial level. Study what they did. Read their work, listen to them, seek their advice.
2. Jim Rohn said, "Find out what failures do, and don't do it."
3. Success formulas and secrets have been known since ancient times. But it's in the *implementation* of the concepts where the rubber meets the road. One quality possessed by every person Napoleon Hill studied was *self-discipline. You must choose to do what you should do, when you should do it, whether you feel like it or not.* Self discipline is also what keeps you from doing what you should not.
4. Read at least one hour a day (tweets and texts don't count). We need longer attention spans, not shorter.
5. If you really desire to be successful at anything, you must engage in deliberate practice doing that thing.
6. Enjoy the little things, because someday you may look back and see they were really the big things.

7. Go *wide and deep*. And no, I don't mean football. I mean life. You may have within you the capacity for several careers and endeavors. But if you must choose between wide and deep, go deep.
8. We all have a purpose in life—a call, if you will. Find yours. Ask for help in achieving it. The only thing that stands between you and what you want is the *will* to try and the *faith* to believe it is possible.

Many years have passed since I crossed the stage over in the old Ferguson Auditorium to receive my diploma. Today, I hope you will begin gaining what Mary Ann Soule called the gifts of age.

She said,

> *If we continue to succumb to modern America's stereotypical vision of aging, fearing the changes in our bodies, resisting the natural transitions of life, and avoiding the unknown territory of death, we will deny ourselves and the whole of civilization the gifts of age:*
> 
> *Mature Perspective*
> *Seasoned Creativity*
> *Spiritual Vision*

Don't delay as I did.

Daniel H. Burnham said, "Make no little plans; they have no magic to stir men's blood. Make big plans; aim high in hope and work."

One more story: Renowned author and investor Alexander Green knows about universal truths. He was browsing in a bookstore with a friend when they encountered Nicholas Taleb, the best-selling author of *The Black Swan*. All three were speaking at a financial conference close by.

Nicholas' announcement that he was planning a book on religion prompted an argument with Green's friend as to whether a particular theological point "was true." Nicholas pointed to the fiction section of the bookstore and asked, "How about all those books over there. Are they true?"

"Of course not," Green's friend said. "They're novels."

Green stepped into the argument. "But they are full of universal truths."

Nicholas smiled with satisfaction and said, "Exactly!"

Nicholas and Green advocate the perennial philosophy. In Green's book *Beyond Wealth*, he says,

> *Perennialists seek enlightenment wherever they can find it. It doesn't matter whether the source is ancient, modern, mythical, foreign, mystical, or verified by the latest scientific findings. It only matters that it's true—and that it has some practical application for more skillful living.*

In his timeless book, *As a Man Thinketh*, James Allen said:

> *Cherish your visions, cherish your ideals, cherish the music that stirs in your heart, the beauty that forms in your mind, the loveliness that drapes your purest thoughts. If you will remain true to them, your world will at last be built.*

I leave you with my own words to remember when you become discouraged:

Enjoy these days of struggle, the best you can. Because almost surely you will look back on them with fondness. Try to hear the music that sings in all of our souls. On some days, success will seem to reside on a mountain that reaches through the clouds—a mountain you sometimes tire of climbing. But then there will be other days when success visits like a firefly at twilight, elusive and distant at once, then brushing your cheek or resting on the back of your hand, too swift to touch. Someday, a firefly will land in your palm. Don't close your hand around it, because the light will go out. Allow yourself to feel the thrill of success changing from stranger to friend, and then let it fly away so you can find it again.

# Lines that Rhyme

## With Apologies to Real Poets

Brenda Black White always poked me with her pencil when I professed to know nothing about poetry. She took offense at my protestations because I had published her book of poetry. But Dr. Fred Tarpley deserves all the credit for that. Still, I have had a few minutes in my life when I felt inspired to make rhyme that may or may not qualify as poetry. Indulge me.

# Unworthy

As I walk out on a cold early morn
A blue heron glides to a diamond-sparkled pond.
Look down in the pasture, silver frost to the creek,
I hear the sound of familiar hoof beats.
He runs up to me, a soft little nudge,
For food or for lovin', who am I to judge.
On my leg comes a soft rub, a faint little purr,
The stray cat we rescued wants fingers on fur.
As a gaggle flies honkin' in that special V,
A feeling of gratitude wells up inside me.
Just as I think it can't get any better,
She opens the shutters soft as a feather.
From her quilting she looks up, sees me outside,
Knows what I'm thinking, she's right by my side.
I feel unworthy, don't deserve so much,
Fine place to live, lovely woman to touch.
We learned life by livin' it, this woman and me,
Course, things are not perfect, neither are we.
For blessings we have, we're on our knees,
Our pledge to Him: We'll try to please.
On this life journey, we've come a long way.
Together forever, till our dying day.

# The Wedding Dress

It's just an inanimate thing, I thought, when they asked if they could see,
Just a dress like any other, how special could it be?
They were planning a wedding, just as we had years ago,
They wanted to see if it would serve again, without a lot to sew.
I said, "Sure, take a look, I know it will be fine,"
I knew that I could speak for her, knew she wouldn't mind.
But as they took it from the closet and brought it down the hall,
I felt a little wistful as its fabric brushed the wall.
And as they held it to the light, I saw a vision from the past,
A vision of my daughter, one that will forever last.
I saw her as the first time, when she left the bride's room at the church,
A vision of loveliness, a feeling for which we all forever search.
And as she took my arm and we started down the aisle,
I knew this was a moment that would forever make my heart smile.
As my throat started to tighten and my eyes to fill,
I knew that all the planning, expense and trouble now mattered nil.
My advice to any father is to always look ahead,
See yourself walking down that aisle, one chance to see your daughter wed.
Think even further, five years down the road,
Be sure you can look back with pleasure and it will lighten your load.
I hope she has fond memories, that I served as Daddy well,
When she needs me for lesser things, I promise not to fail.
So thank you to my daughter for that special day,
I know it belongs to her, but I treasure it anyway.

# Boots with Soul

I TOOK SON DAMON TO GET A pair of boots when he was in high school. He had grown into my size boots, and when we got home, I tried his new pair on. They fit like a glove. I traded him for two pairs of slightly used eel hides for his new pair. Twenty-eight years later, I gave them back on a stand with this poem.

---

An old pair of boots ain't much of a gift,
But the story behind 'em gives me a lift.
Still original soles, almost like new.
Never wore 'em much, cause they really belong to you.
Near thirty years old now, give or take,
I'm passing them to you, for old times' sake.
You were barely knee-high when I bought your first pair.
On the day I bought these, your boots I could wear.
Finding narrow boots can be quite a treasure,
When they seemed to fit you, I tried them for measure.
I pulled them down snug; they fit like a glove.
Ten steps later, I was deeply in love.
And those soft floppy tops folded over so neat,
With quality leather, it's hard to compete.

But these were your boots, not mine to wear,
A swap I proposed, my silver eels for your new pair.
The eels were in style way back then,
For most young boys, they stirred quite a yen.
But used boots for new bothered me some,
From father to son, well, it just ain't done.
So I threw in a second pair, to make things right,
But I still think of you when they come in sight.
I remember that boy around time's bend,
Always my boy, now also my friend.

Jim Ainsworth wore these boots 1983-2011 // Damon Ainsorth 2011-

# Unseen Things

DAUGHTER SHELLY LIKES OLD BOOTS, country and mountain music, vintage collectibles, guitars and most things cowboy.

> *Things are not the same as love and family, but for some of us, they may help survive hard times and fill our souls. They may represent the road we came down and where we may dream of going.*
>
> —Shelly Ainsworth Boles

When I saw that quote on her website, I had friend Jerald build a rustic stand for an old pair of elephant hide boots that meant a lot to me. I gave her the boots with this poem.

---

These old elephants sort of served that purpose for me in years gone by.
They traveled with me in stirrups and in airplanes high in the sky.
They walked the streets of Boston the same as Texas small towns.
Standing toe to toe with Gucci loafers, they never let me down.
As I made those trips to places I didn't really want to be,
I'd look down at these elephant boots and become a different me.
Look back at the roads just traveled and ahead to the ones of dreams,
Chasing steers in pastures and arenas, crossing a river's stream.

They were with me crossing the Brazos as we stepped back in time,
By wagon and horses across Texas, the years to unwind.
The tough hide stayed with me through four heels and soles,
Now I pass them on to someone who heals many souls.
The little girl who looked up to me come what may,
Even when I disappointed her, she never turned away.
So when you look at these old boots and the love they bring,
See hope, promise and inspiration, the best of unseen things.

# A Quilt for Papa Jim

## By Jan Ainsworth

This quilt was started for your special day,
To show you my love in a special way.
This art from my heritage I share with you,
For you are the one that keeps my life anew.
With its end unknown we received the news,
Grandparents... to a bundle in blue.
Your quilt in the corner, you patiently wait,
For a quilt to be made for this heavenly fate.
Before its finish there was more good news,
Three more quilts to be made, but not in blue.
Our precious little girls have fulfilled this life,
But again you wait for the quilt from your wife.
With no more new arrivals coming our way,
I present this quilt to you on your special day.
It is given with love and holds many memories,
For while being made, we were blessed with our babies.

# A Boy, a Man

### By Patricia Ann Ainsworth White

Years ago a baby boy was born,
Parents were poor and lived on a farm.
Chances of achieving status in life
Would mean deprivation, work and strife.
Education? How? Was the question asked,
Could such an accomplishment come to pass?
Determination, goals, and a desire
Suddenly seemed realistic to acquire.
A job quickly led to a small store,
Hard work and respect earned him more.
A larger building with marquee in lights,
His name stood out as approached the site.
More buildings and marquees grew,
Until one day all those non-believers knew.
This poor boy from Klondike, Texas was real.
He said, "No big deal."
Yes, I have been there all those years,
I was the one without doubt or fear.
I knew because he was different from any other,
Because you see, he is my brother.

# Life's Final Songs

William Zinsser, author of the million-selling book *On Writing Well*, tells the story of his first job at a newspaper writing obituaries. He complained to his boss and asked for some decent story assignments. His boss replied,

> Nothing you write will ever get read as carefully as what you are writing right now. You misspell a word, you mess up a date, and a family will be hurt. But you do justice to somebody's mom, you make a life sing, and they will be grateful forever. They will put your words in laminate.

I wish I had read that story before I was asked to deliver my first eulogy. On second thought, maybe not. I am honored each time I am asked to write and present a final tribute to someone who has departed this life. I try to find how each of them made their lives sing so that I can help with their final songs. Most of the time, I already know. I hope reading these will make each of you more cognizant of the words and tune to your own final song.

# High Plains Tribute

## *Hereford, Texas, 2001*

HE DIDN'T ASK FOR MUCH. FIVE MINUTES (people had things to do and places to go), a pair of 501 Levis, some Bob Wills music, a pine box and an old pickup to haul it in. He meant it, too.

As one of his best friends said afterward, you either knew him well or you didn't know him at all—meaning, of course, that you can't judge the interior by the exterior.

Some would say he was old-fashioned, certainly stubborn. He didn't try to conceal his less endearing traits, but his word was always good. He had strong opinions and didn't care too much about being politically correct. His good deeds were many, but done quietly, usually anonymously, and always unselfishly.

At a local restaurant the night before, he had been the main topic of discussion for a small group. "Most unselfish person I have ever known," said one lifelong friend.

"Yes, if he was here tonight, we would have to watch him to keep him from paying the bill for all of us and sneaking out before we knew it," said another.

"Most people don't realize a tenth of the good deeds this good man has done."

Where had they all come from? Miles could be driven without seeing a house, much less a person. Eyes which have seen Texas only through fiction would have nodded approvingly at the sea of black and silver-belly hats. Wranglers and Levis topped boots of oil-soaked cowhide and full-quill ostrich.

A lonesome pair of spurs played a tinkling, sporadic tune when their owner shifted his boots in the cold wind. No time to remove the spurs when he left work or no time to put them back on before returning? More likely, just part of the daily uniform.

Being there was important...dressing up was not. An occasional tie or pair of shoes interrupted the Panhandle dress code, but not enough to notice.

A look at the faces and their expressions confirmed that these were not just characters in a movie or a book—they were real Texans. Many had come from the North Country, some from Germany and other countries, but all had passed the test.

They were Texans to the core—only one or two generations removed from the pioneers who came to this one-time desert to tame it with livestock and crops. Most did not live in town, but the closest town is named for a breed of cattle.

The seventh year of a more or less continuous series of droughts showed that Mother Nature does not tame easily. The continuous struggle had etched deep lines in some faces, but cold determination and persistence were evident in their eyes. Today, those eyes and faces showed pain and respect for one of their own.

The temperature hovered in the thirties with a matching wind speed. The sun was out, but they would have preferred standing in a downpour. They knew that he would have wanted it to rain on his special day.

Some were kin by blood; most were kin by shared hardships, grief, and occasional victories. Hardy stock—the people kind. They stood reverently as a close friend gave the best kind of eulogy, one spoken in plain words—from the heart—and from close kinship.

Afterward, they broke into small groups to share stories of the man's life, his sense of humor, his jokes and stories, his infectious laugh, his generosity, of how he would be remembered.

Without benefit of topcoats or gloves, they stayed in the cold wind until their turn to speak to the family came. A sentence spoken at a time like this does not do justice to a life well-lived, but a hug and a look convey more than words can say.

They made their way across the brittle grass, kept alive by irrigation, to their waiting trucks, leaving the pine box alone on the prairie. They would continue their struggles without him.

His worry about rain and crops was over for now. Was he watching? Was he pleased? It took longer than five minutes, and the pickup had not been practical for hauling the box, but he had his Levis, a tin of snuff was in his pocket, grandchildren had left him remembrances, and Bob Wills music had been played. It was good...it was honorable...befitting a good and honorable man.

Now he was alone on his beloved prairie and snow was in the forecast. Maybe a good crop was in the offing for his family and friends. He would surely want it to be.

---

Arliss Edwards' great and generous heart stopped beating on Christmas Eve, 2001, in the office of his farm shop on the High Plains of Texas where he had lived and worked all his life.

# Aunt Hido

## *Hildred Alexander Ainsworth Shaw*

*Delta Funeral Home Chapel*
*Cooper, Texas, May 28, 2000*

I AM PRIVILEGED TO STAND BEFORE YOU to honor the life of this wonderful person. Uncle Arch and I were sitting in a porch swing in their front yard many years ago talking about old times. We were silent for a while and I noticed he was weeping. I asked him what was wrong and he said "When you get past 50, you get more emotional. When you get past 70, you will cry at the drop of a hat." So if I can't get through this, I hope you will understand. I know for a fact Aunt Hildred would understand.

I am sure everyone here has fond memories of Aunt Hildred. When I first heard she had died, I was seven hours from home by car, so I had a lot of time to think about my memories of her and how you measure the worth of a person's life.

Daddy was sick a lot when we were kids and Mother spent a good deal of time with him in various hospitals. When the absences were really long, she had to find places for all of us to board. Most of my time was spent with Aunt Hildred and Uncle Arch. Sometimes, they had all three of us. Times were tough. With three children of their own, imagine adding one, two or even three extra mouths to feed, laundry to do, etc.

I missed my daddy, but I was used to long periods away from him. A boy that age really needs his mother. She's usually the one who finds the right clothes and packs the right lunch for school. And you can cry in front of her, admit your fears, and not be too ashamed.

Aunt Hildred seemed to know when I needed Mother the most and she did her utmost to fill that role. When she wanted to comfort me, she would be Aunt Hido and I would be Shim. She could always make me laugh and feel better. I never felt like an intruder in her home. Everyone in the family shared with me. They at least pretended they were glad to see me come and unhappy to see me go home. Aunt Hildred would have it no other way. I can only imagine the burden we placed on her, but she never once let it show.

Aunt Hido was also a great cook. I loved her biscuits more than my mother's and was never disappointed at her table. During one of my extended stays at her house, I came home from school and discovered a freshly-made buttermilk pie in her kitchen. I had a strong sweet tooth. Time (or nausea) has dimmed a lot of the details, but I was either alone in the house or my cousin Kay left me alone with that pie.

Either way, the pie was sliced, and I tasted my first piece of the most delicious pie I had ever eaten. I decided that she would not mind if I had another slice. When Aunt Hido told the story over the subsequent years, she maintained that I ate the whole pie. I think Kay helped, and that, using some sort of childish logic, we left only a slice or two for the others.

One thing is certain. I was very, very sick—so sick I could not even glance at buttermilk pie for thirty years. Instead of arriving home to find a warm dessert for the whole family, Aunt Hido found an empty pie plate and a very sick little boy—a real test for the most patient person.

Do you know what she did? After putting a cold wet cloth on my head, she laughed. *She laughed.* I was mortified for doing something so thoughtless and stupid. And, I thought I was going to die for my sin. I was sick enough to wish for it. But Aunt Hido got me to laugh. And we laughed about that until we lost her.

About twenty years after the pie, I returned to my old stomping grounds to open a business. I also began to play racquetball. One of the players (a college professor) turned to me soon after I started playing and asked if my name was Ainsworth. Well, I had just put up a big sign near downtown Commerce and I assumed he had seen it. I guess my head swelled a little when I nodded, expecting congratulations.

But it wasn't the sign that made him recognize my name. "You related to Hildred Ainsworth?" I was proud to say that I was her nephew.

"Well, you must be proud. She is one of the nicest ladies I have ever met. And she bakes cookies that are nectar of the gods."

Yep. He knew her all right. Aunt Hildred was working maintenance at the college and cleaned his office. The professor didn't recognize my name from a big sign or the business I had opened or anything I had done, but by the good humor and good deeds from a very, very fine woman. I learned a valuable lesson that day. My aunt knew what was important. She didn't preach it, she just practiced it.

Remembering that in the truck coming home, I thought about what that said about Aunt Hildred. Acts of good humor and love were typical of her entire life. If that doesn't measure up to the best of standards for a life well lived, then I don't know what does.

Thanks, Aunt Hido—well done.

# She Kept Going

## Nadelle Alexander Ainsworth Hooten

*Delivered in the Sanctuary
of the First United Methodist Church
Commerce, Texas, January 20, 2001*

MOTHER WAS JUST FIFTY-SEVEN WHEN Daddy died. A few weeks later, she asked me to say something nice at her funeral. I did not want to talk about death and funerals. When my brother died three years later, she asked me again. I promised her I would.

How do you put someone's eighty-eight-plus years of living into only a few minutes, especially if that someone is your mother?

She is the last survivor of eighteen children born to Lee and Mary Pearl Alexander. As a child and adult, she was known for her mischief, strong will and sense of humor.

Her life has been full of tragedy, but also triumph over adversity. She married and raised children during the depths of the Great Depression and World War II. She lost her first-born son just before he turned two to illnesses that would be minor problems today. But, she kept going. She had other children, and focused on them and her husband.

She almost died giving birth to con-joined twins who were stillborn. My father was very ill in the same hospital at the time she was giving birth, and had been given little chance to live. They both kept going.

His twenty-year battle with illness devastated them physically, emotionally, and financially. She lost Daddy at fifty-nine. But, she kept going.

Three years later, she lost my brother Eddy in a plane crash. He was only thirty-four. Again, she kept going.

She married Deb Hooten in 1973. Only a few years later, an automobile accident left him partially paralyzed for the remainder of his life. But, she kept going.

She was diagnosed with Parkinson's and lived the last twenty years of her life battling this crippling disease. She had two hip surgeries, thyroid surgery, a brain tumor, numerous hip dislocations, and many fractures, cuts and abrasions caused by her efforts to keep going.

I mention these adversities only to show Nadelle's strength. She persevered. What about the bright side? We grew up dirt-poor. She struggled, along with Daddy, to be sure that we never really suffered. And we didn't. Unless you can call getting rained on regularly in your living room suffering. I remember coming home from basketball games on cold nights and finding the house frigid, but a warmed brick or iron was always in my bed. That was Mother's love.

I was grown before I ever paid any attention to the term "unconditional love," but Mother understood it long ago. She knew how to take our disadvantages and shortcomings and make us believe they were assets. I know she had me convinced that being small for my age was such an incredible advantage I actually felt sorry for the biggest kids.

I have seen *grace* defined as a gift from God—unearned merit—the gift of love we don't always deserve. When I reached adulthood, Mother's grace always gave me more credit than I deserved. I used to joke that if I were ever sent to prison, Mother would say three things:

1. He's innocent and doesn't deserve to be there and I will spend my last penny and the last breath in my body to get him out.
2. He is unquestionably the smartest and best person in that awful place, including the warden.
3. Doesn't he look good in stripes.

She would, of course, say the same thing about my sister or any of her grandchildren or great-grandchildren.

Some years ago, I was going through some of Mother's things. She had been in and out of nursing homes for quite some time. A few material things were lost or given away with each relocation. As I looked through her possessions, it dawned on me that everything she owned now fit into a small chest and ottoman. I was overcome with emotion as I asked, "How could more than eighty years of living be reduced to this?"

But those two pitiful boxes full of material things are not her legacy. She left something much more valuable. This family is her legacy. She filled our lives with grace and unconditional love.

Mother, I know you are listening. I am glad your pain is over. For Pat and myself and all of your family, I say thank you. We love you. Job well done. Rest now and go with God.

# Last Trip to Klondike

## January 2001

AS WE PASSED DOGTOWN ROAD, MY MIND left highway 24 and turned south down the road I had traveled as a teenager—to the house where I had lived during high school and college. My memories of moving Mother from her home there to the nursing home seemed a lifetime ago. That same day, my stepfather moved to a nursing home a hundred miles away. I never saw him alive again. They each wanted to be near their own children, so they could not agree on a nursing home together. I felt it was a little early to move out of the home they shared, that they could manage a little longer, but they were insistent. That still confuses me.

I was riding shotgun to Willie Tucker in a white stretch limo—nervous about his delayed reactions. I couldn't carry on a conversation with my family seated in the back because Willie always thought I was talking to him—his hearing as impaired as his driving reflexes. We were following a white hearse carrying my mother on her last trip to Klondike. The pallbearers, grandsons by birthright and by marriage, followed in a third white car behind us. Having those strong young men represent the future of the family and their bond with my mother and me provided more comfort than I would have imagined.

We passed the three bridges where my siblings and I swam with our father when we were children—the bridges where Star, my brother Eddy's horse that belonged to us all, met his maker courtesy of a milk truck. That, like this one, was a sad day, but I had little notion of real sadness in those youthful days—the kind that can't be cured by a hug from your mother. Now, I knew. Daddy was gone, dead at fifty-nine. Eddy left us too, at only thirty-four. Now Mother.

As we neared the old Reed farm where I spent the first fourteen years of my life, the memories started to flow. I had walked our gravel driveway and down Highway 24 to school at West Delta many times, giving me bragging rights about braving the cold wind, rain and snow to walk to school. I never measured it, but I would guess the school was no more than a mile from the Reed place and I usually rode the bus or in someone's car during bad weather.

But I *had* hitchhiked to ballgames and practices from this spot. Those were bright memories, but looking down that gravel road to the old barns and the spot where the house once stood, the memories seemed bittersweet—memories seldom talked about at times like these. On second thought, maybe only at times like these.

Those memories are cloudy, like the picture on our old black and white television. Today, I couldn't relish them like I wanted, because we still had a job to do. I felt that job getting in the way of the experience. I felt sure I should be immersed in the past, but couldn't get too far out of the present. Willie's driving and the job at hand made sure of that. The job, of course, was to bury Mother beside Daddy and her two sons, say the final prayers and let her go.

Jan and I made the same trip twenty-four hours later. I wanted to try once more to experience the things I felt one should experience when a last parent dies. I couldn't do that in the funeral procession. Connecting to them through remembering the past should somehow be healing. I felt my breath come in short gasps and I got a catch in my throat when we pulled off 24 onto the old Klondike highway. When we entered the Klondike cemetery, Mother's was the only new grave. No visitors were in the old graveyard.

As I left the car, the stark dreariness of the weather struck me. Yesterday had been sunny and cold, my kind of weather—thankful for that. Today, thin clouds blocked any cheerfulness or warmth the sun might have offered and made it seem colder than it was. The sky was gray and that grayness made the surroundings seem even bleaker. It was the dead of winter, though, and I had been here when the sun was warm and birds sang. Today, only a soft wind sang, interrupted regularly by the call of crows. Do crows caw, call, cry or sing? Lots of people don't like their sounds, but I always have. They are lonesome, but peaceful, like the sound of a train whistle. I wondered if that was Mother's or Daddy's way of speaking to me.

I stared at the mound of dirt over her grave. Flowers covered part of it, but it was still ugly. If I had been looking at this plot of land as a potential purchase, I would have called it just a sorry piece of dirt. We had had several days of wet weather and the fresh dirt was muddy. This was the second coldest winter on record and one of the wettest, but that old clay still hung together in huge clods. Will they ever smooth out? I always wondered why Daddy had chosen this place to bury his first-born son and his parents. It was called the  New Klondike Cemetery back then. Now, calling it new seemed a contradiction, but the sorry piece of dirt had changed into a place of healing.

I was twenty-six when Daddy died. I tried to put time into perspective by comparing myself to my father. Daddy was twenty-five in 1936 when he and Mother lost my brother Richard just before he turned two. Daddy lost his mother only three years later. Now, I almost understood their pain, but hoped I would never fully understand. Helping to handle Daddy's funeral arrangements seemed like a blur to me now. What he must have gone through to bury a son and a mother only three years apart.

I tried to recall the story about the Ainsworth plots. How many had he bought and why? Had Daddy bought enough to bury all of his family members or had Papa Hiram bought some? Now, two of my siblings are buried in those plots beside my parents. Also, my grandfather and grandmother and an aunt and uncle. That's eight. How many more sites are there? Why did he buy so many when he had only one child to bury and no other children at that time? I know money was short. Whatever the reason, I was grateful he had been so responsible.

I couldn't help but picture Mother in that casket in her red flannel gown. It was perfect for her and she looked exceptionally pretty. It seems that in the absence of pain, her beauty had returned. But I couldn't keep her fear of dying out of my mind. I think her fear stemmed from having to leave her baby in that cold, damp ground sixty-five years before. I have heard her refer to the horror of that many times. I felt remorse for having left her here. I know there was no choice, but it didn't ease the feeling of guilt. My faith told me Mother's soul and spirit were not there, only her body. But I loved that old, frail, worn out body, too.

In the hospital a short two days before, as I watched Mother draw her last breath, our long odyssey rushed through my mind. More than a decade of various health problems, a crippling disease, broken hips, fractured bones, cuts, abrasions, surgeries, research hospitals and emergency rooms, nursing homes. We had another operational procedure scheduled in three months if she had lived. Her problems were overwhelming, her body was worn out, but at that moment and until now, I want to bring her back for one more genuine hug, one more conversation, one more I love you. I need her to say it to me as much as I need to say it to her. I want to say I am sorry for all the times I was impatient and short with her—all the times I resented her for intruding in my life. I wish I could have been more compassionate, gentler, more consistently loving.

Jan said that in the minute before I returned to Mother's bedside, a single tear rolled down her cheek. Was that just a physical reaction, or was it emotion or pain? Had she heard the myriad of conversations with doctors and nurses about how hopeless her condition was, the conversations about feeding tubes, insurance and Medicare and hospice care? We tried to speak out of her hearing, but we were all guilty of being careless. Did she decide she was too much of a burden and will herself to die?

As I went through the procedures of signing death paperwork and dealing with the funeral home minutes after her death, I irrationally expected to have one more conversation with her. She had come back from expected death before. I waited in the hall and watched as they rolled her out of the room, covered with a gray shroud. I followed as she went out the back of the hospital, and then got in my truck to follow the hearse down the street. Finally, I turned south to head home to call my sister and my children as Mother turned north. The road was blurry as I said goodbye to her one more time.

As the wind blew softly and the crows called, I stood before that mound of dirt where my Mother's body lay. I thought, "She's in a better place. I did the best I could." But I didn't. I could have done better. She told me many times how much she appreciated what we did for her and how she hated to be a burden, and I am sure she is saying now that we did well. Mother's gift was unconditional love. But I think her last gift to me may be a lesson in living—be more patient, more compassionate, more giving, more loving and more expressive of that love.

# The Treasure

## Jackson (Pop) Thomas
### West Oaks Funeral Home Chapel
### Sulphur Springs, Texas, 2002

I AM A PROUD MEMBER OF THE F.O.P. SOCIETY. I suppose all of us here today are. Maybe you just didn't know the group you belong to had a name. I don't know how many members are in F.O.P., but there are many. If you haven't guessed by now, F.O.P. stands for *Friends of Pop*. F.O.P. is an eclectic and unusual group. Members include the downtrodden and handicapped, the highly educated and the uneducated, the rich and the poverty stricken. Members' ages range from toddlers to very senior citizens. You can find them working in gas stations, junk and salvage yards, convenience stores, repair shops, Walmarts, antique stores, trader villages, schoolrooms, college campuses and just about any place else you might look. They are concentrated in this part of Texas, but I know the F.O.P. Society has an even broader reach.

There were no forms to complete to join F.O.P, no dues to be paid, and there were no scheduled meetings, although members looked forward to each encounter with the founder...Pop Thomas. Membership was not entirely voluntary, however, because once you met Pop, you became a lifetime member.

When the family honored me by asking me to speak on his behalf, I struggled with the awesome responsibility of trying to sum up a good man's life in a few minutes. This was a man who lived simply and happily without worldly comforts, but loved his treasure-trove of "swappers and traders." A complex man who did not appear that way.

As I stumbled to find the right words to describe him, Pop laughed and whispered in my ear. "What's wrong with you, Jim? I've already done the work for you." I laughed as I always did when I spoke with Pop. He was right, you see. I don't have to sum it up. His legacy will eclipse anything I say here today. His memory will be cherished by his family and other loved ones, and the members of F.O.P.

Let me just say a few things, then, to celebrate the life of Pop Thomas. I think everyone who knew Pop would agree he was a unique individual. So what made him unique? Was it what he did for a living? Maybe. He was, after all, an airplane pilot, a race car driver, mechanic, carpenter, construction foreman, a dealer in heavy engines, parts and equipment, a skilled craftsman who could make or repair most things, a jack-of-all trades, but most of all, a trader. He also caddied for Lee Trevino when he was just a golf course hustler. A unique lifetime of careers? I think so. Pop had also reached a level of awareness in life that allowed him to live simply, without the so-called comforts many of us consider necessities. Most of us fail to reach that plateau.

I first met Pop through his oldest son. Jerald built a desk and some bookshelves for me and I was amazed not only at his ability to understand what I wanted from a crude drawing, but to actually build it from very raw materials in the style I envisioned—always going one better than I required. When I met Pop, I gained a better understanding of where Jerald got the wonderful gift of understanding how to create something out of nothing, of how things work—even things never seen before. As Jerald said often (usually out of Pop's hearing), "Pop taught me what I know." I had the privilege of watching the two of them interact for more than a decade. The jokes they played on each other and their arguments never masked their obvious love.

I asked for stories about Pop. I got many. They brought a lot of laughter and fond memories. Unfortunately, most can't be repeated here today. There were lots of stories about the Good Samaritan that Pop was, stories of his buying junk from the disadvantaged in order to help them without taking away their dignity. Most of the junk had to be tossed because it was useless. The rest, he gave away. There were stories of appliance and engine repairs, carpenter, plumbing, and electrical work that he did for neither recognition nor reward.

I remember two stories from my own experiences with Pop. He was helping Jerald and me put down a floor on a second-floor porch at my barn. Jerald was standing on a ladder under the porch with a screw gun and screws. Pop and I pushed the boards together and stood on them to hold them in place while Jerald screwed them to the steel underneath. When we placed our last board, I turned to walk down the stairs. Pop turned to follow, but dropped to one knee. Only one foot would move. Jerald had screwed the sole of his boot to the floor. The boots were new, and Jerald got a tongue-lashing. The more Pop vented, the more Jerald and I laughed.

My wife, Jan, recalled the story, I think, that describes Pop best. Jan and I were hosting a United Way benefit at our barn only a few weeks after Pop's boot had been screwed to the floor. Some of the arriving guests were turning in the driveway to our house instead of going on down the road to the barn entrance. It had rained a lot recently and it was hard to turn around there, so Jerald persuaded Pop to leave the barn, where all the fun was taking place, to sit alone, outside, at our driveway, directing traffic to the barn. We joked that it was cruel and unusual punishment, but Pop turned the tables on us. When we took him some refreshments, Pop's magnetism was at work. He had convened a large meeting of the F.O.P. New members had been recruited and old ones had stopped to visit. People on the way to the party, including my son-in-law and son, had stopped to visit with Pop and stayed. Others had already brought him an ample supply of refreshments.

So what words describe Pop best? Mischievous? Generous? (He was always offering me this or that as a loan or a gift.) Loving? Caring? Sense of humor? (He certainly had a good one). Well, he was all of those things and more. But I like to think of him as a treasure. He was a treasure to downtown Commerce, to his family and loved ones and to the lifelong members of F.O.P.

Jerald and sister Debbie were with Pop in his final hours. Pop knew they were there and knew what they were saying. They are comforted that they held him and said the words that all fathers want to hear. "You are my hero, and I love you."

Jackson (Pop) Thomas, father of my great friend, 2002

# A Bright Torch

## William W. (Bill) Venable
*First Baptist Church
Commerce, Texas, June 2006*

BILL VENABLE WAS MY FRIEND. I'M PROUD of that. He had qualities I admire. Qualities that seem to have become rare today.

When friend June Dunn sent word that his condition had worsened, I asked her to tell him a little story for me. Daughter Robin asked me to share it with you. Many of you know that my son, Damon, worked for Bill for many years. Damon will tell you that Bill is one of the main reasons he is in the construction business today. He tells the story of the time Bill caught him idle in the store one day. Bill asked what he was doing. Damon honestly replied, "Nothing."

Bill replied, "Come with me." When Damon finished all the tasks Bill assigned, he vowed never to be caught "doing nothing" on Bill's payroll again.

When Damon was in school, he came home with a class assignment to write about people he admired. At the supper table that night, he asked me whom I admired. Without thinking more than a few seconds, Bill Venable came to mind. I named a few more, but our discussion focused on Bill. I admired Bill because he had qualities I respect most in people.

Bill's word was good. He did what he said he would do.

He did it well.

He did it *when* he said he would do it. And...you could count on it every time.

Bill may have been a mere mortal like the rest of us, but he stood tall among his peers. He was just plain admirable.

Woody Allen takes credit for saying 90% of success in life is showing up—but he was far from the first to say that. Bill Venable always showed up. I believe that discipline is freedom, and Bill was a disciplined man. He was at work when people arrived in the morning and when they left at night. Some might say he worked too hard, but Bill understood what was required to run a business and he wasn't afraid or ashamed to do it. He turned a fledgling lumberyard where it was hard to find a straight 2x4 into one of the best hardware and construction supply stores in the nation. Yes—I said best in the nation. I still have never been to one better. I miss it. When I went in, I almost always ran into Bill. He helped me so many times. I know he did the same for thousands of others. When the community or a charity or any good cause needed support, Bill was always at the front of the line—giving of his time and resources.

Sure, he made sacrifices to provide for his family and to run a good business, but he also understood the necessity of balance in his life. He was a devoted husband and father and a good friend. He was not a gushing parent, but when he spoke to me of his children and grandchildren, his voice and expression changed. I knew that every word was from his heart. He loved and was loved by those closest to him. I knew it and he wanted me to know it.

Bill accepted responsibility. For himself, for his business, for his family and for his community. It is too bad we sometimes don't appreciate these rare qualities anymore. Bill Venable had them. I believe Bill's life exemplified these words from George Bernard Shaw:

> *This is the true joy in life:*
> *To be used for a purpose recognized by yourself as a mighty one.*
> *By being a force of nature—instead of a feverish, selfish little clod of ailments and grievances complaining that the world will not devote itself to making you happy.*
> *I am of the opinion that my life belongs to the whole community.*
> *And as long as I can live, it is my privilege to do for it whatever I can.*
> *I want to be thoroughly used up when I die.*
> *For the harder I work the more I live.*
> *I rejoice in life for its own sake.*
> *Life is no brief candle to me.*

> *It's a sort of splendid torch which I have to hold up for the moment. And I want to make it burn as brightly as possible before handing it on to future generations.*

Bill, thanks for handing on a very bright torch.

# The Man Had Sand and Salt

### Jay Palmer
*Lynch Funeral Home Chapel*
*Greenville, Texas, 2007*

ALL SORTS OF CLICHÉS RAN THROUGH my mind when I was asked to say something about Jay Palmer's life on the day of his final tribute. Straight shooter; no-nonsense; tough cowboy; they don't make 'em like that anymore; gravel in his gut; blunt talker; the man had sand.

Jay was salty. With his physical limitations, most men would have given up on horses a long time ago. Jay, however, was listed as trainer for two horses at Lone Star Park as recently as two weeks ago. He's been salty all his life. There was that time in Albuquerque in the fifties when he took a rank mare and trained it to outrun three world champions. He served his country in many theaters all over the world for nine and one-half years. He had to stuff himself with peanut butter sandwiches to meet the minimum weight of 120 pounds when he volunteered.

This good man maintained a crusty exterior and fit all of the terms we use to describe a man's man, but he was much more. Here are a few other words that describe Jay Palmer:

GENEROUS. I'll wager there are several seats in this house filled with someone who has benefited from Jay's generosity. He helped people in need, but did it in such a way that the person being helped was not demeaned. Some people will hold a debt over you and boast about who they have helped. Not Jay. You had to find these things out from somebody else, because he would not tell you.

PRAGMATIC. A lot of people here knew Jay better than me, but I know we hit it off from the first time we met. I think that was because Jay was my kind of fellow. He had tons of good old-fashioned horse sense. If it didn't make sense to Jay, it probably was not sensible. He understood how the world worked and seldom repeated his mistakes. When he did repeat a mistake, he had a purpose (helping somebody else, usually) and would make fun of himself while he was doing it.

What word describes the opposite of politically correct? We need to come up with a term that is the antonym for political correctness. When we do, I think we should place the words in the dictionary and make Jay Palmer the definition. Irreverent is the closest word I could think of. I, for one, admired his irreverence. He had little tolerance for stupidity and made no bones about expressing his opinion. I think the world would be a better place if more people were like that.

When I received the call about Jay Wednesday night, I was in the middle of a poker game with five other fellows about fifty miles from here. When I announced that Jay had died, four of the five men there knew him or knew of him. Only two had ever owned a horse. It seems almost everybody knew the man.

When my son called and told me to be on the lookout for a horse for my granddaughter, I thought of Jay Palmer. When we took a covered wagon across Texas in 1998, we met a fellow on the Brazos River called Oaks Crossing Slim. He knew Jay Palmer. Jay told me about Slim's habit of not snapping the cuffs on his shirts.

My favorite Jay Palmer story involves, however, a septic system. He told Benny Herman and me this story on the way to a team roping many years ago. The fellow who had installed Jay's new aerobic system was explaining the wonders of it to Jay. Jay, like I would have, grew increasingly irritated as the man explained the inspection fee that would have to be paid, the pills that would have to be used, the maintenance of the sprinkler heads, and on and on.

When the man demonstrated the sprinklers, Jay asked. "How do I know when they're going to come on?'

Answer. "You don't."

Jay said, "I don't get around as good as I used to. What if I'm out here in the yard and get sprayed?"

"Oh, don't worry. What comes out of those sprinklers is as safe as drinking water."

"You really believe that?"

"Yes, sir."

Jay looked at the man for a few seconds and started for the house.

"Where are you going?"

"To get you a water glass. I want to see this."

# She Rode to the Whistle

*Brenda Black White*
First United Methodist Church
Commerce, Texas, 2010

THOUGH I FIRST MET HER WHEN I WAS a soda jerk at the City Pharmacy downtown almost fifty years ago, I really got to know Brenda during the last ten years. I remember every one of her "high teas" that I attended, but especially the first one. I arrived in my customary boots and jeans—definitely not looking like a literary...or a tea type. I sat down to tea with Brenda and legendary professors Dr. Fred Tarpley, James Conrad, Charles Linck, and others who did qualify as literary. They even looked the part.

    I remember looking around the room and suppressing a chuckle at the eclectic group. What a sight we must have made, sipping tea, eating key lime or ice cream chocolate pie, munching cookies, all under Brenda's watchful eye. She brought us all together, stimulated the conversations, directed the event as if it were a stage play. There were to be many such delightful occasions. But never enough.

    Brenda did for me what no teacher or college professor had been able to do before. She got me interested in poetry—made me appreciate it more through her often edgy, often humorous, often dark, always deeply felt verses. She could provoke a range of emotions with her words. And you just knew every word came from her heart.

    The best testament I can offer personally is this: Fred Tarpley and I each had to do important introductions on separate occasions a year apart. Our words had to be incisive and informative and hopefully, inspirational. There was no time for redundancy. Yet, we each, in our own way, had to finish with feeling and a proper flourish. Whose words did we choose to provide that polish, that flourish? Brenda Black White's.

Brenda had a credo, a philosophy, a doctrine for living that she expressed in a poem called "Life." With her customary simple but profound words, she equated her life to riding a wild stallion (saying she was *on till the whistle*).

Brenda did, indeed, ride to the whistle. I have been to a lot of rodeos, seen lots of rides to the whistle, but none did it as well or as long as Brenda.

When I heard of her passing, I sent up a short message to all the angels in heaven. Brenda is coming. Be ready.

# Riding a Fine Horse in New Country

### William Ben Herman, Jr.
West Oaks Funeral Home Chapel
Sulphur Springs, Texas, July 2011

WHEN THE FAMILY HONORED ME BY asking me to help celebrate Ben's life, I was more than a little intimidated. Summing up almost eighty-eight years of living in a few minutes is a daunting, if not impossible task, but it is worthwhile to try. I knew that Ben Herman was going to be especially difficult to sum up. Some might have called him a simple, uncomplicated man, but I found him to be exceedingly complex. I admit I never quite figured him out. But some things I do know.

I'm about to describe a man with many admirable qualities, a man who loved his family and a man who had many good, close friends. But let's just get all the bad stuff out of the way, so everybody will know that I really knew Ben Herman. He was quick to anger, slow to forgive, mule-headed, bulldog stubborn and set in his ways. When he made up his mind, he was almost impossible to budge. I am reminded of what Jake Spoon said about Woodrow Call in *Lonesome Dove* when Call decided to drive a herd of cattle and horses from Texas to Montana. Jake said, "I forgot how determined he can get, once an idea takes root."

Ben was quick to judge, but usually right about his judgments, especially of people (a necessary trait if you are doing much buying, selling and trading). When he was wrong, it was hard to get him to change his mind, but when the evidence piled up, he occasionally relented.

But he was also very quick to laugh. I can recall many gatherings when I knew he was there from the time I stepped out of my pickup. The sound of his robust laughter carried like the sound of a baby calf calling its mother travels down a bottomland creek. I heard him laughing with me, consoling me, encouraging me, as I wrote and rewrote this tribute. I hear him chuckling now.

And Ben loved stories. He loved hearing them, but he loved telling them more—and he knew lots of them. Many of us here today have heard them many times. One of my favorites is about the time he had to babysit the twins when they were babies. When one started to cry, he reversed them in the crib and stuck a toe in each mouth. Apparently toes work well as pacifiers when you have twins.

Telling stories is one thing, but living stories worth telling is quite another. I think that it's fair to say Ben Herman lived more than his share of extraordinary stories.

Ben and Nita were children of the depression, their children baby-boomers. Ben lost his mother at an early age, and I expect that had a momentous impact on the course of his life. When I began forming my thoughts as Ben neared the end, I visualized his life as a highway with guardrails on both sides. Ben starts down that highway as a teenager in a Model A Ford. He's driving it pedal to metal. The old car gradually changes to a fifty-something new Ford, then a new pickup with a matching horse trailer. All the time, Ben has got the accelerator all the way down. Sometimes...well, okay, pretty often, he veers far enough off the road to bump against the guardrails. A lot of us do that. Occasionally, Ben really scraped against those rails for long patches. Eventually, however, he always found the right path again.

Now, I know he would not like that analogy, because he took great pride in his driving skills and in his vehicles, but the road is a metaphor for his life and Ben Herman ran at life full speed. Who knows what would have happened if he had not had his compass, his navigator, and his anchor along for the ride. Nita always served as his tether to the right path, pulling him back each time he scraped the rails.

Ben had a code he lived by but sometimes found it difficult to explain that code to anyone else. It was a common sense code, so obvious to Ben that he had no patience with anyone who did not live by it. I don't think he would mind if I take a crack at explaining at least part of that code. He did what he said he would do; he paid his bills on time; his handshake was his contract; he kept his word, and he certainly expected the same of others.

Ben didn't have a high school diploma. But he had a knack for turning a buck. I personally know of several occasions when he spent a day out buying, selling and trading, and came home with more money than most educated men make in a month. And Nita made sure he kept most of it. Many do not understand the frugality of children of the Depression. It seems that today, society has made frugality a vice rather than a virtue, but, make no mistake, it is a virtue. Ben and Nita understood scarcity and wasted nothing, and knew value when they saw it. They didn't throw money around, but I'll bet there are many people here today that can recall an aspect of Ben and Nita's generosity.

I will wager also that many of you have had the same experiences I had in the years I knew Ben. Ever just say the name Ben Herman when there are several people within earshot? In almost every case, somebody will hear it and approach you. Maybe not today, but on most days before and after today, one or more will grin, another will get a twinkle in his eye. With me, they usually start with, "You Ben Herman's son-in-law? I remember one time me and old Ben..." Of course, I can't repeat many of those stories today, but I can say they are always punctuated with laughter. How many of us will be able to claim our lives inspired so many retellings of stories, so much laughter?

During his final years, he found that right path and stayed on it. In the end, I think he finally began to explain himself to himself. He knew what really mattered—love of friends and family and of course, his beloved Nita. Ben also leaves behind his greatest gift—four generations of descendants.

He loved nothing more than to spend time in son Rod's barn, listening to music and telling old stories or sitting in son Benny's barn, watching him train horses. In his final days, Joan leaned over and kissed her daddy's cheek and he said, "Hello, Shug." She had never realized until then how much she cherished that term of endearment.

He had nicknames for most of his grandchildren, and he loved watching them all. At every holiday, he wanted every one of his thirty-four descendants to come and join in the celebration. Counting spouses, the number coming together sometimes edged close to a hundred. When they gathered, the favorite spot for grandchildren was at the foot of Ben's chair.

In the end, Ben fought death the way he lived life, with gusto and dogged determination. Someone gave him a soft rubber ball when he became bedfast. As his voice grew weak, he used that ball to get your attention. A few days ago, he was struggling for breath and dealing with pain that we can only imagine. The family thought it was the end. But, only a few minutes after the struggle with death, one of the kids walked back into his room, and that ball sailed past their nose. Now that was *vintage Ben Herman*.

On the final day, you couldn't hear his voice, but you could feel him urging and helping Nita to choreograph his final exit. His children and grandchildren gathered and told stories...with Ben as the star of them all. They laughed and cried together, he said goodbye and heard goodbyes from his children and grandchildren, then peacefully drifted away.

Any tribute to Ben would be incomplete without some mention of horses. Ben loved them all of his days and passed that on to his children. Jan said her father became a different man astride a horse. I expect that's right. Onboard a horse going down a trail or chasing a calf down a roping arena, Ben was confident and happy. I recall that Benny and I team-penned with him after he was in his seventies. He had not lost his knack with cattle or horses and performed as well or better than we did. When he communicated with a horse, he stayed between the rails of life.

As that great fictional philosopher Augustus McCrae said in *Lonesome Dove*, "Ain't nothin' better than ridin' a fine horse in new country." Well, Ben's in new country now. I like to think he's riding a fine horse.

# A Country Funeral

## Cross Trails Cowboy Church, 2012

I ATTENDED A FUNERAL A FEW WEEKS ago, an increasingly common occurrence in my life. I knew the deceased, but not well enough to really expound on the quality of her life and legacy. I won't even mention her name, because these are my private feelings and I'm just not qualified to speak with authority about her or her family. Many things about death are public, but I think the most important things are private.

I knew all of her children (there are eight) and most of their spouses—some just by sight, some through business or social interaction. It's fair to say I was friends with one or two. One once worked in my small western wear store many years ago; another two or three were my clients when I had a CPA firm. I have bought goods and services or transacted business with a couple more. I'm not sure the rest of the children would recognize me on the street. I state all of these non-qualifications because they matter to what I am about to say. These are thoughts more from an observer than a participant. I went to the funeral expecting to pay my respects to the deceased and her family. But I received much more than I gave.

As the family filed into the Cross Trails Cowboy Church, I tried to get a glimpse of the children I knew but had not seen in a long time. Then something changed in the big sanctuary. It wasn't the music; I think it actually stopped; it wasn't anything anybody said. For me at least, it was as if the family brought not only their sorrow, but their shared memories of happiness, sadness and hardship as they filled the big room with an aura that went to the ceiling, settled, and gently spread itself on all of us.

Yes, I know that usually happens for close friends when families enter at the beginning of a service. But that's why I mentioned those non-qualifications before. It surprised me when the warm feeling settled on me and I felt a sense of reverence and awe.

I don't know how many were seated before the family entered, but I would guess there were at least three hundred, probably more. The family filed in for a long time (eight children, nineteen grandchildren and thirty-eight great-grandchildren, the obituary read). With spouses, the immediate family had to be close to a hundred. Now, the church was not only almost filled to capacity with people, it was filled with memories.

The children and grandchildren told stories of a fun-loving and just plain-loving wife, mother and grandmother. By the time the service was done, the family had succeeded in bringing together a Church of Christ pastor, a Mennonite choir, and the Cross Trails Cowboy Church, a Southern Baptist Outreach.

As I heard the eulogies and stories, I felt a strong message was being conveyed, that there were many lessons to be learned from this woman's life. Yes, I know there are lessons we can learn from every life, but something special was conveyed to me that day. Maybe it was because of my country upbringing and the culture I revere and love. I'll bet my hardscrabble—tough times—raised in poverty upbringing with just about anybody and raise them a plate of red beans and cornbread. You can only beat me if you had parents who did not love you. On that score, I was a rich boy. This woman's children probably also suffered more than their share of deprivations, but they were also raised rich on love.

Another thing. I'm country and proud of it and this funeral made me even prouder, because I think it's fair to say this woman, her husband and most (or all) of their children were and are country, too. And they are justifiably proud of it. I know at least one son is cowboy to the core. I hardly recognized him without his hat. He's figured out how to make a good living doing something he is good at and loves.

And look at what this country couple accomplished. Eight children. I have no way of knowing, but I'll just bet they didn't start out to raise eight. One was on the way or had just been born when the husband was reported killed in the service of his country. That turned out not to be true, of course, but he did lose an eye. Can you imagine the pain of loss she endured until he was discovered alive? And what about his sacrifice, loss and pain?

Those of us who have raised kids or are raising them know the financial burdens and the tremendous time involved in raising two or three (yes, the rewards are greater than any sacrifice), but eight? Times were tough, but they raised them all. That meant the children all had to pitch in and help with their own upbringing and I'll just bet that is one of the reasons this family is so close. After the kids were all grown, the family managed to pull together a fun-filled family reunion every year, diligently attended by most of the descendants and a few dozen of their closest friends. This couple showed you don't have to be rich or famous, urbane, or even sophisticated to make your mark in this world, to have a positive impact. They showed that in the beginning, during the process, and at the end, it's all worth it. What a legacy and lesson for us all.

# The Jerry Don Test

## Jerry Don Lambert
*Church of Christ*
*Commerce, Texas, 2012*

JERRY AND I HAVE BEEN FRIENDS FOR over fifty years. Our paths have diverged and crossed many times. During times when we had more in common, we traveled the same paths for long periods. We helped each other get through stressful periods in our lives. Then he would go off and do his thing and I would do mine. Our interests changed, but I always knew I had a friend in Jerry, a friend I could call on who would come running and bring all his tools and equipment. A friend who was not afraid to get his hands dirty helping out.

I first met him when I worked at City Pharmacy in downtown Commerce. He had left the job I held at the drugstore to become a men's clothing salesman for Jim Clark's down the street. He sat down at the counter one day about closing time as I was wrestling with the wooden pallets behind the soda fountain. He made some suggestions as to how to do it more efficiently. I looked over at this handsome fellow all decked out in a tie and sport coat. That's the first time I remember seeing Jerry Lambert. I admit I was a little irritated at his unsolicited advice, but he soon proved himself to be sincere and friendly and shared a few more helpful hints about the job he had held before me.

Our kids grew up together. Kim and Shelly have maintained a friendship from about age 6 to now. I won't mention how many decades that covers. Jerry and Derek built the fence around our yard almost thirty years ago and it is the only fence that I have never had to repair.

When I first heard that Jerry Don was ill, several things came to my mind immediately. One is the way Jerry liked to get "up close and personal." We were about the same height, but he usually managed to get himself up under my chin, even going so far as to bump his shoulder against my chest or a hand on my arm when he was talking to me. I noticed it was his habit to talk to everyone that way. He liked looking you right in the eyes. That's just one of the ways Jerry Don showed how much he liked people and why he had such a loving family and so many friends.

When I went to see him at home the first time after hearing he was not going to survive, he seemed like his usual exuberant self, not much subdued from pain or medication, ignoring the elephant in the room—the forecast of his impending death. I listened to him describe the path his illness had taken, the decisions he had made, the courageous path he had chosen in how to live the last days of his life.

We were sitting side by side on barstools and when he turned to look at me directly, I asked him if I could tell him a few stories—if I could relate the memories that had flooded my mind and stayed there. But first, I told him about another friend I had visited a few years back who was in a similar situation. I admitted as I drove away after seeing that friend for the last time, I knew he had done more for me than I could ever do for him. I had not had any eloquent or soothing words for that friend and I regretted I did not have any for Jerry. All I had were memories. He asked me to tell the stories. I think they say a lot about Jerry Don Lambert.

The first has to do with the dune buggy he used to own. After being chained to a desk twelve hours a day for twelve weeks of tax season, I always thirsted for the outdoors. Jerry, in his usual generous spirit, always loaned me the Volkswagen he had converted to a dune buggy.

One year, I found a particularly good stretch of off-road to my liking and, exercising what I viewed as superior driving skill, plunged that VW into an embankment, bending at least one wheel. I feared the entire front-end would have to be replaced, definitely repaired.

I got it to the shop, called Jerry, offered profuse apologies and promised to repair the damage. His cheerful response: "Don't worry about it, partner. That thing is for having fun. It's made to take rough treatment."

Then there was the ping pong tournament. Many years ago, we were in New Mexico on a skiing trip with our families and a few more and found ourselves in an after-ski joint that had a ping pong table. There were four or five of us guys, so I suggested a tournament. Before we started playing, Jerry picked up a paddle that quickly looked like a natural appendage to his arm. He tapped the paddle on the table and said, "I have to warn you, boys. I cut my teeth on a ping pong table."

I smiled, thinking of the hundreds of lunch periods I had spent in the rec. room of a defense contractor I worked for, playing ping pong, pool and shuffleboard. But we all quickly found that Jerry was not exaggerating. He *had* cut his teeth on a ping pong table and had lost little or none of his hand-eye coordination.

Jerry played his first hole of golf with me. Neither of us remembers the exact details, but I had a set of cheap clubs, had just finished nine holes and was ready to head home as dark approached. I saw Jerry in the parking lot and told him he should start playing with me sometime. With his usual enthusiasm, he said, "How about now?"

Well, it was almost dark and he didn't have any clubs. Not to mention the flip flops he was wearing. He looked down at his feet and at the rising moon. "Can I borrow your sticks? We'll have time for at least a couple of holes. With that moon, we might play nine."

I hit the first ball off the tee to show him how it was done. I cringed a little as he teed up the ball and took a couple of practice swings that seemed dangerously close to his toes. Then he hit one, turned to me and said, "Is that how you do it?"

I winced when I saw his ball in the middle of the fairway about thirty yards past the one I had hit in the rough. "Yep, that's how you do it."

He developed this habit of forecasting his shots that I found annoying at first. What made the habit annoying was that, about half the time, he was right. I quit playing a few years after that. Gave up in frustration. But Jerry kept going. His golfing buddies tell me Jerry kept forecasting where the ball was going to go and actually making it go there. Occasionally, he would hit one in the rough and leave himself a really tough lie behind a tree or two. Instead of playing it safe, taking a stroke and punching one out into the fairway and taking a bogey or, in my case, a double bogey, he would choose the more difficult path.

"Okay, boys. I'm gonna hook this a little to get past that first tree, make it duck between the two limbs on the second, then fade it right. I figure about three bounces will put me on the edge of the green. With a thirty-foot putt, I can get it in for a birdie." His buddies stopped laughing at those predictions a long time ago—because Jerry almost always made the ball perform just as he predicted. He was usually the smallest guy in the group, but often hit the ball the longest distance.

My favorite story as we talked was the footrace. Jerry and I compared notes on this story, so if there is anyone here who ran in the footrace or remembers it differently, forever hold your peace. Jerry and I agreed that this is the way it was. This story also begins at Sand Hills—also at sunset. A close round of golf had left some young men's competitive challenges unsettled. Horseplay and boasting soon led to more challenges, more boasts about who was better, stronger and faster. It was too dark to settle their scores playing more golf, so the young men settled on a foot race.

As we recalled, Jerry and I were only spectators up to that point. When we went outside to watch the race, Jerry started to roll up the legs to his jeans. I asked him what he was doing. He said "I'm gonna run in this race." He sat down on the #1 tee box and started removing his shoes.

Even I was surprised. "Barefoot? Have you thought about goatheads?" Jerry ignored me as he took off his socks. The race was from the tee box to the green and back as we recalled—a distance of about 700 yards. "Have you looked at these guys? They're all taller and have longer legs than you. Plus they're a lot younger."

He started to limber up. "Yeah, well, I probably won't win. But I used to be pretty fast barefoot." I remembered the ping pong remark, but hand-eye coordination is one thing, stamina and running barefoot for long distances is another.

Well, the excitement was surprising and contagious as the runners left the tee box. All of us spectators were caught up in this unplanned event. It was too dark to see the runners touch the flag on the #1 green, but I soon heard the sound of their shoes clomping on the grass on their return from the green to the tee box.

But I could not hear bare feet, so I worried Jerry might have cut a foot or given up and was walking back. No shame in that, I thought. It was too dark to make them out at first. But, eventually, the dim lights of the parking lot and clubhouse revealed a set of arms pumping, knees going high and strong. I will never forget my surprise (make that shock) when I saw the guy without shoes was out in front.

Without ever mentioning it, Jerry was a natural at visualization. It helped him in his golf game to verbalize what he saw in his head. He saw himself winning that footrace, too. He used the same technique in hunting and fishing. He saw in his mind, where, when and how he was going to hunt or fish, what type of equipment he was going to use and how he was going to use it. That often resulted in his harvesting the most fish or quail, the buck with the biggest rack.

The final story has to do with a flat bed trailer. I lived in town in those days, and had no place to park a flat bed trailer, so I didn't own one. But almost everyone has an occasional need for one. I, along with people from at least four counties, borrowed Jerry's. I have seen that trailer all over Delta, Hunt, Fannin, and Hopkins counties, often overloaded, always pulled by someone other than Jerry. Sometimes, it came back much the worse for wear. But I never heard Jerry complain about it.

Those other stories exemplify Jerry Lambert's gregariousness and adventurous spirit, his affectionate nature, his love of people. The trailer exemplifies the man's kindness and generosity. There are many more examples of all those things. There are dozens of hunting and fishing stories, for example. All of us here today could tell Jerry stories for hours.

One other thing, I don't recall ever seeing Jerry get angry. I have seen him a little upset, but never just plain mad. He seemed to like people too much to harbor any type of grudge. I am sure there were times and events I am not aware of, but they must have been rare.

When we finished with the stories that day, Jerry leveled with me about the heartache and struggle facing him, reiterating his long-held conviction that material things don't really matter much when it comes down to it. It's love that counts, particularly love of family. He was not ready to say goodbye to Joan, to Derek and Rhonda, to Kim and Joe and their families. And he wanted to see his grandchildren grow up. There were other things he was not ready to give up, but he was determined to make his peace with it.

I know he had already started checking things off his bucket list. I know that his loving family made it possible for him to check off a few more before departing this life.

It's obvious to everyone who knew him that Jerry also had a lot of good friends. He and Joan entertained regularly, opening their home to a pretty steady stream of guests. Jerry wasn't ready to give that up, either.

One of the measurements of a man's life is the people whose lives he touched in a positive way. By that measure, Jerry Lambert stands tall.

The stories over, our chuckles subsiding, I took his hand to say goodbye. The handshake quickly turned into a hug, our laughter to tears. And as I headed home, I realized that, though my intentions were good, Jerry had done much more for me than I had done for him. I expect this room is full of folks who can say exactly the same thing about Jerry Lambert. Now that's a legacy any person would be proud to leave behind.

Immediately after the visit and for all the days since, I use his visualization technique and imagine Jerry talking to me each time I found myself complaining about some task I have to do or some minor misfortune or inconvenience that comes my way.

I vowed to subject each of those tasks and misfortunes to what I call the "Jerry Don test." Given his situation, would Jerry Don be doing this? Would he worry about this misfortune or laugh at it, recognize it for how little it really matters? He always has a good answer. It's a test I hope to continue for the rest of my days.

Another part of the legacy of a good, kind, and generous husband, father, grandfather and friend.

Jerry Don Lambert left us with our memories and a warm feeling in our hearts November 8, 2012.

# Not Ordinary

### Ricky Lynn Thomas
*Presented under the Oak Trees*
*at Cowhill Council, 2013*

RICKY LYNN THOMAS LIVED ON THIS earth from January 13, 1956 to June 13, 2013. He is survived by his wife, Alana, son Jimmy, daughter Crystal and five grandchildren; his mother, Aline Malone Thomas; five sisters: Linda Sue Parker, Tina Horton, Debbie Risener, Dena Thomas and Donna Shepherd; three brothers: Jerald Thomas, Roger Sluder, and Kenneth Shepherd, and many nieces and nephews. He was preceded in death by his father Jackson E. Thomas and brothers Billy Jack Thomas and Ricky Sluder.

Ricky was a carpenter and was a member of Local Union 198.

Jerald asked me to present a short eulogy for Ricky. I am a member of the Cowhill Council, a group of seasoned gentlemen who meet right over there when the weather is good and inside the round building when it's not so good. Jerald and I met out here sporadically until Ricky moved here. Then we made it a regular thing. Others soon joined in. I searched and searched for a quote or two from some eloquent writer or speaker that might describe Ricky. But I couldn't find a single one. Of course, my search was hindered by the sound of Ricky laughing at me. I could hear him saying, "What are you going to say about me now, Mr. Jim?"

I recall a conversation Jerald and I had out here a few years back. Jerald, Ricky's brother, described himself with terms like ordinary, normal, everyday. I laughed out loud and said, "I have known you well for several years, and I still don't know how to describe or even understand you. But one thing I am sure of, you are not ordinary."

I think the same could be said of Ricky. He was not normal in the ways that most of us think of as normal. But being average or normal is not always the best, certainly not the only way to live. That still leaves a void in describing how Ricky was unusual in his own unique way. Let's start with some undeniable traits. He had a great sense of humor and laughed a lot. He saw humor in situations where I often did not, but, sometimes, his laughter was contagious. He loved fast cars, motorcycles and fast times.

He loved to tell stories and, like a lot of us who regularly meet out here, had such a fondness for a few he felt compelled to tell them over and over. I am reminded of the man who was told he was repeating a story he had told many times before.

He said, "I know that, but it's such a good story, I wanted to hear it again myself." I know I have told that one more than a few times.

Ricky loved to play the guitar and sing. I don't think his feelings would be hurt if I say he wasn't very good at either. But to his credit, it didn't keep him from trying.

Ricky loved his family and often spoke fondly of them. I know he expressed gratitude almost every day to his brother for picking him up when he was down and keeping him up. He described how Alana never deserted him even though he probably deserved to be deserted. And of course, Mom, who stood by him, defended him and loved him through thick and thin.

In one of the few serious conversations we ever had, I told Ricky that he was a classic underachiever, that I had seen his natural intelligence peek through more than once. He never made full use of it, never pursued achievements he seemed capable of. I asked him why he did not polish it up, let it shine. Ricky told me that developing his natural abilities might have gotten in the way of a good time. I don't pretend to understand why he chose that path, and I am not about to judge him because I never walked a mile in his moccasins.

So, we're not here to judge him today. We're just here to honor the life of a good man, to celebrate his life, not just mourn his passing. Ricky was kind and gentle to people and animals. He had a soft heart. I never saw the slightest tendency toward cruelty of any kind. I seldom saw him angry, though he and I did engage in a few heated arguments. Those were always forgotten by the next day.

I will remember Ricky for what he was, not for what he did or did not accomplish in life. One thing is for sure. I will never forget Ricky Thomas, and I'm sure that none of you will either. He was an unforgettable character. I'll just bet all of us would be happy to have that said of us at our own memorial service. Ricky, rest in peace now, free of pain.

# He Made All Things Seem Possible

## Dr. Fred Tarpley

*Presented in the Sam Rayburn Student Center on the campus of Texas A&M University-Commerce March 8, 2014*

I CAN'T, OF COURSE, DO JUSTICE TO THE LIFE of this great man today, not even if I had a week. There is not time to list all the titles and offices he has held (usually president) and all the honors he has received from at least twenty organizations (that I know of). He is Professor Emeritus of Literature and Languages at Texas A&M-Commerce, a Gold Blazer and Distinguished Alumnus, a Texas Piper Professor.

I have had the privilege of introducing Dr. Tarpley on many prior occasions. As I returned to my files each time for his resume, I always had to add a page for his most recent remarkable accomplishments.

Now, I have the honor of saying a final goodbye. His body may be lost to us, but his influence will last longer than any of us, much longer.

His insatiable thirst for knowledge led to graduation from high school at sixteen and later becoming the youngest PhD on the faculty of this university, even after serving his nation during the Korean War.

Fred said he loved practically everything about his public school education except what he was taught about East Texas. History teachers told him nothing of note ever occurred in this part of our state. That sent him on a lifelong quest to change that perception. His books *Jefferson: Riverport to the Southwest*, and *Jefferson: East Texas Metropolis* were a good beginning.

He told me that a lot of academia branded our corner of Texas as a literary wasteland, and that only New England produced worthwhile American reading. Fred responded with articles on the literary heritage of the region and a traveling photographic exhibition and lectures featuring twenty-five East Texas writers. I think at least one of those authors is here today, maybe more.

When academics said that Northeast Texas speech was the most appalling of all American talk, Fred answered with more books, *From Blinky to Blue-John: A Word Atlas of Northeast Texas*, *Place Names of Northeast Texas*, and *1001 Texas Place Names*.

Another gauntlet for Fred came when people called the bois d'arc a trash tree. He wrote *Wood Eternal: The Story of Osage Orange and Bois d'Arc*, the most comprehensive book ever written about the tree that is native to Northeast Texas. He co-founded the Commerce Bois d'Arc Bash almost thirty years ago and was named Citizen of the Year.

He started a literary criticism contest for the University Interscholastic League and directed that contest for a quarter century. He manned the *Origin of Family Names* booth at the Texas Folklife Festival in San Antonio for twenty-five years.

Fred Tarpley wrote or co-authored nine books, three media scripts, scores of articles, hundreds of reviews, two one-act plays, six screenplays and numerous academic papers and articles. He plowed the fertile ground of his home territory to help others discover the richness of our heritage. Through his writing and teaching, he has preserved for the ages a wealth of information that might otherwise have been lost. Indeed, much of it was lost until Fred Tarpley came along.

His own writing is exceeded only by his encouragement and mentoring of other writers (myself included). He guided aspiring authors through editing, teaching writing classes, and leading writing organizations. He shepherded writers with dreams into the realities of stories and essays, articles, poems and books. He also brought back to life long-forgotten manuscripts from the estate of Eusibia Lutz, a professor of French at this university.

In his seventies, Dr. Tarpley told me that he really needed a staff to keep up with his burgeoning career. In my travels with Fred, I noted a book in his hands was not just held, it was caressed, as he prepared to feed it into his great, always-thirsty mind.

He was faculty sponsor of the Tejas Social Club, later to become Sigma Phi Epsilon. How many fraternal or social organizations maintain close relationships with faculty sponsors for more than a half century? The lifelong friendships he nurtured are a testament to his leadership. Hosses and Bosses are well-represented here today, every one carrying a wealth of stories about Fred.

A writing course he taught on this campus several years ago was so successful and well-received that it evolved into the Silver Leos Writers Guild and that led to many, many books and helped to fulfill the dreams of many writers. Most are also here today.

Yes, his list of accomplishments is too long, too complicated. But I think I know what Fred would say to me. "Tell them stories, Jim. People remember stories."

My favorite story of Dr. Tarpley involves his visit to Washington, DC, to continue his research at a library across from the Smithsonian. He conveyed his needs to a willing research assistant who went back into the canyons of the library and returned with two of Fred's own books. In his usual modest style, Dr. Tarpley smiled and pushed the books back across the counter saying, "I don't believe this author can be of much help to me."

Fred taught me Freshman English fifty years ago, but not until I asked for his help with a manuscript almost forty years later did he became my mentor and close friend. I was intimidated during the entire editing process. When he used his influence to get me speaking engagements, I dreaded the hours on the road for our first trip, wondering what I would say to the great intellect with whom I had almost nothing in common.

I needn't have worried. He kept up a non-stop lively, interesting, and informative conversation all the way there and back. Every time we crossed a creek with a name, he would tell me its history and rich stories of the heritage of the area. I learned he was not only a fountain of knowledge about literature, but also history. He also had a lot to say about local events and told a lot of funny stories. I learned that an hour spent with Fred was more informative and entertaining than most books.

For the next decade, we talked four to five times a week and traveled to events all over Texas, most arranged through Fred's contacts and influence. When I needed credibility, I just mentioned that I came with Fred. It was like traveling with a celebrity.

The only problem was that he kept telling people I was a publisher as well as an author. I would stand behind him, wave my arms, and shake my head. I asked him to quit, worried that people might be misled. But Fred went on undeterred. That's when I discovered his tenacious capacity for getting things accomplished. His powers of persuasion were always polite and subtle, but extremely effective. So pretty soon, I found that we were in the publishing business together. We did seven books in two years.

I knew little about Fred's health problems in the beginning, because he never mentioned them. In all that traveling and visiting and phone conversations, he never once, not once, complained. I learned only later that he suffered a lot of pain and discomfort.

I never saw him show more than a second or two of mild irritation. He was unfailingly optimistic and enthusiastic even when he was critiquing an event, a book, a movie or a manuscript.

Wherever I speak to a group, I am always approached by someone who knows Fred—and they all speak of him with the utmost respect, many with awe and admiration. His touch has been far-reaching, deep and profound, immeasurable.

When I decided to switch from writing nonfiction to novels, I found the publishing world unwelcoming and littered with broken dreams. I prayed for a mentor, someone who could guide me through this new minefield. About two years into those requests, I heard a soothing thought as I drifted off to sleep one night. It said, "You are working with one of the giants of literature in this country. What more could you want?" I was ashamed for being late in recognizing the great gift I had been given.

I knew from those days as a freshman on this campus that Dr. Fred Tarpley was a great intellect. What I discovered later was he was also a great conversationalist, a man of much compassion and unfailing enthusiasm... not just a man with a great mind, but a man with a great heart.

After I had introduced him at one event, someone approached me and said it seemed almost unbelievable that one man could accomplish so much in a lifetime. He said it sounded as if I were describing a fictional character, a perfect man.

Fred wasn't perfect, of course. Fred and cars, for example, sometimes did not get along. A few years back, he called me on an early spring morning. When I arrived at his house, his car was smashed, the driver's door jammed, the gear shift hung as a useless appendage from the steering column. And the engine was running at a fairly high speed. Fred stood out in his yard, wiping blood from a few injuries. The crash had apparently triggered an alarm system in the car and I had to speak to him over the sounds of approaching sirens.

We will never know if what happened was an automobile malfunction or a Fred malfunction, but his car had crashed into a utility pole, cutting off power to his house.

When I crawled into the car to cut the engine and try to back it off the pole, I noticed a trail of blood from the front seat to the back door. Fred had extricated himself from the steering wheel, crawled over the seat and out the back door—a good acrobatic maneuver for a man half his age.

But what will always stay with me about this story is what he said and how he said it when he called me... while still stuck behind the steering wheel with the engine roaring and the gearshift useless, bleeding profusely, he said, very calmly and cheerfully, "Hello, Jim. I think I may need your help." He had the gift of what I call effortless serenity.

A few years back, we had a snow and ice storm. Fred had an appointment in Greenville for dialysis. Road conditions were severe, but I told him I could get him there in my four-wheel drive Jeep.

Jeeps like mine sit fairly high and are not easy to get into and don't ride like Fred's Cadillac. But he piled into the passenger seat without breaking conversational stride. He kept me entertained on the treacherous drive and helped me to relax a little about road conditions... until we reached Greenville. I-30 was backed up—eighteen-wheelers as far as the eye could see.

I didn't want Fred to miss his appointment and I had an appointment of my own back in Commerce that I really needed to keep.

I said, "Fred, this looks like it could take an hour or more to clear up.

What do you think about crossing that ditch and getting on the service road?"

Fred looked straight ahead as if he were enjoying the excitement of sitting in a traffic jam and said cheerfully, "I'm in no particular hurry."

I shifted into four-wheel drive. "Well, I am."

I looked both directions for law enforcement and headed across the ditch. The Jeep tilted as it went down the side of the ditch, splashed mud and slush when we crossed the middle, and then tilted opposite as we climbed the other side. Headlines flashed through my mind: *Reckless Driver Injures Local Legendary Professor*. We made the service road only to find a truck jack-knifed across it. This time, we had to drive down the middle of an even more treacherous ditch. When we finally made it back to the main road, I looked over at Fred, expecting to see a face white with terror. Instead, I saw only relaxed demeanor. I don't know what he said, but I realized he had never stopped his lively conversation during two ditch crossings. Somehow, I think that says almost as much about this good man as all of his books.

Then there was the afternoon he phoned to tell me he had received a call from Horton Foote, winner of the Academy Award, an Emmy, and other little things like the Pulitzer Prize. Mr. Foote was asking for advice. There are other stories—stories of renowned author James Michener and other famous people that have been touched by Fred Tarpley, but time does not permit.

Yes, he was a great intellect and will forever be remembered as such. But I, for one, am now, and forever will be, amazed by his strength, vigor, boundless enthusiasm and good humor in the face of adversity.

I have struggled to sum up the magnificent scope of his positive influence, but know I cannot. I can say to his children, Ted, Marie, Mark and Colleen, his seven grandchildren, and his sister Dorothy, that he spoke of you often with love and tenderness in his voice and eyes.

No, I cannot do him justice, but poet and author Brenda Black White may have done it as well as it could be done in a card she wrote to Dr. Tarpley during the time we were publishing her last book of poetry.

Brenda, as many of you know, suffered the effects of a debilitating disease for more than forty years. She showed me the card she sent to Fred:

> *Dear Dr. T.,*
>
> *There is something inspiring about you that arrests my ebbing energies... something that supports my commitment to transcend my maladies. When I talk with you, I feel all things are possible. You are kind in a hundred ways... sharing your joy for the little treasures you find—a fact... a place... a deed... a book... or a person. I want you to know that I appreciate how uniquely wonderful you are. I am blessed to have you in my life.*

We are all blessed to have had Dr. Fred Tarpley in our lives.

---

NOTE: The above was written for oral presentation. Any departures from standard grammar and punctuation are intentional and were made for that purpose. (Fred would have advised this notation).

# Believing in a Grand Thing

## Stories of Faith

*All I have seen teaches me to trust
the Creator for all I have not seen.*
—Ralph Waldo Emerson

# When the Student Is Ready, the Master Will Appear

EVER HAD A CHILD, SPOUSE, CLIENT OR FRIEND talk about a book read, a seminar attended, a lecture heard, that revealed some great secret or answer to a question they have been pondering for a lifetime? Ever listen to their enthusiasm, all the while wanting to shout that you have been trying to tell them this secret for years? Don't blame them. The author, speaker, or teacher they heard spoke to them. You may not have. It could have been because they knew you too well or just that the message had to be delivered by a stranger. In my old business, we often referred to an expert as a person with a briefcase who has traveled more than a hundred miles. There's a lot of truth to that. We listen to these experts while we fail to hear the same wisdom from familiar sources. Even Jesus said, "*Truly I tell you, no prophet is accepted in his hometown.*"

We all know the old proverb, "*When the student (pupil) is ready, the master (teacher) will appear.*" I dabbled around the fringes of C. S. Lewis's writings for many years. I quoted him in many seminars and training sessions, even though I had read only excerpts from his work (I plead guilty). I decided it was about time for "the teacher to appear."

Clyde Staples Lewis preferred to be called Jack. If you are not familiar with him, I suggest starting with the movie *Shadowlands*. Anthony Hopkins plays Lewis in this excellent rendition of a part of Lewis's life. I collect quotations about writing and reading and use them to defend my writing habit during times when there seems to be no rational justification for it. This movie provided one of the best. "*We read to know that we are not alone.*" We also write to find out if we are alone. What does that mean to you?

To me, it means we read to vicariously experience situations such as illness, death, murder, betrayal, great business success or failure, and athletic or artistic accomplishment. We need to see how characters in books react to situations we may have experienced, want to experience or just wondered about. We see also that other people in other places might have troubles worse than our own. We see places where they live, places we will likely never visit. This provides regular reassurance that "we are not alone."

C. S. Lewis is probably best known for his *Chronicles of Narnia* series (*The Lion, the Witch and the Wardrobe*, etc.). He was also close friends with J. R. R. Tolkien of *Lord of the Rings* fame. Both were on the English faculty at Oxford. But the book I am writing about is *Mere Christianity*. I perused it many years ago, but didn't apply myself. I picked it up about a year ago and read it again, this time with a highlighter and post-it notes. I wondered, for heaven's sake (a cliché meant to be taken literally here), why I had not done so before. After all, a boy's struggle to understand was partially revealed in this early passage from *Rivers Flow*.

> *After nine weeks of perfect attendance at Sunday school and church in Klondike, Jake heard the teacher ask the question he had been dreading. "Please raise your hands if you have been saved by accepting Jesus Christ as your personal savior." All of his classmates raised their hands. Jake sat on his.*

And there is this later passage where Jake is in church again.

> *As the sun rose higher, one of the spiraling dust tunnels focused on Jake, and he felt himself floating above the congregation, his mind drifting back to events that seemed so long ago.*

Several things sparked my revived lifelong need to understand (most would not interest you). I have written previously about the Cowhill Council, a group of seasoned sages who meet regularly for coffee. I make no pretense that our discussions are usually highly intellectual, but occasionally we try. One morning, we were fortunate enough to have two evangelists and a fellow in the middle of the rigorous training required to become a Catholic Deacon present for our meeting. I stuck my neck out and asked if anyone could explain the Crucifixion, Resurrection and Atonement in terms that an ignorant mortal like me could understand and spiritually absorb.

Everyone stared at me as if I had just arrived on planet Earth and never set foot in a church. But then, their faces lit up as they launched into vigorous attempts to comply. It led to a vibrant and enjoyable discussion, but their explanations were the same ones I had heard all my life. I was reminded of what Pastor Rick Warren said about the Holy Trinity, "*To deny the Holy Trinity is to lose your soul. To explain it is to lose your mind. God is God, I am not.*"

C. S. Lewis speaks to me. He lost his mother at nine. Raised in the Church of Ireland, he turned atheist at fifteen, even became interested in the occult, quoting Lucretius, "*Had God designed the world it would not be, a world so frail and faulty as we see.*" But he slowly re-embraced Christianity, influenced by his friend Tolkien and by his own "teacher" G. K. Chesterton and his book, *The Everlasting Man*.

In *Mere Christianity*, Lewis explains the Atonement and Resurrection this way:

> *The only person who could do it perfectly (repentance) would be the perfect person—and He would not need it. But supposing God became a man—suppose our human nature which can suffer and die was amalgamated with God's nature in one person—then that person could help us. He could surrender His will, and suffer and die, because He was man; and He could do it perfectly because He was God.*
>
> *You and I can go through this process only if God does it in us; but God can do it only if He becomes man. Our attempts at this dying will succeed only if we men share in God's dying, just as our thinking can succeed only because it is a drop out of the ocean of His intelligence. But we cannot share God's dying unless God dies, and He cannot die except by being a man. That is the sense in which He pays our debt and suffers for us what* **HE NEED NOT SUFFER AT ALL.**

Read that last sentence aloud. That explanation makes sense out of deep complexity.

And as for my wondering about God's punishment, Lewis has these words:

> *A Christian is not a man who never goes wrong, but a man who is enabled to repent and pick himself up and begin over again after each stumble—because the Christ-life is inside him, repairing him all the time, enabling him to repeat (in some degree) the kind of voluntary death Christ Himself carried out...the Christian thinks any good he does comes from the Christ-life inside him. He does not think God will love us because we are good, but that God will make us good because He loves us.*

There are many, many more explanations, of course. But that one does it for me. God recognized our weakness and knew we would continue to sin in spite of being shown miracle after miracle, with the most miraculous being the Resurrection and Ascension. So does that mean we mortals can just keep right on sinning because Jesus provided a permanent pathway to forgiveness? Yes and no. Yes, because we have been given a path to forgiveness. No, because purposeful, careless sinning means we don't really believe. If we have faith, we will exert every effort to live our lives following the example Jesus left for us. Yes, we will continue to be buffeted by doubts and be confronted with evil; we will continue to sin because we are weak, but we will recognize evil, recognize our sins, confess them, and ask for forgiveness with love. Sincere prayer will protect us. We must recognize our sins by studying God's Word and ask for forgiveness in **FAITH.** We must believe.

# Is There Evidence of Life After Death?

*We have little to lose by believing, and everything to lose if we don't.*
—Dinesh D'Souza

DINESH D'SOUZA EXPLORES THIS QUESTION in his book, *Life After Death: The Evidence.* I admit a certain attraction to the word *evidence* in the title. I knew the author first as a secular think tank intellectual. I have seen him debate the now deceased atheist (but brilliant) Christopher Hitchens, who acknowledged D'Souza as a world-class advocate for the Christian faith.

Rick Warren, author of *The Purpose Driven Life*, wrote the introduction to this book. *Death:*

> The mortality rate on earth is 100 percent. This book by my friend Dinesh D'Souza is a brilliant investigation of the fascinating and crucial issue of what happens when we die. It is an inquiry based on scholarship and reason and it provides a convincing answer that is explosive in its impact.

D'Souza deftly turns the table on scientists who say, "If they really believe in a life after death, why not conduct sound experiments to establish it?" D'Souza answers that religious believers don't believe in the afterlife based on scientific tests. He then challenges them to come up with some tests to prove or disprove it. Without such tests and empirical evidence, how can true scientists reject it? Atheists say that the absence of evidence is evidence of absence. D'Souza answers by saying *not found* is not the same thing as found not to exist.

*Life After Death* also explores near-death experiences including the out-of-body phenomenon, the tunnel of darkness, the bright light, the sensation of love and warmth, the life review, and subsequent life transformations. Evolution? Yep, D'Souza covers it, saying,

> *...contrary to atheist boasting, evolution cannot provide an ultimate explanation for life because evolution itself presupposes specific environmental conditions and specific entities with specific properties. The human cell, thousands of times tinier than a speck of dust, has the processing power equivalent to the largest supercomputer. So how did we get cells? How do they self-replicate? Darwin does not attempt to answer.*

In a later book, D'Souza explores another question he poses in debates with atheists: Why did it take mankind more than 85,000 years to figure out he could effectively communicate, make useful tools, and settle in one place to grow crops? Humans accomplished virtually nothing for ninety-eight percent of our existence, then abruptly in the last two percent, produced everything from the pyramids to Proust, Newton to nanotechnology.

D'Souza also says that evolution does a good job of accounting for why we are selfish animals, but it faces immense challenges in accounting for why we simultaneously hold that we *ought not to be selfish*.

In a chapter called "Good for You," D'Souza refers to William James, the founder of modern psychology. James makes the point that while belief in life after death poses the risk of adopting a position without complete proof...unbelief poses the risk of missing out on the blessings of immortality that are promised to believers. Makes sense to me. Who was it who said irreverently but also logically, "Why take a chance?"

> *Believers are provided with hope at death and a way to cope. For atheists, death is a disaster. Belief infuses life with an enhanced sense of meaning and purpose. Belief gives us a reason to be moral and a way to transfer that morality to our children. Finally, there is strong evidence that belief in life after death makes your life better and also makes you a better person.*

On page 166, I found my favorite words from D'Souza.

*Here is my pre-suppositional argument for life after death. Unlike material objects and all other living creatures, we humans inhabit two domains: the way things are, and the way things ought to be.*

Why is it my favorite passage? Because on page three of *Rivers' Flow*, Griffin Rivers says, "*Flow is the difference between the way things are and the way they ought to be.*" I promise not to sue D'Souza for plagiarism. I'm kidding. Just a little more proof that similar threads run through all our stories, binding us together.

# Why Does God Let Bad Things Happen?

I HEAR THIS QUESTION STATED MORE OFTEN as a statement by non-believers and others trying to come to grips with their faith. "How does one believe in a God that would let these kinds of things happen?" Remember Lucretius's quote that C. S. Lewis used when he was an atheist? *Had God designed the world it would not be, a world so frail and faulty as we see.* The quote does raise some doubts. If God is perfect, then why did he not design a perfect world? Why do bad things still happen?

Another book by Dinesh D'Souza, *God Forsaken: Bad Things Happen. Is there a God Who Cares? Yes: Here's Proof* addresses this question with boldness. Lucretius challenges our belief in a God who could have made a perfect world, but chose not to. D'Souza says the Divine Architect could not have made a perfect universe and have us human beings in it.

> God intended us to be here to marvel at his architecture and get to know the Architect and enter into an intimate relationship of mutual love with Him.... He built the universe in the only way He could to get this result.
>
> Christians praise God when good things happen to them, so should they also blame God when bad things happen to them? The book of Job has been recognized as one of the deepest, most candid examinations of the problem of evil and suffering. Yet remarkably, it never occurs to Job or to anyone else in the story to question God's existence. What Job questions is the character of God.

D'Souza says that omnipotence does not mean the power to do anything, but rather the power to do *what is possible*. And there is only one possible way to create a universe containing rational, conscious creatures like us—creatures who are prone to sin, evil and corruption. If the world was perfect, we wouldn't be allowed in it.

Do we suffer punishment here on earth for evil deeds? Do we get what we deserve? I explored this through Jake's character in *Rivers Flow* in this scene with Claire Hurt when Claire tells him,

> *Oh, I shook my fist at God, raging at His injustice to us. We were in church every Sunday morning and Sunday night, yet we lost our only child.*

Most of us, believers and non-believers who have lived long enough, know there is almost no direct correlation between pain and hardship and our virtues and vices. Earthquakes and tsunamis make no distinction between the just and unjust.

Rabbi Harold Kushner says in his book, *When Bad Things Happen to Good People*, "It's simply a fact." Kushner also says that *God doesn't stop the bad things because He can't. So he does what he can to reduce evil and suffering, and He identifies with the victims*. But Dr. Charles Stanley says Scripture tells us that God has absolute authority over the world and lets evil enter the world because He desired love from the human beings He created. Love must be given freely, so God had to offer humans a choice. The only other choices were to not create or to create robotic-like humans without choice. The views of these religious scholars seem to conflict, but Kushner might be saying that God can't stop evil...because He allowed choice.

More confusion. Does this mean prayer can't work because God can't stop bad things from happening? No. The two words to remember are faith and love. If we pray with faith and love, we have made choices and then God can interfere, because these are the two things He wants from us. In *Rivers Flow*, Claire lets Jake explore his own anger at God, his feelings that he and his family did something to cause their loss. She answers him thusly:

> *We have a right to be hurt, even angry. Life is unfair, and God is*

*there to help us when unfair things happen to us, not to prevent them from happening.*

Kushner says that God is as outraged by it as we are.

In the *Shadowlands* movie, Anthony Hopkins as Jack Lewis lectures to various audiences about the good that comes from suffering. In his book, *Theodicity*, Gottfried Leibniz says if not for evil and suffering, how would we appreciate painlessness and good? We need the one to appreciate the other, just as we need the night to appreciate sunrise.

Why does God let us sin? D'Souza says God sought to create a creature (us) that could reciprocate his love. Now, it is in the nature of love to be free: love cannot be compelled. He made us free so that He could love us and we could love Him in return. But free will also brings sin. *Freedom is the necessary prerequisite for virtue.* Coerced actions have no moral value.

Why does God mostly hide himself from us? *If He made his presence obvious, then humans would, in a sense,* **be forced** *to believe in Him.* Because His presence would be so overwhelming, even atheists would believe. And He wants us to believe of our own free will.

# Why Me, Lord?

AS A WRITER OF LITTLE NOTE, I DON'T HAVE the nerve to say this about my own writing, but I am pleased that Pat Conroy *(Prince of Tides, Beach Music,* my personal favorite *The Great Santini,* etc.) did express it in a recent issue of *Writer* magazine.

> *A novel is my fingerprint, my identity card, and the writing of novels is one of the few ways I have found to approach the altar of God and creation itself. You try to worship God by performing the singular courageous and impossible favor of knowing yourself.*

Some of us were brought up to believe politics and religion were not proper topics for group discussion. I beg to differ. How can we learn if we don't openly discuss? I received several copies of an e-mail titled *Look Up.* It says in part, *Sorrow looks back, worry looks around, but faith looks up. Live simply, love generously, care deeply, speak kindly, and trust in our Creator—Who loves us.* I see myself as functionally illiterate on the subject of religion and faith. My bet is there are a lot of you out there in the boat with me. So I write not as an expert, but as someone with a deep desire to learn. I apologize to all you biblical scholars, evangelists, pastors, priests, and other preachers out there.

When I was a boy, religion in our home was tender to the touch, sometimes maybe even raw. Our forays into organized religion were subject to fits and starts. I heard a lot about a vengeful God from hellfire and brimstone preachers. I feared His wrath, and knew with some degree of certainty that I deserved it. My parents lost three of their six children. And it never (well, almost never) rained from the time I was six until I was twelve. As I watched our crops and cattle suffer and our pools dry up and our financial predicament regress from poor to desperate, I wondered what we had done to deserve such punishment. And were our neighbors also guilty of making God angry?

I described one of our sporadic embraces of religious fervor in a tent revival scene in *Rivers Flow*.

> *One man seated in the back of the tent bolted from his seat and ran down the aisle.... the man's tongue shot out of his mouth and flopped on his chin. He fell backward as if pulled by an invisible rope, flopping on his back and grinding his body against the grass. Jake could smell the dust and the bruised goat weeds the man was wallowing in.*

We were believers, but family tragedy and extreme hardship made religion uncomfortable to talk about. We simply did not understand. My Sunday School lessons began to take on some minor degree of clarity when Aunt Lilas gave me her son Jerry's set of children's Bibles when Jerry left for the service (both Testaments in color and pictures). I still occasionally refer to them.

During a motivational seminar more than twenty years ago, I was asked to name the times in my life when I reached a pinnacle of achievement in any task, no matter how small; times when I had been in what athletes call the zone; when I had done something well beyond my perceived capabilities. I couldn't name a single one at the time, but they began to come to me later. I read *Flow: The Psychology of Optimal Achievement* and began to understand. But only when I started writing and making flow a theme for four novels did I see that achieving the pinnacle called flow or zone comes only when we are one with the Holy Trinity. It usually comes when we are deeply engaged in some type of mental or physical endeavor that requires intense focus and creativity and when are being of service to others. Flow is God's presence talking to us, loving us.

As I grew older and tried to build and fortify a belief system that would set the course for the remainder of my life, I examined the primary principles Christians must accept, believe, and *understand*. I was a "show me" kind of person. Even a person of weak faith (as I was) can hardly deny that Jesus Christ changed the course of human history more than any human before or since. And He did it in a short lifespan without traveling very far from home.

Considering those facts, a logical thinker has to accept that a higher power had to be involved and the Immaculate Conception, Crucifixion, and Resurrection became easier to accept as possibilities. But to my everlasting shame, I could not get my logical brain around how and why Jesus died for our sins and how His Crucifixion forever affected all of our lives. One preacher corrected me when I referred to Jesus as a human, saying He was God. True, but He was also human. He ate, tired, slept, hurt and bled. But why? And why did He ask God to take away the extreme pain He knew was in store (*"remove this cup from me"*) before He was put on the cross? I could not reconcile that with an all-powerful being. That opened the door for C. S. Lewis to explain it was because He was human. Makes sense now, but I could not see the logic in it for a long time.

Although tens of thousands of books and millions of words have been written on religion, spirituality and faith by scholars and experts, there are still many who have questions they are afraid or ashamed to ask, doubts they dare not express. Writing about these things may help them, and it will almost certainly help me.

As I was refining the pages of this section, I received the following message by e-mail from Dr. Charles Stanley's *In Touch Ministries* magazine. It said, "Don't discredit yourself or count yourself out. You can walk through the open doors God has placed before you and have a significant part in reaching the world with the good news of Christ." I saw that as reason enough to push on.

I do ask God to inspire my written and spoken words. Then I ask myself, "Who am I to ask such a thing? Why would God choose me?" During quiet times, I hear the answer, "Because you asked."

So does that mean all of my writings have been divinely inspired? The obvious answer seems to be a resounding no. Okay then, which ones, which books, which articles might have been inspired? And why are inspired words all mixed up with my own inferior human efforts? Are there just a few paragraphs of inspired words mixed in with the millions of words I have written?

The only answer that comes close to satisfying my need for clarity is that God is teaching me as I go along, and I am certainly not, and likely never will be, a finished product until the end. *He who began a good work in you will carry it on to completion* (Phillipians 1:6, NIV). Allowing me, even encouraging me to write and occasionally throwing in a little divine inspiration is His way of teaching me.

So how does this inspiration come? Do I hear God's voice? Do I see visions? No, at least not in the normal senses of sight and sound. I do believe, however, that God speaks to me often, just as He does to everyone else who asks to hear His message. Guidance may come in a dream, a random thought, a phone call, a chance encounter with a stranger, a passage in a book, an assigned chore, a conversation with a loved one, a book that drops off the shelf at the right time, or in any one of hundreds of ways.

I have traveled down a lot of blind alleys, taken wrong paths, failed many times, and hurt others by my actions. When I drove life's car into the ditch, somehow I learned from the mistake and got back on the road again. Soren Keerkegarrd said of such occasions,

> *The true significance of what happened would inevitably become clear to me and I would be numb with surprise: I have done many things in my life that conflict with the great aims I set for myself and something has always set me on the true path again.*

The mistakes I made helped me to develop a belief system, a set of principles to live by. Yes, I still veer from those principles, still occasionally amend them, but I never abandon them. I ask for forgiveness and get back on the right path. My life has undoubtedly been blessed. Prayers have been answered. I am ashamed to admit that, for the most part, I neither properly recognized nor expressed gratitude for such blessings until long after they were received. More often than not, I did not even recognize the blessings when I received them. Why? Because they seldom came on the timetable I requested, and usually not in the way I expected. More often than not, I attributed the blessing to my own personal efforts. And yet, I was forgiven for my ingratitude. And that defines God's grace.

How were my eyes opened? More than thirty years ago, I began writing. At first, it was just a journal, then essays about my private feelings, nothing for public consumption. Then I began writing for lectures, seminars and workshops. The writing caused me to reflect, to look back, to be still and listen. Psalms 46:10: *Be still, and know that I am God*, took on new meaning for me.

So how does God speak to me? His voice sometimes comes to my mind as clearly expressed thoughts. I used to half-seriously ask, "God, could you please deliver your inspiration at more convenient times—like when I have pen and paper handy, or when I'm not driving or dozing off at night?" Those requests entered my mind involuntarily, because even I knew better than to question an inspired gift from the Almighty. But one night, quite unexpectedly, God answered. "I have repeatedly asked you to be still, to be quiet, to clear your cluttered mind, but you have ignored Me. So I take opportunities as they present themselves. By the way, a thank you might be nice."

I got the message. Some of you are probably thinking I am hearing what I want to hear. Others are saying these words are only my imagination at work. Right on both counts. I do want to hear it. But sometimes, I hear things I really don't want to hear. And, I believe that my imagination (subconscious, if you will), is God speaking through The Holy Spirit, in language I can clearly understand. That is what I call faith.

As I read the words above, they still seem arrogant, self-serving. Why me? What qualifies this sinner, this man who ignored blessings when they were received because I could not be still long enough to recognize them? My answer: Why not me? Why not you? I used to envy those with invincible, unwavering, lifelong faith, the preachers who seem to have all the answers. Mine has been a meandering search along a path littered with doubt, even cynicism. My saving grace is that I never stopped searching. I just looked in a lot of wrong places.

In the final pages of this book, I will try to detail the wrong and right paths I followed and how I tried to find answers to questions that kept me from building my faith. I still occasionally struggle with these questions as life's paths lead in directions I never expected, but I have learned how to deal with them.

# Self-Help vs. God's Help

MANY RELIGIOUS LEADERS SCOFF AND EXPRESS disdain for the "self-help" shelves in bookstores, explaining that real answers to the most important life questions can only be found in the religious section. They are right on some level. However, self-help gurus and their books, seminars, and recorded messages provided a gateway to the religious section for me. I deeply immersed myself into a world where prayers are called affirmations; where the subconscious is recognized, but not as a deity; a world where God and The Holy Trinity are seldom or never mentioned but "invisible forces" and "the powers of the universe" are. The teachers in that world made religious writings easier to understand, easier to see their practical applications to my life. I later learned many of my mentors in that world were, in fact, biblical scholars who saw themselves as providing a portal for skeptics like me to enter into a more spiritual world, the world of faith. I was just late.

I told a college graduating class to seek wisdom wherever you can find it, excluding neither the self-help nor religious sections. And please do not exclude the ancient texts or wise people just because they might have lived centuries ago. And don't adopt a rigorous requirement that any principle must be supported by the latest scientific findings. Science has been wrong many times on many subjects for long periods of time throughout history—often on purpose when money and power interfere. But if science is your only belief system, then look at several scientific studies and books about NDE's (Near-Death Experiences) by Paul Perry, Ramond Moody, MD, PhD and Jeffrey Long, MD. The evidence of an afterlife in their voluminous research and many books is ample.

The Bible is filled with stories and examples of God's awesome power. These stories have been told for centuries. When I talk with non-believers, I ask if there are not at least two or three miracles they could consider believing. If they can't accept He raised humans from the dead, healed the sick and afflicted; then, how about feeding four thousand with seven loaves and a few small fish, maybe feeding five thousand with five loaves and two fish? Does the fact these miracles were witnessed by thousands and have endured for centuries impress you at all?

Doubts and questions plagued my own meandering journey toward faith. I have often imagined what God might say if He were telling the story of my life. "When he was a boy, he saw Me as vengeful and angry because of what he heard from others and what happened in his own family. He was frightened of Me. As a young man, he was weak, sinful, and cynical. In middle age, he wanted to live a good life, be a better man, and have a strong faith, but he still did not understand. He diligently searched for answers to the questions that plagued him, 'Why am I here? Am I doing what I am supposed to do?' He looked in some wrong places, came to some wrong conclusions, but I had patience and forgave him because he was trying very, very hard, and because I love him. In old age, he walked through the doors I had always left open for him, studied my words, and came to Me. He began to understand I am a God of love, not vengeance."

# Free Will vs. God's Will

HOW MANY OF US HAVE HEARD A TRAGEDY or untimely death explained as "God's will." I still struggle with this one. I think it's because I have spent the better part of my life believing in personal responsibility and that seems to run counter to the idea of "God's will." Some believe in predestination (fate)—that God has planned each of our lives in advance. I have always believed in free will. If we don't have choices, how can we earn our eternal rewards?

A recent unattributed article says,

> *The Potter has power over the clay. He can do what He chooses. We humans do have limited free will, but God's will is greater. So even if we try to resist His sculpting hand, He continues to work toward His purpose. The master Craftsman has set out to achieve a particular design in us, and He has a plan to make it take shape.*

I don't disagree with that, but it leaves questions unanswered and confuses me a little. Since His will is greater, will He shape us all to His purpose, no matter how much we resist? I think not. Otherwise, we're all going to heaven. The author goes on to say,

> *…human clay sometimes shifts off-center and becomes misshapen. Just as clay can be fashioned only when it sits precisely in the middle of the wheel, Christians must be in the Father's will to grow spiritually. The Potter maneuvers the drifting believer back into position and begins remolding. He never discards His vessels but tirelessly works to perfect them.*

I think the key words here are, "*Christians must be in the Father's will to grow spiritually*" and "*He never discards his vessels.*" I believe God has a will for each of us, but we must try to continually return to the "*middle of the wheel,*" and we must do that through asking for His guidance. If not, we will get misshapen and stay that way. One pastor believes there is a difference between God's *determined* will and His *desired* will. That speaks to me. Certain things are going to happen because God has ordained them; He wants other things to happen, but they will only if we hold up our end.

I still have to remind myself daily to let go and let God. I have trouble surrendering, because there are so many days when I am still unsure if I am doing what God intends for me to do. Surrendering is not giving up or letting life carry us along on *any wind that blows*. Letting go means having faith; trying to live our lives according to God's teachings; asking for forgiveness when we fail; using the gifts God gave each of us; and asking for guidance to fulfill our reason for being—our purpose in life. When we are confused, we must believe, pray, and just do the things that come into our minds. When we are unsure if we are doing the right things, we must believe. We must have faith that we are being guided, that even if we do not understand today, we will understand tomorrow, next week, or next year. We must keep taking the steps our conscience tells us to take.

Even though I can look back on my life and see example after example of His guidance, I have to remind myself daily to have faith, ask, and then surrender. If I do those things, He will help me to apply my particular gifts to the highest possible purpose for me. He will bring the circumstances, events, and people into my life to bring about His will for me. And I have to accept I may not understand what has happened until I look back. Again, life is lived forward, but understood backward.

I still ask myself about the times when I did, spoke, thought, or wrote the wrong things. Who inspired those times? Where was God? Where was my faith? Writing and the reflection necessary for writing helped me to understand those times. My selfish nature had allowed me to take credit for every success and blame circumstances or others for every failure. I let ego take control. When I intensified my search for answers, when I accepted with certainty there are forces in the universe much more powerful than us mortals (even though I gave those forces wrong identities at first), I was rewarded through grace. My mistakes happened because I did not fervently ask for God's guidance in making decisions, in achieving what I wanted, charging on, thinking I was fully capable of taking care of it myself. I did not meditate, get still, and listen.

# How and Why Do We Pray?

I CAN'T ANSWER THAT QUESTION, OF COURSE. Each of us must find what works for us. As a child, I was often embarrassed by public prayer. I feared raising my head or opening my eyes at the wrong time. My first reading of scripture in a children's Bible gave me comfort.

> *But when you pray, go into your room, close the door and pray to your Father, who is unseen. Then your Father, Who sees what is done in secret, will reward you.* Matthew 6:6

I felt redeemed and determined all public prayer was somehow misguided. I no longer think that, but still believe private prayer is what we need most.

I was also plagued with the questions most of us wrestle with. Is it wrong to ask for material rewards or success in our careers, for example? One pastor writes our prayers should be more about what He wills than what we want. I find that advice confusing, especially if one is unsure of God's will for our lives. I prefer to turn it around and ask for guidance, faith and strength to conform my desires to His will. And I ask for help in my continued quest to build invincible, impenetrable, unwavering faith so that I can surrender and know that God will use me to carry out His will for my life, to help me achieve my reason for being. And I try to remember to express gratitude for God's patience, love and forgiveness in every prayer.

I have read many articles on the subject of prayer, tried various methods of prayerful meditation, failed many times at finding the right words and thoughts. I have written many prayers, copied many from other sources, and memorized many lines.

> *When you pray, don't babble on and on as people of other religions do. They think their prayers are answered only by repeating their words again and again.* Matthew 6:7

> *Do not be quick with your mouth, do not be hasty in your heart to utter anything before God. God is in heaven and you are on earth, so let your words be few.* Ecclesiastes 5:2

Still, I think writing the best words I could create or copy from more learned sources helped me. I wanted my prayers to say what was in my heart and I needed a pen and paper and keyboard to refine exactly what I needed to express in my prayers. Over a period of several years, I have refined (and memorized) my prayers, so that I will not leave anything out I need to say. Trying to be eloquent in thought or voice at prayer time without that crutch sometimes caused my mind to wander, my memory to fail, or my tongue to tie itself in knots. I don't believe God expects eloquence, but seeking the right words helps me to give voice or thought to daily prayers that don't confuse me or make my mind wander. I still make mental and physical notes of people or events I need to pray about. And now that I have what I think are the best words at my disposal, I seldom recite the memorized prayer because the process of writing it helped me to feel as if I can open a thought or verbal dialogue with God more easily.

I try to be worthy of a relationship with the Holy Spirit filled with love and forgiveness. That is what I want and what I believe God wants. I also believe we must schedule a time and place regularly and often, or else the relationship will suffer.

Does God answer? Maybe not how or when we want Him to, but yes, He does. I try to see His face in the eyes of good people and animals, my loved ones, in clouds; to feel His touch in the kiss of a raindrop or snowflake, the soft embrace of a gentle breeze; hear His voice in the roll of thunder or a bird's song. I don't hear a booming voice, but I do hear thoughts and I do see signs, especially when I pay attention with an air of expectancy and faith. I try to remember I am not Moses or Paul. Remember what was asked of them when God revealed himself to them?

Does prayer work? Yes. For me, it helps to solve one of the most difficult parts of the Christian life—letting go and surrendering to God's will without knowing for sure what God's will for my life is. Prayer helps me to continually recognize surrendering does not mean abdication of responsibility. Instead, it means acceptance of the even greater responsibility to carry out God's will for my life. I still sometimes have to suppress the urge to take charge, to take full responsibility and credit for what happens. Prayer strengthens my faith, helps me to surrender and to understand better how the Holy Spirit works in my life.

Do we need to be on our knees? If it works, then do it. A submissive posture works best for me. It helps me to focus and concentrate and it conveys respect and love. Of course, many pray just fine lying, sitting or standing. Where do we need to pray? Anyplace will do, but I like a completely dark closet to help me focus. I can't recall where I read them or who said them, but these words helped.

> *The Holy Spirit prays with us and for us. We do not pray alone. Regular prayer helps us to bask in the presence of the Holy Spirit, to become closer and more intimate with God, to better understand the Trinity and why Jesus left the Holy Spirit with us.*

# The Bible in a Few Words

AS A LAYPERSON AND ADMITTED FUNCTIONAL illiterate on Scripture, I undertook (embarrassingly late in life) a study of both Testaments. Oh, I read children's versions of both when I was young and have sporadically read at both as an adult. I bought and read many short-cut books to learn about the Bible when I became frustrated with reading actual Scripture I found confusing. And I don't just mean archaic language. I tried several translated, simplified versions.

I was confused by what seemed to be contradictions between what God said vs. what He did, especially in the Old Testament. I was also confused by timelines, i.e. when did this happen? Why are both Testaments not presented in chronological order? Why do the same people have different names? Why are the same stories told by different people? And why does God do things in the Old Testament that seem to defy the teachings in the New Testament? I even embarked on several suggested Bible study courses, reading certain passages on consecutive days. It didn't work for me.

So I decided to read both Testaments from start to finish. My sense-of-order brain insisted, of course, that I start with the Old Testament. Lots of people have many different ways to learn. I have learned what does and does not work for me. This approach made sense to me. Although it seemed sort of sacrilegious at first, I highlighted and made margin notes in the Bibles on this reading journey. I read consistently and I read for fairly long sittings. That helped.

I kept a small notebook beside my reading chair and made notes of the various passages that had always confused or interested me—passages related to the Holy Spirit, The Holy Trinity, how to pray, why bad things happen, why and how the Crucifixion and Resurrection paid for our sins, baptism, finding life's purpose, the afterlife, Satan and hell, etc.

I also found passages and characters in the Bible that I had never noticed before. Melchizedek, for example—who is this man who had the power to bless and minister to Abram (Abraham) and whom Abram gave a tithe? I breezed right by him in my first reading, thinking he was just one more hard-to-pronounce name in a long line of kings and prophets. But I noticed him in the second reading (see how rereading increases comprehension?). I found him in Genesis, Hebrews, and Psalms. He was King of Salem, from which Jerusalem was named. Salem also means peace. David said, *"Thou art a priest forever after the order of Melchizedek."* It was also said that he was *"without mother, without father, without descent."* What does that mean? I found myself starting to read Scripture like a novel.

And who was the *beloved* disciple, the one referred to in John as the *"one Jesus loved"*? Exploring the answer to these and other mysteries made things much more interesting.

I stuck to my disciplined approach through three readings of both Testaments in three different versions. It took me a little over two years. I have started the fourth read. This time, I am rereading the New International Version Student Bible. So, do I consider myself now educated on Scripture? Sorry, but no. Reading the Bible three times made me realize I have only scratched the surface of understanding. Yet, I am not discouraged. Just the opposite. For the scratch I have made offers the richest bounty life has to offer. I have learned a lot, developed a lot of questions, and the reading goes much faster now and my comprehension rate is going up exponentially.

Of course, there is the distinct possibility my interpretation of what I am reading is very flawed. On second thought, there is little doubt that it is probably flawed, but is it totally wrong? Several ministers certainly disagree with my opinions (or I disagree with theirs). But then again, reading has brought me the comfort of allowing myself to refine my own belief system with each reread. I believe God is okay with that, as long as I grasp the essentials. I reconciled (mostly) the seeming contradictions in the Old Testament by listening closely to explanations and researching what others have written about the subjects.

When I switched from nonfiction to fiction writing, I was introduced to loglines, book jacket summaries, and synopses. A logline (sometimes called an elevator speech) is a one sentence description of the book you have written. A book jacket summary is a few lines printed on the inside flap of a book jacket meant to entice readers. In this age of digital printing, such summaries are even shorter and are printed on the back of the book. Imagine reducing 100,000 words to 100 words that will persuade a reader to buy and read the book. A synopsis is a summary (usually 250 to 500 words) that tells the entire story of a novel. We reduce four hundred or so pages to one or two. Synopses are usually required by potential agents and publishers. I find these things very difficult to write, especially for character-driven novels.

But as I started my third read, I started to imagine what a logline or synopsis for the Bible would be like. How would I explain the Old and New Testament if I were forced to reduce each to a few paragraphs? Should we even try to do that? I, for one, need that type of thing firmly in my mind so the details will come easier. I prayed for forgiveness as I tried to do it.

## *The Old Testament in Three Paragraphs*

God makes man in His own image and gives Him free will and almost complete freedom. He places Adam and Eve in a world of beauty and almost perfect peace and harmony where they want for nothing. He promises them dominion over every living thing on Earth. They only have to follow a few simple rules (some would say one rule, but I believe there were at least two). But they disobey and mankind keeps disobeying for about fifteen hundred years, until finally God can find only one righteous man on earth. He sends the Great Flood to destroy humanity except for Noah and his family. After the flood, descendants of Noah populate the earth and the great biblical stories and characters evolve. God promises a childless and old Abraham he will be the father of many kings and nations. God continually shows His power and asks only that mankind have faith and know that He is God. Over a thousand years after the flood, He sends

Moses to lead the Israelites out of slavery in Egypt. When ten plagues and the awesome power of God finally force the pharaoh to accede to Moses' plea to let His people go, Moses leads his people out of Egypt and slavery (The Exodus). God parts the Red Sea and drowns the pursuing army.

With clouds during the day and pillars of fire by night, He leads his chosen people toward the Promised Land and to freedom. He feeds them with manna from the sky. Yet, after all these miracles, many still do not believe, proving that impressive displays of God's power will not guarantee faith and many humans are short-term thinkers with a "What have you done for me lately?" attitude. Approximately 430 years after his covenant with Abraham, God delivers the Ten Commandments and other laws through Moses, but Moses discovers the people have created things to worship while he was on the mountain rather than worshiping the Creator. After forty years in the wilderness and because they continually disobeyed and showed lack of faith, only two Israelites over the age of twenty, (Joshua and Caleb—not even Moses) crossed the Jordan into the Promised Land.

For fourteen hundred more years, God's chosen people engage in wars with the tribes of the Promised Land. They experience many defeats, many victories. They lose and regain God's Temple and the Ark of the Covenant, become oppressors and oppressed. They ask for a king to lead them, and God gives them Saul. Saul's reign is a failure, but he is followed by David and Solomon who restore the Temple and return the Ark. For over nine hundred more years, a succession of kings leads the Jews into and away from idolatry, slavery and power. Great prophets such as Elijah, Elisha, Isaiah, Jeremiah, Ezekiel, and Daniel continue to bring God's message to His chosen people and to their kings.

## *The New Testament in Three Paragraphs*

The Old Testament has many prophesies of the coming of Jesus. God knows His creations will continue to sin and lack faith, that no human will follow rules perfectly, and all who try will ultimately fail. Twenty-five hundred years after the flood, John the Baptist is born to prepare the way for Jesus. A short while later, Jesus, a descendant of David the giant slayer and a King in the Old Testament, is born. At approximately thirty, Jesus puts down His tools, walks away from His father's carpentry shop and begins His ministry. He is baptized by his cousin John the Baptist and gathers the disciples. For the next three years, He heals the sick, raises the dead, speaks in parables, and delivers the most important sermons of all time to multitudes. There are no miracles on a massive scale, just enough positive demonstrations of His power to spread the Word. He asks only one thing—*Believe in Me and in my Father.* It is said that He never travels more than two-hundred miles from his home, yet He changes the world in ways not seen before or since, has a greater effect on mankind than all the kings, emperors, warriors and scholars who came before or after. He is God in human form, the Christ, the Messiah, yet He comes in humility and lives His life as a servant. He takes Peter, James, and John, His closest disciples, to a high mountain where He is transfigured *(and He was transfigured before them, and His face shone like the sun, and His garments turned white as the light itself)*. Moses and Elijah appeared by His side and God's voice thundered from heaven, "*This is my beloved son, in whom I am well pleased.*"

Jesus joins the procession to Jerusalem for Passover but stops in Bethany to raise His good friend and follower Lazarus from the dead. Because He is a threat to the establishment Jews, He is nailed to a cross between two thieves. He endures the most agonizing of deaths and suffers in ways only humans can to prove He is human. Then, in the greatest miracle of all, He rises from death, proving He is also God. He reveals himself to his disciples and a few others and gives them further instructions on how to spread His Word, the Good News that is the Gospel. Forty days later, He ascends into Heaven, leaving behind The Holy Spirit to dwell within us and with us, to comfort us and guide us, and leaving a pathway for weak mankind to sin again and be forgiven. We only have to have faith, ask for forgiveness, and believe. This is the New Covenant, a covenant destined to last forever. He leaves us with the greatest commandments saying,

> *Love the Lord your God with all your heart and with all your soul and with all your mind. Love your neighbor as yourself. All the Law and the Prophets hang on these two commandments.*

He instructs His disciples to teach all nations to observe His commandments. The disciples, and later Paul and others, go forth and continue to tell and write the story of Jesus. Finally, in Revelation, a man named

John writes of visions he has while imprisoned in an Alcatraz-like Roman prison on a rocky island called Patmos. Because his visions are filled with symbols, grand imagery, and unique numbers, they have been subject to many conflicting theories as to their exact meaning. But there is little doubt the writer named John who was being persecuted for his Christian beliefs was revealing his visions of the cosmic significance of the return of Jesus Christ when followers of Christ will be made safe at last.

---

Oversimplified, even flippant? Guilty. I needed simplicity to help me study the details, the many stories, parables, prophets and kings, famines and wars that surround and support this basic premise for me. The confusion I had when I read the Old Testament gained clarity as I sorted out the differences between the Old Covenant and the New Covenant. One was a covenant that killed and the other gave life. One was a covenant written in stone, the other written on the heart of man. When I become confused, I go back to this summary. You should try doing your own synopses. It would undoubtedly be different than mine. By the time this is printed, I will have probably changed my own several times. The more I study the Bible, the more books written about Christianity by true Bible and religious scholars mean to me.

# Final Thoughts

FREDERICK BUECHNER'S MEMOIR, *Telling Secrets*, sat on my books-to-read shelf for a long time, possibly a decade. I don't recall why or when I bought it and can't explain why I never read it until recently. Maybe it was waiting until I needed it. Maybe it was one of those times when inspiration comes when we need it most. This book did literally drop to the floor when I was rearranging a shelf. That happens a lot.

The book is difficult to describe. The author is an ordained minister who writes fiction and nonfiction. This memoir is in three parts. The titles seem allegorical, but Buechner delves into very real, personal and tragic events in his life which I won't spoil here. Even if his stories had not worked for me (which they did), these quotes made the book one I will never forget.

As a writer, this was a favorite gem.

> ...*a book you write, like a dream you dream, can have more healing and truth and wisdom in it at least for yourself than you feel in any way responsible for.*

I especially liked the author's open, almost self-deprecating style, not what we usually expect from an ordained minister. As a husband, father and grandfather, I also enjoyed the way he integrated the meetings of a particular group to bring readers a valuable lesson. Buechner does not mention the group by name, but you will recognize it when he eloquently describes their meetings.

> *They have slogans, which you can either dismiss as hopelessly simplistic or cling on to like driftwood in a stormy sea. One of them is 'Let Go and Let God'—which is so easy to say and for people*

> like me, so far from easy to follow. Stop trying to protect, to rescue, to judge, to manage the lives around you—your children's lives, the lives of your husband, your wife, your friends—because that is just what you are powerless to do. Leave it to God. It is an astonishing thought. It can be a life-transforming thought.

And as a believer, this is my favorite:

> Even if there be no hereafter, I would live my time believing in a grand thing that ought to be true if it is not.... I will go farther, and say I would rather die forevermore believing as Jesus believed, than live forevermore believing as those who deny him.

---

NOTE FROM AUTHOR: The original manuscript ended here. But on the day after I made the final changes, I went for a morning horseback ride to have coffee with friends. One the way back, I found two sheets of paper in the ditch across the road from my old friend and mentor Dr. Fred Tarpley's house. His redwood house sits way back in the woods like a reclusive author or professor's should (Fred was the opposite of reclusive) but not so far that I could not see two large dumpsters appear in his yard a few weeks after he died. I don't know what is in them, but I suspect a lot of Fred's research and books had to be discarded. Many had suffered water damage and fire damage when his house caught fire many years ago.

When I saw the yellowed and tattered sheets, I immediately thought of Fred. The wind had probably carried them out of the dumpster, across the road and into my horseback path that particular morning. The two sheets of paper were printed on both sides and I could tell from the missing page numbers they had been part of a book or manual for teachers in a religion course of some kind. A date in the margin told me they were printed more than half a century ago.

If you read my notes at the beginning and got this far, you know I struggled with the last part of this book. As I said in the opening notes, I struggled to write about things very personal to me and to offer opinions on subjects I may be unqualified to write about. I considered deleting the last section of the book many times. I was still considering deleting it when I dismounted and picked up the sheets. I found these words:

> *If Christianity does not begin with the individual, it does not begin; but if it ends with the individual, it ends.*

I had particular problems with the "How to Pray" section, because I am still figuring it out. In the yellowed, tattered sheets, I found these words:

> God hears the meditations of our hearts, rather than the words of our mouths. If we pray one way with our lips and another with our true feelings, which is the true prayer?

I might be making too much of what may be a coincidence, but if I have learned anything in this life, it is to pay attention and to engage in deliberate practice of the things we want to get better at. God sends signals we may miss if we are not paying attention. Finding those two pages told me to leave the last section in.

In his book *Letters to My Son*, Kent Nerbern says,

> *Once you love an art enough that you can be taken up in it, you are able to experience an echo of the great creative act that mysteriously has given life to us all. It may be the closest any of us can get to God. Spiritual growth is honed and perfected only through practice. Like an instrument, it must be played. Like a path, it must be walked. Whether through prayer or meditation or worship or good works, you must move yourself in the direction of spiritual betterment... only a fool refuses to walk in the sunlight because he cannot see the shape of the sun.*

This has been my effort to walk in the sunlight. What more can I say? Thanks. It's been quite a ride.

# Index

Abilene Ranch Rodeo 92
Abilene, Texas 79, 82, 84, 86, 92, 102
Abilene Western Heritage Classic 82, 102
Abraham 313–315. *See also,* Abram
Abram 313. *See also,* Abraham
Academy Award 285
Adam 314
Adams, Carroll 177, 215–216
Aden, Greg 66
Adrian High School 89
Adrian, Texas 84, 89, 91, 98–99
Ainsworth, Arch 105, 242
Ainsworth, Bailey 194
Ainsworth, Caden 191, 192, 193
Ainsworth, Damon 191–194, 232, 256
Ainsworth, "Doc" 9, 12. *See also,* Ainsworth, "RA"; Ainsworth, Richard; Ainsworth, "Teadon"
Ainsworth, Eddy xv, 172–173, 179, 245, 248–249
Ainsworth, Hiram "Papa" 42, 251
Ainsworth, Jan Herman 17–19, 26, 28, 39–41, 44–45, 55, 71, 136–137, 142, 148, 150, 155–156, 182–184, 194, 196, 209, 213, 220, 235, 249, 251, 255, 267
Ainsworth, Jim H. iv, vi, viii, 70, 79, 83, 175, 232, 243, 277, 282, 284
Ainsworth, Marion Shepherd "Shep" 30, 81, 101–103, 105–107, 109, 111–114, 181
Ainsworth, Nadelle Alexander (Mother) 5–6, 8–11, 84, 148, 172–173, 176, 184–185, 207, 214, 242, 246–252
Ainsworth, Pat 103
Ainsworth, "RA" 12. *See also,* Ainsworth, "Doc"; Ainsworth, Richard; Ainsworth, "Teadon"
Ainsworth, Richard 12, 214. *See also,* Ainsworth, "Doc"; Ainsworth, "RA"; Ainsworth, "Teadon"

Ainsworth, Richard Lindon 250
Ainsworth, "Teadon" (Daddy) xv, 5–11, 43, 53, 84, 105, 172–176, 181–183, 214, 242, 245–246, 249–251. *See also,* Ainsworth, "Doc"; Ainsworth, "RA"; Ainsworth, Richard
Akers, Jody Allgeier 155, 157
Alaska pipeline 96
Albany, Texas xiv, 77, 79
Alexander, Lee 245
Alexander, Mary Pearl 245
Allard, Jerry 300
Allard, Lilas Alexander 300
Allen, James 225
Allen, Rex 57
Allen, Woody 257
Allgeier, Gela 155, 156
Allied Forces 139
Alpine, Texas 66, 81
Alumni Center 150
Alvin York Bridge, 49
Amarillo, Texas 69–70, 84–88, 98, 160, 222
*American Cowboy* 68, 80, 134
American Indian and Cowboy Artist's Society 117
"America the Beautiful" 80
*Anne of Green Gables* 143
Ark of the Covenant 315
Arnold, Eddy 64
Arnspiger, V. Clyde 176
Artist of the Year 67
*As a Man Thinketh* 225
Ascension 292
Aspermont, Texas 105–106
Atkins Diet 86
*Atlantic Monthly* 54
Atonement 291
Autry, Gene 57
Badger 119
Balladeer xiii, 63, 65–67
Baltimore, Maryland 66, 203–204
Bar Nun Ranch 55

Bard xiii, 38, 63–67
baseball 19, 27, 29, 98, 143, 177
basketball 8, 176, 212, 214, 246
*Beach Music* 299
Bell, Alexander Graham 222
Bent Door Cafe xiv, 98–99
Bertani, Stephanie viii
*Best American Mystery Stories* 54
*Best American Short Stories* 54
"Best Little Whorehouse in Texas" 56
*Best New American Voices* 54
Bethany 316
*Beyond Wealth* 225
Bible xvi, 148, 300, 305, 309, 312–314, 317
Big Bend 82
Big Texan Steakhouse 87
Billy Bob's 57
Billy the Kid 87
biscuits 27–28, 106, 108, 163, 169, 174, 181–183, 243
*Biscuits Across the Brazos* iv, 59, 81, 181
Bivins, Julian 98
Black, Baxter 66
Black, Lucas 77
*Black Swan, The* 224
*Blinky to Blue-John: A Word Atlas of Northeast Texas* 281
*Bloodworth* 52
Boggs, Bob Lee 158
bois d'arc 155, 160, 210, 281
Bois d'Arc Bash 281
Boles, Grayson Ridge "Gray Boy" 189, 196, 214
Boles, Peyton 193–194
Boles, Shelly Ainsworth 148, 193, 233, 271
Bonney, William 87
Booker, Tom 48
Boot Hill 98
*Bootlegger's Other Daughter, The* 157
Borgnine, Ernest 137, 142
Bosses xiii, 17–19, 282
Boyd, William 140

Boy Scouts 137
Boys Ranch 85, 98
Brannaman, Buck 140
Brazos River iv, 59, 81, 101–103, 107, 163, 181–182, 234, 260
brogans 7, 10, 11, 208
broker–dealer (BD) 20, 21, 24
Broom, Perry 177
Brown, Earl 91
Brown, Roscoe 137
Brown, Sam 70, 87, 91, 99, 107
buckaroo 64–65, 140
bucket list xiv, 104, 115, 123–125, 275
Buechner, Frederick 318
Burkett, Sandy 104
Burnham, Daniel H. 224
Burns, George 151
Bush, George W. 67, 138
Caan, James 143
Cain, Susan 200
California 66
*Callahan County* 60
Callaway, Huey 69
Call, Woodrow 264
Campbell, Texas vi, 209
campsite 127, 130
Canadian, Texas 222
Cannon, Hal 66
Canton, Texas 63
cappuccino 15, 28
Carnegie, Andrew 222
Carrington, Jace 17, 19
Casa Manana 56
Cash, Johnny xv, 181, 183
Cassidy, Hopalong 140
castrated 95, 113
*Cattleman, The* 117
cattlemen 80, 115
Cauble, Bill 77
cedar breaks 111–112, 115. *See also,* mott
cellar 211
Chalaire, Tommy 103

Chalaire, Trish Ainsworth 103
Champion 171
Chiang Kai-shek 139
Channing, Texas 84
Charles Goodnight Award 77
Charlie 119
Charolais 94
Chekhov, Anton 189
Chennault, General Claire Lee 139
Chester A. Reynolds Award 140
Chesterton, G. K. 291
Chicago, Illinois 99
chicken house 211
Chief Joseph Scenic Trail 125
Childress, Texas 85
Chili Cook Off 82
chinks 91–93, 95
Choctaw 50
Cholla 94
Christ 290, 292, 300–301, 316–317
Christian 292, 293, 310, 317
Christianity 290–291, 317, 320
Christmas 15, 170, 241
*Chronicles of Narnia* 290
chuckwagon 81, 102, 106, 112, 114
Churchill, Winston 34
Church of Christ 269, 271
Church of Ireland 291
Cimarolli, Mary 157
cistern 189–190, 212
City Pharmacy 30, 59, 176, 262, 271
Clift, Montgomery 142
Clooney, George xv, 57, 181–182
Clooney, Rosemary 57
Cochran, Mike 57
Cody, Wyoming 125
coffee 15, 24, 26–28, 46, 50, 59, 76, 92, 105–106, 115, 169, 208–209, 290, 319
Colorado 64, 85, 96, 125, 131, 136
Colorado and Southern Railroad 85
Columbia, Tennessee 50
*Comes a Horseman* 143
Commerce, Texas 29, 53, 55, 59, 65, 67, 104, 139, 176–177, 204, 243, 245, 255, 256, 262, 271, 281, 284
Connally, Gov. John 57
Connors, Chuck 57
Conrad, James 61, 262
Conroy, Pat 299
Coon Creek 49
Cooper, Gary 131, 142
Cooper High School 30, 216
Cooper, Texas 19, 29–30, 67, 172, 174, 209, 242
Coors Ranch Rodeo 87
Corbin, Barry 137
corral 95, 99, 103, 106–109, 113
Corsicana, Texas 58
Covenant, New 316–317
covered wagon 26, 30, 36, 56, 67, 81, 101, 181, 260
Cowboy 64, 65
cowboy CPA 76
*Cowboy Ethics: What Wall Street Can Learn from the Code of the West* 115
*Cowboy Gear* 76
Cowboy Hall of Fame 66, 78, 116, 135, 138, 140, 142
cowboy poet 64, 87, 99
Cowboy Poetry Gathering 81
*Cowboys and Indians* 134
*Cowboy's Faith, A* 76
Cowgirl Hall of Fame 56
Cowhill Council xiii, 26–28, 46, 277, 290
CPA 27, 30, 76, 79, 216, 222, 268
Crane, Stephen 164
Cross Trails Cowboy Church 268–269
Crucifixion 291, 301, 313
Csikszentmihalyi, Michael 163
Cumby, Texas 209
Cutter Boy 119
dairy barn 169–170, 211, 214
Dalhart, Texas 85, 97
*Dallas Morning News* 67
Dallas, Texas 55, 66, 76, 172–174, 208, 215

# INDEX 325

Damon, Matt 142
Daniel 315
Darwin, Charles 294
David, King 313, 315
Dearborn heater 207
Decatur, Texas 36, 67
Decoration Day 201–202
Delaney, Clayton 72, 151
Delta County 19, 67, 101, 150, 190, 275
Delta County Champion Indians 150
Denver Road 85
Devane, William 137
Dewhurst, Colleen 143
Dewitt, Geral 150
disciples 316
Distinguished Alumnus 280
Dixie 119
Dobie, J. Frank 70, 139
dogtrot 169
Dolittle, Jimmy 139
"Do Not Stand" 203–204
Dorrance, Bill 140
Dorrance, Tom 45, 140
Douglas, Kirk 142
Dowell, Bob 177, 216
*Dreams and a White Horse* 57
D'Souza, Dinesh 293–298
Dufresne, John 149
Duncan, Arthur 57
Dunkel, Jill J. 80
Dunn, June 256
Dusard, Jay 86, 132
Dust Bowl 7
Eastland County 67
East Texas Historical Association 208
East Texas State College (ETSC) 175, 178, 214
East Texas State University (ETSU, ET) 17–19, 53, 178, 213, 217
Ecclesiastes 310
Edwards, Arliss Lee 100, 147, 158–160, 241
Edwards, Don 38, 63–68, 116
Edwards, Jimmie Dee Alexander 185

Egypt 315
Elam, Jack 137
Elijah 315–316
Eliot, T. S. 212
Elisha 315
Elko, Nevada 66, 68
El Paso, Texas 138
Emerson, Ralph Waldo 222, 288
Engler, George "Stanley" 130–131
Engler, Phil "Buck" 126–128, 130–133
Engler, Randy "Rangey" 130, 133
Enloe, Texas 209
Epton-Seale, Jan 70–71
eulogy 4–6, 11, 238, 240, 277
Eve 314
*Everlasting Man, The* 291
Exodus, The 315
Ezekiel 315
Fabulous Forty Motel 99
Fairlie, Texas 55
faith 22, 155, 216, 224, 251, 292–293, 296–297, 299–300–301, 303–305, 307, 309–311, 314–316
Falcon, Rooster 92, 94–96
Fannin County 275
Farley, Cal 98
Farnsworth, Richard 137–138, 142–143, 182
Ferguson Auditorium 224
Field House 176, 214
Financial Planner 76
*Find the Flow* 152
First Baptist Church 6, 256
First National Bank 79
First United Methodist Church 245, 262
Five Acres, The 26
*Flow* 163
*Flow: The Psychology of Optimal Achievement* 300
Flying Tigers 139
*Follow the Rivers Series* 42
Fonda, Henry 142
Fonda, Jane 143

Foote, Horton 285
F.O.P. Society 253–255
Forrest, Nathan Bedford 50
Fort Worth and Denver Railroad 85
Fort Worth Cowboy Gathering 66
*Fort Worth Star-Telegram* 57
Fort Worth Stockyards 66–67
Fort Worth Symphony Orchestra 38
Fort Worth, Texas 56–57, 66–67, 85, 116, 208, 215
Forum Arts 176
Four Lads, The 178
Four Sixes (6666) 104–105
Fowler, Zenita 204
Frost, Robert 215
Frye, Mary 203–204
Ft. Davis, Texas 82
Fulton, Joe Kirk 86, 96–97
Fulton, R. H. 96
Gage Motel 82
galluses 208
Gambler 118–121
Gardiner, Mike 222
Garrett, Gary 104
Garrett snuff 189, 212
Gay, Enola 28
Gay, William 49–51, 53–54, 183
Genesis 313
*Georgia Review* 54
Germany 240
Gervers, Jake 29, 31, 185
Gervers, Pauline 185
GI Bill 18
Giles Hotel 99
"Give What's Left of Me Away" 205
*Glass House, The* 157
Glawson, Wanda Myers 150
Glen Rose, Texas 118
God ix, xvi, 63, 143, 148–149, 154, 164, 246–247, 291–292, 296–316, 318–320
*God Forsaken: Bad Things Happen. Is there a God Who Cares? Yes: Here's Proof* 296

*Go Down Looking* iv, 70, 147, 150–153, 158, 174, 179
God's will 306, 309–311
God wink ix, 63
Godwink 63–65
Gold Blazer 280
Golden Globe 143
Golden Spur Award 77
Golightly, Annie 55–58, 76. *See also*, Milford, Ann
*Goodbye to a River* 163
*Good Old Boys, The* 69
Good Samaritan 254
Gospel 316
Gottschall, Johnathan 2
gramma grass 94
Grand Tetons 128
Graves, John 163
graveyard 73, 201, 204, 206, 249
Great American Cattle Drive 56
Great Depression 7, 138, 245, 266
*Greatest Secret in the World, The* 221
Great Flood 314
*Great Santini, The* 299
Great Western Performers 137, 140
Green, Alexander 224–225
Green, Billy 80
*Grey Fox, The* 143
Grinders Creek 51
Grinders Switch, Tennessee 54
Gros Ventre Wilderness 125
*Gunsmoke* 65
Guthrie ISD 101, 115
Guthrie, Texas 102–103, 106
gyp water 106, 115
Hackett, Buddy 68
Hagen, Julie 131–134
Haggard, Merle 209
Hagler, Skeeter 28, 104
Half Circle One Ranch 68
Hall of Great Westerners 138–139
Hall, Tom T. xiii, 16, 57, 72, 151
Hampton, R. W. 87
Handy, Charles 163

Harper's 54
*Hate to See That Evening Sun Go Down* 52, 54, 183
*Havana* 143
Hawkes, Howard 203
hay barn 170, 211
Hear the Music 152
Heaven 316
Hebrews 313
Hereford, Texas 239
Herefords 94
Herman, Benny 260, 266
Herman, Nita 265–266
Herman, Rod 266
Herman, William Ben Jr. 264–267
Hico, Texas 68
Highland Park, Texas 71
High Plains xiv, xv, 88, 147–148, 239, 241
Hill Country 86, 96
Hill, Napoleon 221–223
*Historic Ranches of Texas* 76
Hitchens, Christopher 293
hitchhiked 249
Hohenwald, Tennessee 49–50, 54
Holbrook, Hal 52
Holy Spirit 303, 310–311, 313, 316
Holy Trinity 291, 300, 304, 313
"Homecoming" 72
Homecoming 194, 201
*Home from the Hill* 204
*Home Light Burning* iv, 70, 111, 115
Honey Grove, Texas 209
Hooten, Deb 245
Hooten, Nadelle Ainsworth 245. See also, Ainsworth, Nadelle Alexander
Hopkins, Anthony 289
Hopkins County 275
Horchem, Charles 29–31, 116
horseback 26, 42, 56, 67, 95, 101, 103, 111, 114, 125, 136, 194, 319
horse breeding 104
horsemen 115, 125–126

*Horse Whisperer, The* 48, 140
Horton, Tina 277
Hosses xiii, 17–18, 282
houlihan loop 109
Hughes, Jamie 3, 146
Hull, Morgan 103
Humphrey, William 204
Hunt County 275
Hunt, Ray 140
Hurt, Claire 297
Icahn, Carl 136
Idaho 64
Immaculate Conception 301
*In Search of Excellence* 221
*Interwoven* 79
"In the Jailhouse Now" 182–183
*In the Rivers Flow* iv, 19, 70, 189
*In Touch* 3, 301
Ireland, John 142
Isaiah 315
Israelites 315
"I Wish I was Eighteen Again" 151
Jack, Bill 177, 216
Jackson, Wyoming 125, 133
Jade 39–41
James 316
James A. Michener Memorial Prize 54
James, William 294
Janes Clinic 172
Janes, Olen 174
Jeep 15–16, 24–25, 49–51, 54, 194, 209, 284–285
*Jefferson: East Texas Metropolis* 280
*Jefferson: Riverport to the Southwest* 280
jellybean 191, 197
Jeremiah 315
Jernigan Creek 170
Jerome, John 163
Jerry Don Test 271, 276
Jerusalem 313, 316
Jesus 46, 289–290, 292, 300–301, 311, 313, 315–317, 319

Jews 315–316
Jim Clark's 271
Job 296
Jobs, Steve 222
John 316
Johnson, Ben 45
Johnson, Elton 176–177
Johnson, Graham 178, 215–216
Johnson, Jeremiah 131
Johnson, Michael 61
John the Baptist 315–316
Jonesborough, Tennessee 67
Jordan River 315
Jubilee 45, 119
Keerkegarrd, Soren 302
Kelton, Elmer 69–70, 82, 84
Kennemer, Carroll 177
Kentucky 104
King, Bill 216
King Ranch 139
King, Weldon 177
Kirkpatrick, Jane 70
Klondike Cemetery 203, 208, 249–250
Klondike, Texas xv, 6, 29, 201, 204, 208, 216, 236, 248, 290
Knaur, John 28
Koko 171
Korean War 280
Kristofferson, Kris 52
Kushner, Harold 297–298
Ladonia, Texas 209
Lambert, Derek 271, 275
Lambert, Jerry Don xvi, 271–276
Lambert, Joan 275–276
Lambert, Rhonda 275
Lambshead Ranch 77, 79
*Last Innocent Summer* 204
Lawrence, Trice viii
Lazarus 316
Lea, Tom 138
legged up 43, 102
Leibniz, Gottfried 298
*Letters to My Son* 320

Levis 176, 239–241
Lewisberg, Tennessee 50
Lewis County, Tennessee 50
Lewis, C. S. 3, 50, 149, 289–292, 296, 298, 301
Lewis, Meriwether 50
"Life" 60, 263
*Life After Death: The Evidence* xvi, 293–294
*Life* magazine 139
Linck, Charles 61, 262
*Lion, the Witch and the Wardrobe, The* 290
Little Beaver 45
Little Jennie Ranch 131
Little League 10, 19, 29, 150
Little Swan Creek 51
*Lonesome Dove* 137
Lone Star Park 259
*Long Home, The* 54
longhorn cattle 56
Long, Jeffrey 304
*Lord of the Rings* 290
Los Angeles, California 99
*Lost Country, The* 52, 54
*Love of Horses, The* 76
Lucretius 291, 296
Lufkin, Texas 151
Lutz, Eusibia 281
Lynn, Loretta 117
MacAdam/Cage 54
Mackie, Asa 118–121
Maclean, Annie 48
Madison, Guy 117
*Magnificent Seven, The* 125, 130, 133
Maltz, Maxwell 222
Mandino, Og 221, 222
"Man of Constant Sorrow" 182
*Man Who Listens to Horses, The* 140
Marathon, Texas 82
Marfa, Texas 82
Marlboro Man xiv, 135, 136
Marshall County, Tennessee 50
Marx, Groucho 18

# INDEX 329

Matador Ranch 85, 99, 101
Mathews, Lucille 78
Mathews, Sally Reynolds 79
Mathews, Terry 56
Matthew 309–310
Matthews, Watt 77–80
Maury County, Tennessee 50
Maury, Tennessee 49
May 119
McAnally, Emmett 177
McCall, Alexander (Smith) 163
McCarley, CT xiii, 20–25
McCarley, Maggie Jo 23–25
McClendon, Bill 147
McClendon, Penny 147
McCord, Ken 177, 216
McCord, Sam 216
McCrae, Augustus 267
McCrea, Joel 45, 142
McCullough, David 77, 164
McNamee, Lawrence 177, 216
McQueen, Steve 143
Melchizedek 313
Memorial Student Center 178
Mennonite choir 269
*Mere Christianity* 290, 291
mesquite 93, 112
Messiah 316
Metroplex 29
mettle 88, 119
Michener, James 285
Mid-Point Cafe 99
Miles City, Montana 56
Milford, Ann 55. *See also*, Golightly, Annie
Milford, Dale 55
Miller Grove, Texas 209
Miner, Bill 143
Minnesota 125
*Minstrel of the Range, The* 64
*Misery* 143
*Missouri Review* 54
Mitchell, Larry 102, 116
Mitchell, Waddie 38, 64–66

Moline, Bob 64–67, 116–117
"Moments to Remember" 178
Montana 48, 56, 64, 131, 264
Moody, Ramond 304
Moore, Kay Ainsworth 243
Moorhouse, Bob 101–102, 105
Moorhouse Ranch 37–38, 101–108, 111, 114
Moorhouse, Togo 106
Moorhouse, Tom 101–102, 104–109, 112–115
Moses 310, 315–316
Moss, John and Peggy 18
Mother Road xiv, 98
mott 111. *See also,* cedar breaks
Mt. Zion Church 201, 207
mules 36, 102, 130
Murphy, Joseph 222
Murphy, Michael Martin 137, 140
*Myself and Other Important Matters* 163
Nabers, Hannah 196
Nabers, Landon 195
Nabers, Taylor 195
Nashville, Tennessee 54
Natchez Trace Parkway 50, 54
National Cowboy and Western Heritage Museum 135
National Cutting Horse Association 78
National Storytelling Festival 67
*Natural, The* 143
Nerbern, Kent 320
Nevada 64–66, 68
New England 64, 281
New International Version Student Bible 313
New Mexico 64, 96, 125, 272
*New Stories from the South* 54
New Testament 312, 314–315
Newton, Isaac 294
New York, New York 60, 96
Nicholson, Jack 143
Nightingale, Earl 221–222

Noah 314
Norris, Bob 136
*North American Cowboy: A Portrait, The* 132
Northeast Texas 6, 19, 57, 101, 158, 160, 281
Nugget 15, 16
Oaks Crossing Slim 260
Oasis of the Panhandle 222
O'Brien, Rich 67
*O' Brother Where Art Thou* 182
O'Connor, Flannery 53, 177
"O' Death" 182
Odessa, Texas 139
*O. Henry Awards Prize Stories* 54
Oke City 135
Okies 135
Oklahoma City, Oklahoma 135
"Old Dogs and Children and Watermelon Wine" 16
Old ET 213, 217. See also, East Texas State University
"Old Hag" xiv, 130–131, 133. See also, Julie Hagen
Old Jail Art Museum 79
"Old Rugged Cross, The" 5
"Old Stud" 83
Old Testament 312, 314–315, 317
Oliver, Rosalie viii
*On the Western Trail* 150
*On Writing Well* 238
*Open Boat, The* 164
*Ordways, The* 204
Oregon 70
Orwell, George 42
outdoorsman 23
outhouse 211
Outstanding Original Western Music 140
overalls 7, 10, 11, 73, 173, 201, 211, 216–217
Owen Wister Award 138
Oxbow Saddle Shop 67
*Oxford American* magazine 53

Oxford University 290
packhorses 128, 130–131
Padre Island, Texas 23–24
Paine, Thomas 186
*Paint Horse Journal* 117
Palmer, Arnold 57
Palmer, Jay 259–261
palm leaf hat 83, 94
Panama hat 92, 94
Panhandle xiv, 29–30, 83–86, 88, 101, 158–160, 222, 240
Panhandle Professional Writers Conference 84
Papa Jim xv, 194, 209, 235
"parable of the talents" 148
Parker, Linda Sue 277
Parkinson's disease 246
Parks, Minnie Ainsworth 181
Parramore Ranch 106
Passover 316
Patterson, Paul 81–82
Patty (trail cook) 130–131
Paul, Donna G. viii
Paul, St. 310, 316
Peale, Norman Vincent 222
Pearl, Minnie 54
Pecan Gap, Texas 18, 30, 209
Pennzoil 136
Perry, Paul 304
*Persimmon Hill* 135
Peters, Billy 88
Peters, Calvin 83–84, 86–97, 99, 107
Peters, Linda 86, 90
Peter, St. 316
Peters, Zack 88–89, 91
Peters, Zane 88, 91
Petty, Kathleen 148, 155–157
Phillipians 302
Pickens, Slim 57
Pickering, Danny 101, 103–105, 115
Pickering, Jennie 103–104
Pickering, Welton 104
pine box 80, 239, 241
Piper, John 3

# INDEX

Pitchfork Ranch 102, 105
*Place Names of Northeast Texas* 281
plagues 315
*Plainview Daily Herald* 70
Plainview, Texas 150
poet 60, 64, 70, 87, 99, 132, 150, 285
pool 31, 113, 211. *See also,* tank
*Power of Positive Thinking, The* 222
*Power of the Subconscious Mind, The* 222
"Prairie Land" 80
*Prairie Portrait, A* 38
prayer 202, 223, 292, 297, 309–311, 320
Prince Albert tobacco 208
*Prince of Tides* 299
Princeton 77
*Progressive Farmer* magazine 54
Promised Land 315
prophet 289, 316
Proud Cut Saloon 125
Proust, Marcel 74, 294
*Provinces of Night* 49, 52–54, 183
Psalms 302, 313
Psycho-Cybernetics 222
Pulitzer Prize 28, 57, 77, 104, 285
Purdy, Bobbie 216
purple sage 94
*Purpose Driven Life, The* 105, 293
push mower 201, 208
Quien Sabe Ranch xiv, 81, 83–85, 87–88, 91–92, 94, 97–99
*Quiet: The Power of Introverts in a World That Can't Stop Talking* 200
quilt 41, 155, 164, 184, 194, 222, 235
Ranger, Texas 67, 78, 101
Ray, Chrystelle 31
Ray, John 29–31
razor strap 7
Reagan, Ronald 34, 67
*Red Badge of Courage* 164
Redbone, Leon 66
Redford, Robert 140, 143

*Red River* 142
Reed, Jimmy 18
Reid, Ace 57
religion 28, 224, 299–301, 319
remuda 38, 106
Republican National Convention 138
Resurrection 291–292, 301, 313
Revelation 317
riata 66
Rimrock Cowboy Church 102
Rio Grande 138
Rio Grande Valley, Texas 70
Risener, Debbie 277
Rivers 39
*Rivers Crossing* iv, 174, 190
*Rivers Ebb* iv, 85, 99, 158, 174
*Rivers Flow* iv, 19, 70, 150, 174, 189, 290, 297, 300
Rivers, Gray Boy 169–171
Rivers, Jake 19, 52, 85, 153–154, 158, 169–171, 174, 189, 290, 297, 300
Rivers, Mattie 45, 169–171
Rivers, "Papa" Griffin 42, 295
Rivers, Rance 43, 169–171, 174
Rivers, Trish 169–170
Robbins, Marty 64
Roberts, Monty 140
Robertson, Dale 45
Robnett, Stella 185
Rockefeller, Nelson 57
Rockin' Vintage 196
rodeo 83, 87, 102, 142
Rodgers, Jimmie xv, 49, 63, 181, 183
Rogers, Roy 57, 140
Rogers, Will 34
Rohn, Jim 221, 223
Roland, E. W. 177, 216
roundup 37, 71, 77, 94, 101, 106–107
*Roundup* magazine 138
Route 66 98–99, 159
Rowdy 43, 102, 104, 106–115, 119
Ruidoso, New Mexico 45
Rural Youth Day 31
Rushing Creek 49

Rushnell, Squire 63–64
Ryan, Ken 151
Ryon's Saddle Shop 117
*Saddle Songs* 63, 65, 68
Sam Rayburn Student Center 280
San Angelo, Texas 78–79
Sand Hills Country Club 274
saucered-and-blowed coffee 208
Saul 315
Saylor, Joe 177, 216
Scar xv, 119, 169, 171
scleroderma 59
Scripture 297, 312, 313
*Seven Days in Utopia* 77
*Seven Habits of Highly Effective People* 221
*Seven Pleasures: Essays on Ordinary Happiness* 164
Sevenshoux Ranch 66
Sewanee, University of the South 53–54
Sewanee Writers Conference 54
*Shadowlands* 149, 289, 298
Shaw, George Bernard 257
Shaw, Hildred "Hido" Alexander Ainsworth 174, 185, 242–244
Shepherd, Donna 277
Shepherd, Kenneth 277
Shiloh Cemetery 147
Shiloh Community 29
Shooter 42, 44–46, 119, 155
Shortcut 119
Shott, Hugh I. 177
Sigma Phi Epsilon 18, 282
Six Flags Over Texas 66
Sluder, Ricky 277
Sluder, Roger 277
*Smiling Country* 69
Smith, Charlie viii
Smith, Mary 216
Smithsonian Institute 139, 282
Smith, Tumbleweed 28
smoke house 211
Snicker 119

Soggy Bottom Boys 183
songwriter 48, 72, 151
Sons of the Pioneers 140
Soule, Mary Ann 224
South Dakota 99
Southern Methodist University (SMU) 177, 215
Spanbauer, Tom 165
Spiegelman, Willard 164
Spindletop 136
Spinks, Louis 91
Spoon, Jake 264
Sprayberry, Tommy 108
spurs 79, 82, 91–93, 134, 170, 240
Stanley, Charles 297, 301
Stanley, Ralph 183
Stanley Walker Journalism Award 57
Star xv, 169–170, 248
Starvation Point 70
State Fair 31
Steagall, Red 66, 140
Steinbeck, John 162
Stone, W. Clement 221
Stoney, Texas 103
*Straight Story, The* xiv, 142–143, 182
Stringer, Joan Herman 266
*Success Magazine* 221
Sugar 119
*Sulphur Springs News Telegram* 56
Sulphur Springs, Texas 253, 264
Sweetwater, Texas 79
*Swim With the Sharks Without Being Eaten Alive* 221
Szansz, Thomas 219
tack 43, 82–83, 105–106, 108–109
Taleb, Nicholas 224–225
*Tales of Wells Fargo* 45
tank 113. See also, pool
tapaderos 93
Tarpley, Colleen 285
Tarpley, Fred 17, 60–61, 99, 164, 177, 215, 228, 262, 280–286, 319
Tarpley, Marie 285
Tarpley, Mark 285

Tarpley, Ted 285
Tascosa, Texas xiv, 85, 87, 98
Taylor, Buck 65, 67
T-Cross Ranch 136
team roping 37, 45, 67, 71, 82–83, 101, 112, 117, 260
Tejas Social Club 17–18, 282
*Telling Secrets* 318
Ten Commandments 315
Tennessee Hill Country 51
Tennessee River 49
Tennessee Williams Scholar 54
Terlingua, Texas 82
Texaco 136
Texas A&M University-Commerce 17, 213, 217, 219, 280
Texas A&M University 104
Texas Bicentennial Wagon Train 116
*Texas Books in Review* 71
*Texas Cattle Barons* 76
*Texas Cowboys* 76
Texas Folklife Festival 281
Texas Folklore Society 201
Texas Institute of Letters 57, 61, 139
Texas Piper Professor 280
Texas Poet Laureate 70
Texas Professional Artists 117
Texas Ranger Hall of Fame. 117
Texas Tech Red Raider 96
Texas Wesleyan University 57
Texline, Texas 85
*Theodicity* 298
*Thing About Me, The* 61–62
*Think and Grow Rich* 221
Thomas, Alana 277–278
Thomas, Aline Malone 277–278
Thomas, Billy Jack 277
Thomas, Debbie 255, 277
Thomas, Dena 277
Thomas, Jackson "Pop" 26, 253–255, 277
Thomas, Jerald 15–16, 26–28, 63, 68, 254–255, 277
Thomas, Jimmy 277

Thomas, Ricky Lynn 26, 28, 277–279
Thompson, William "Bill" 157
Thoreau, Henry David 146, 163
*1001 Texas Place Names* 281
*Thriving on Chaos* 221
Tolkien, J. R. R. 290–291
*Tombstone* 65
*Tom Horn* 143
Tongue River Ranch 105
*Too Good for the Mainstream* 64
Tracy, Brian 221
trailhead 126–127, 130, 133
Trevino, Lee 254
Trigger 171
Trinkle, Jim 57
*True Grit* 142
*True Unity* 140
TT 103–104, 106, 108–112, 115
Tucker, Willie 248–249
Tulsa, Oklahoma 208, 215
Turner, Stephen 150
*Twilight* 52, 54
Twister saddle 120–121
*Two Jakes, The* 143
United States Artists 54
USA Ford Foundation 54
USS Hornet 139
Utah 64, 66
Van Gogh, Vincent 51
Vega, Texas 91, 159
Venable, Robin 256
Venable, William W. "Bill" 256–258
Verghese, Abraham 164
Voss, Paul 28
Wagstaff Land and Cattle Company 132
*Walk the Line* 183
Walter A. Dakin Fellow 54
Warren, Rick 105, 291, 293
Washington, DC 139, 282
Wayne, John 203
Weatherford, Texas 66, 68
Webber, Joe Jr. 275
Webber, Kim Lambert 271, 275

Welch, Buster 117
West Delta School 29–30, 174, 249
West Texas State University 91
Western Heritage Awards banquet 135
*Western Horseman* 68, 87
Western Music Association 67
Western Writers of America 138
West Oaks Funeral Home 253, 264
West Texas 91, 101, 110, 113
West Texas Post 110
*When Bad Things Happen to Good People* 297
*When God Winks* 63
White, Brenda Black 59–62, 228, 262–263, 285
White Elephant Saloon 66, 67
White House 55
White, Patricia Ann Ainsworth 213, 247
Whitlock, Elaine 150
Whitlock, Larry viii, 150
*Why I Write* 42
Wichita Falls, Texas 85
Williams, Hank 73
Williams, Tennessee 54
Wills, Bob 239, 241
Wilson, Laura 77

Winnsboro, Texas 29
Wisconsin 70
Wittliff, Bill 137
Wolfe, Thomas 207
*Wood Eternal: The Story of Osage Orange and Bois d'Arc* 281
woodstove 27, 51, 169, 207
World War II 139, 245
Worthington Hotel 67
wrangler 107
Wrangler jeans 61, 66, 92–93, 240
Wright, Kendall 19
*Writer* magazine 299
*Writers Digest* 84
Wyoming 64, 125, 131
XIT Ranch 99
"Year that Clayton Delaney Died, The" 72
Yellow Dog 119
Yellowstone River 125
*Yippy Yi Yea* 65–66, 116
York, Alvin 49
*You Can't Go Home Again* 207
Yowell, Texas 55
Yucca 94
Ziglar, Zig 221
Zinnser, William 238
ZZ brand 88

www.ingramcontent.com/pod-product-compliance
Lightning Source LLC
Chambersburg PA
CBHW020323170426
43200CB00006B/252